RASA YATRA

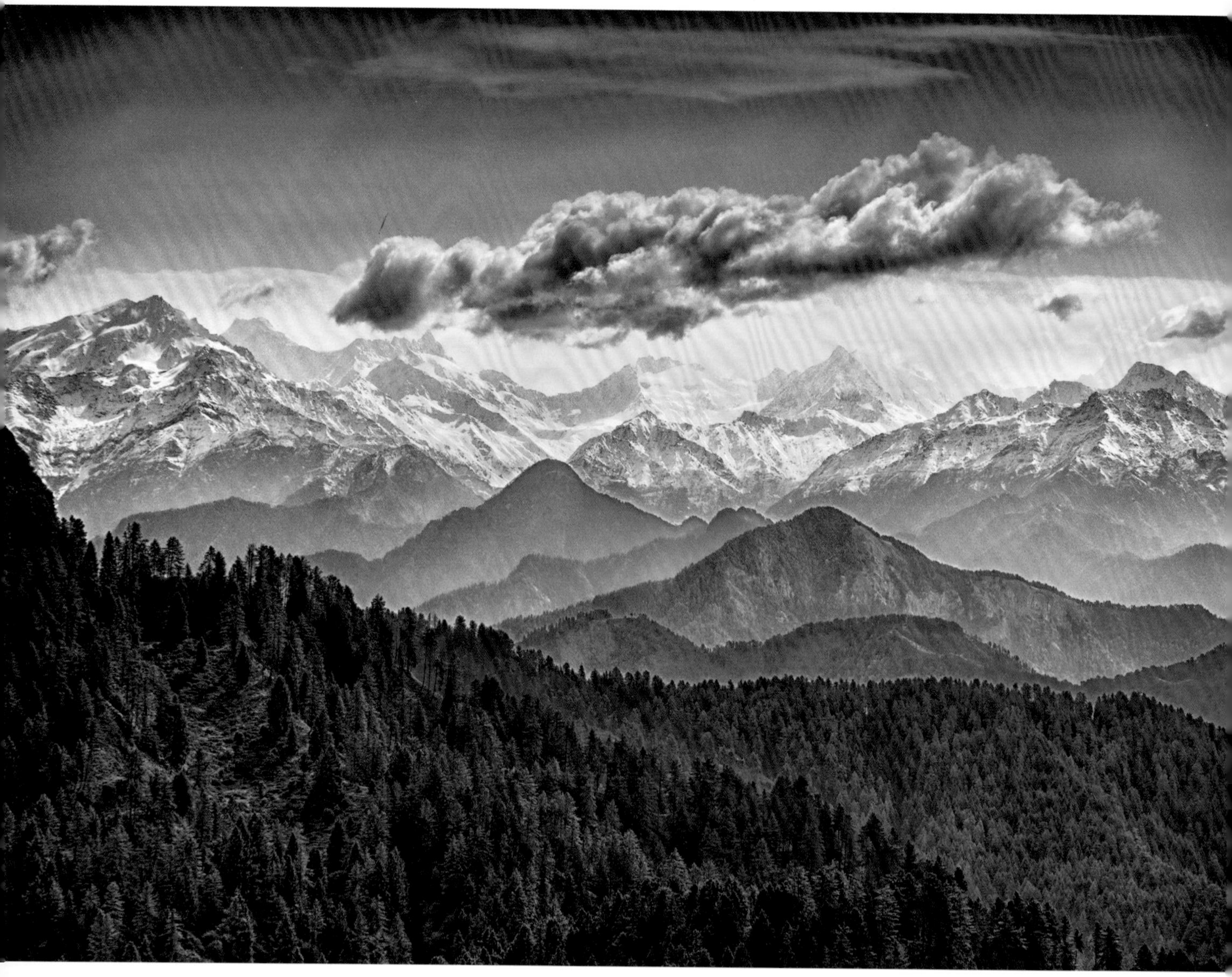

On Cloud Nine

Indian Art Series

RASA YATRA

A pilgrimage into the heart of India

PARAM P. TOMANEC

MOSA
MUSEUM OF SACRED ART

NIYOGI BOOKS

Overseas Distribution

USA and Canada
ACC Distribution
email: sales@accdistribution.com
www.accdistribution.com

United Kingdom, Ireland, Europe and Africa
Kodansha Europe Ltd.
email: info@kodansha.eu
www.kodansha.eu

Cambodia, Burma, Laos and Thailand
Paragon Asia Co. Ltd.
email: info@paragonasia.com
www.paragonasia.com

Jointly published by

MUSEUM OF SACRED ART

MOSA Belgium
Petite Somme 5,
6940 Septon,
Durbuy, Belgium
Tel: +32 (0) 86 43 30 22
Email: info@mosabelgium.com
Website: www.mosabelgium.com
http://www.radhadesh.com/

MOSA Italy
Via Scopeti 106/108,
San Casciano in Val di Pesa,
Florence, Italy – 50026
Tel: +39 (055) 820054
Email: info@mosaitaly.com
Website: www.mosaitaly.com
www.villavrindavana.net

NIYOGI BOOKS
D-78, Okhla Industrial Area, Phase-I
New Delhi-110 020, INDIA
Tel: 91-11-26816301, 49327000
Fax: 91-11-26810483, 26813830
email: niyogibooks@gmail.com
website: www.niyogibooksindia.com

ISBN: 978-93-83098-74-3
Publication: 2015

Printed at: Niyogi Offset Pvt. Ltd., New Delhi, India

CONTENTS

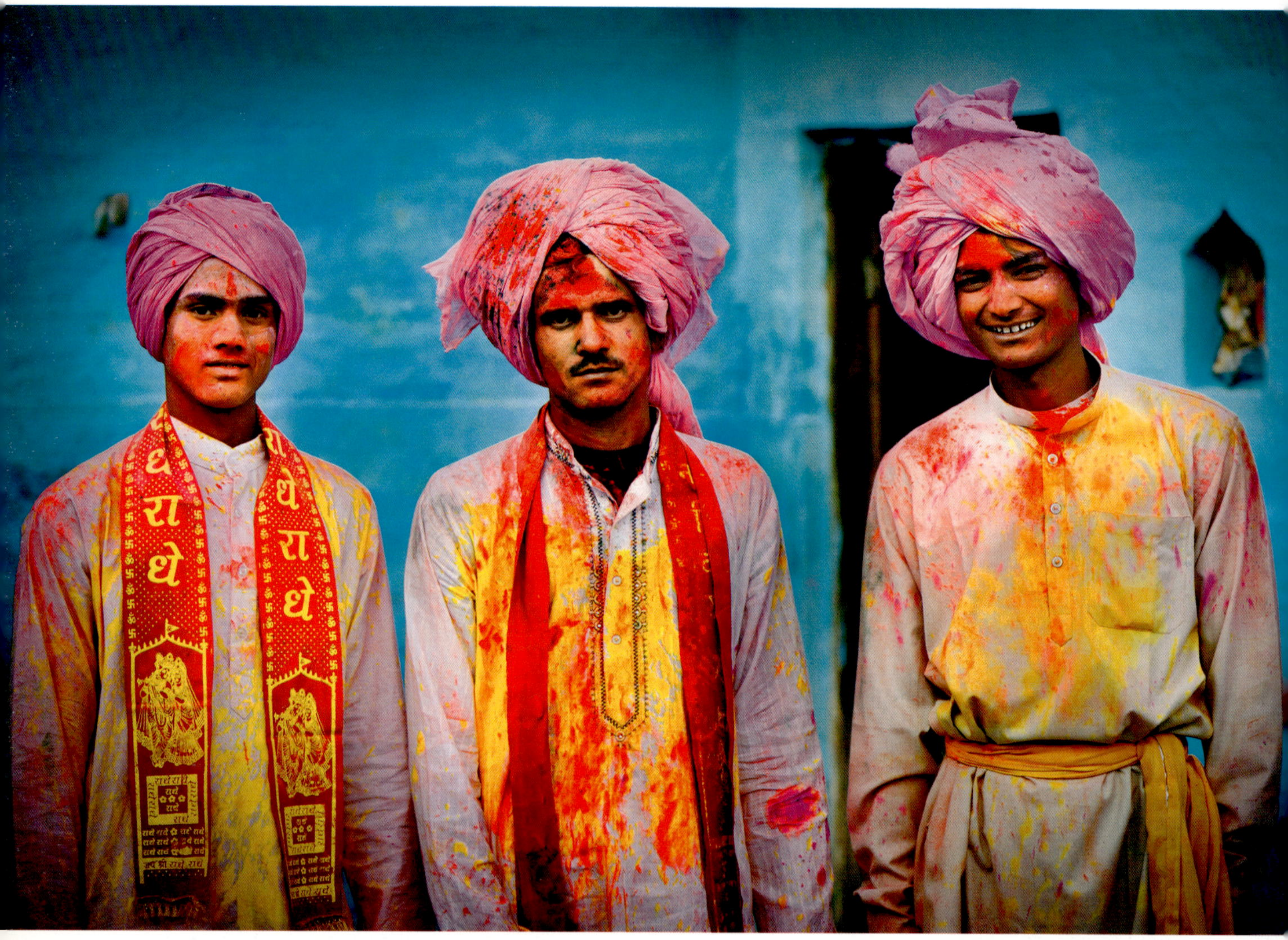

Mohan, Raj and Brajesh

FOREWORD

A panorama of ethereal images with an innate spirituality that evokes a sublime, blissful experience engages you as you encounter Param Tomanec's Rasa Yatra photographs. With their focus on eternity, rather than a momentary reality, his photos offer you an inner journey, a pilgrimage beyond the obvious and the physical or bodily toward the meditative, spiritual, and blissful-: sat-chit-ananda.

The devotional iconography that is replayed visually by this artist suggests in-depth meditation, study, and research, which the artist confirms preceded his experimentation. About fifty carefully framed photographs and an art film in the collection feature some amazing portraits of people, pilgrims, and priests beside pristine sites, in engaging situations, or behind the scenes. Various primeval landscapes, sacred mountains, incessant waterfalls, and flowing holy rivers (some illuminated in moonlight or star light), live performances, temples, celebrations, and festivities that connect people with nature all figure in his work.

Param gave up a promising commercial career in films to live a monastic life and embark on a spiritual journey of self-discovery. The confluence of cultures that Param has encountered across Africa, Asia, and Europe is reflected in his current repertoire, with its meditative leanings and philosophical layering.

Param's empathy for the natural environment, cleaner air, and mother Earth figures prominently in his imagery. The beauty and bounty of nature resonate through his photo montage, which presents the world as a pilgrimage, where people come and go. But the earth and the environment, his work seems to urge, must be sustained for future generations. The characters and visuals he presents, remarkable for their spontaneity and soulful silence, and the artist's emotional rapport with his subjects and various situations, penetrate the viewer's innate feelings, beyond what the naked eye can see.

The artist uses fairly complex cinematographic neutral lights, density filtration and optics to explore the relationship between the time impression of moving and still images. His visuals evoke physical beauty and the soul of the image. Param tells me he spends hours on location, looking and waiting, till his eyes and mind meet with that of the subject. And they talk, trying to understand each other, before the photography really happens. What he captures then is not just the physical persona but sensitively photographed portraits, landscapes, mind-frames, scenes, and celebrations that transcend the obvious. The subject is figured holistically, with subtlety, soul, and character in place.

A multi layered mythology and intricately entwined narratives, featuring people and iconic landmarks, inundate Param's art-scape. Aesthetically rendered in amazing compositions and palettes, his photos call for nurturing nature and preserving the environment. His work invites you to meditate and penetrate deep within and beyond the surface, to soak in the image and celebrate life, while also doing some introspection. Param's Rasa Yatra takes one on a pilgrimage into the heart of spiritual India, a metaphor for sat-chit-ananda.

Sushma K. Bahl

(Author of *5000 Years of Indian Art* and Former Head of, Arts and Culture, India for the British Council in India, Sushma K. Bahl, based in Delhi, is an independent arts adviser and curator of cultural projects.)

PREFACE

It is a delight to present *RASA YATRA: A Pilgrimage into the Heart of India* as the first temporary exhibit of the Museum of Sacred Art (MOSA). MOSA is nested in a picturesque Ardennes, Belgium and it has two main galleries in the Château de Petite Somme, also known as Radhadesh.

I launched the Museum in 2009. Since then its art collection has grown significantly. The collection has grown so significantly that today it offers close to 1600 pieces of Indian tribal, traditional and contemporary works, such as paintings, sculpture, film and photography celebrating the idea of devotion. A brand new MOSA gallery has been recently opened in Villa Vrindavana mansion, just five miles from the historic town of Florence in Italy to better serve the artworks.

Our photographer and filmmaker, Param Tomanec, is a talented artist with a unique vision. Throughout his work the viewer can discover the vibrant spiritual culture that endures in India. He reveals as well some of the major challenges India faces today as consequence of fast-paced, often forced modernization. Working with Param for the past several years, it has been for me a learning event, as he has the natural ability to make you see things you are used to see from a quite different yet coherent, enlivening perspective, which is an invaluable asset for the visual poet.

We are fortunate to have several distinguished writers contributing texts: Sushma K. Bahl, Joshua M. Greene and Silke Lange. I envisage for the show to travel to other museums and cultural centers worldwide. Rasa Yatra truly is an odyssey where the viewers can experience deep emotions as if one would visit such sacred places as an insider. I am happy that the Museum of Sacred Art can offer you a pilgrimage into the heart of India in this book.

MARTIN GURVICH
Director

IMAGE AS PILGRIMAGE

Joshua M. Greene

First, a confession: I'm biased against photography as art. Even prints from the masters have always struck me as a poor second to the work of gifted painters and sculptors. A camera steals from nature what artists must search their souls to find: details, colors, composition, and emotion created from internal rather than external resources.

Meditating on the photography of Param Tomanec reminds me that biases often turn out to be founded on flimsy assumptions. Apart from his mastery of its tools and conventions, Tomanec brings to the art of photography an ability to discover consciousness operating below what the eye sees and an artist's skill at conveying its subtle presence to viewers. In India's *bhakti,* or devotional tradition, perception of consciousness—awareness of something transcendent lying just beneath the appearance of things—is called darshan, or "vision of truth." That vision is one purpose of pilgrimage, and contemplating Tomanec's work evokes for me emotions I have known journeying to holy places in India. Darshan differs from pointillism's ability to convince the eye it sees a solid where there are only dots. Darshan evokes hidden dimensions existing past the eye's visual range. The word applies to what visitors experience when looking at temple deities.

To "have darshan" of a deity at a place of pilgrimage is to move beyond ordinary seeing into subtle dimensions where the soul communes with the divinity. As a young man in the 1970s, I made my first pilgrimage to Vrindavanaa—one of the subjects in this exhibition—and found myself displaced by what I saw: humans and animals at peace with each other, sharing food and space; temples unchanged since the Middle Ages, some towering and magnificent, others no bigger than a hole large enough for an attendant, small deities, and the accoutrements of worship; forests and rivers that have withstood the ravages of centuries; and human beings like me but completely unlike me, men and women and children alive with faith, casual with the mysteries of the universe. Sociologist Emile Durkheim described such displacement as "anomie," the sensation of being at loose-ends or mismatched with the surrounding environment. Anomie is what happens when you cannot make sense of your experiences, when what was previously comfortable reveals itself as something more, different; the only way to react is to leave behind whatever notions you had of yourself and to enter abstract realms, like the characters in Samuel Beckett's play *Waiting for Godot.* Let me give you some practical examples of how that sensation occurs for me as I meditate on Tomanec's work.

Take "Jitendra Dasa" the only photograph in which the subject has his eyes closed. The worshiper is half submerged in a sacred river.

We do not know him, but we know something about him: he communes with truths that are within him. He may be a businessman or a farmer, married or single, rich or poor, but in this moment with his eyes closed to the familiar world he is a citizen of the universe. Should I not also stop long enough to go within and acknowledge my place in the cosmos?

Look at "Yogini Forest." As portrayed by Tomanec, here is a place every bit as multidimensional as Pandora, the paradise depicted in James Cameron's film *Avatar.* Meditating on this image transported me out of the gray landscapes of my everyday world and reminded me that our material eyes see so little of the miracles that surround us. The images of "Gauri Kund Lake" suggest that our ordinary perception of the sacred Ganges overlooks the power and majesty lying beneath the pollution, that this is a river of divine origin which flows from the top of the universe in color and choreography to which we have access only when guided by someone like Tomanec, who knows how to have the river's darshan. The photo of cowherd woman "Rishi Ma," her smile as paradoxical as the Mona Lisa's, made me wonder whether I understand what it means to care for cows, to share their lives, and to find in humble vocation the soul's union with infinity.

"Janardan," a former IT manager turned sadhu, lives with his two sadhu friends like with his own sons in the holy land of Vrindavana. Tomanec has captured something universal: a father's love for his sons. The three men are watching me watching them, and I thought of my own children and wondered if I would be as capable as Janardan was of inspiring them to leave the world and all its empty promises behind and live with me to live in a village without malls, without movie houses or fast food, and to spend our days chanting and dancing with God. Here are photographs that invite introspection of a particular kind: how much of ourselves, they oblige us to ask, have we sacrificed to live the life we have? Tomanec reminds us that self-questioning can happen before a photograph as readily as on a pilgrimage, provided the photographer is a rasik, the Sanskrit term for someone attuned to the nuances of spiritual emotion. The challenges for a rasik photographer such as Tomanec are twofold: first, to capture an image that engages the physical eye; second, to capture the underlying rasa of that image, its emotion of divine communion. Tomanec succeeds on both counts. In his work we are drawn first to what is visually and aesthetically recognizable: nimbus clouds challenging immovable mountains, warm faces staring out from under exotic markings, children huddled beneath a driving rain of flower petals. Look again, and Tomanec takes us deeper—away from the literal observation to a rasik or emotive level. It is on that level that a photographic image, like a pilgrimage, can stimulate awareness of our place in the greater mystery of creation.

On the rasik, or spiritually evocative level, things are symbolic in a way that differs from the everyday sense of symbols. Usually, a symbol represents something other than itself. A wedding ring symbolizes the union of two people. The small, concrete piece of jewelry represents a larger abstract concept. The ring is less than the idea it represents, since the marriage does not dissolve if the ring is lost or stolen.

India's rasik or devotional philosophy goes past this secular sense of symbolism to say something quite different about objects and their meaning. From the rasik point of view, the creation around us not only symbolizes the greater concept of God, but is simultaneously one with and different from God. Nature is the virata-rupa, the Universal Form, the Divine manifest as trees and rivers, rocks and waterfalls—not symbolic of God but God present as creation in forms our limited senses can perceive. Devotional vision reveals that nothing is different from God. Care must be exercised in distinguishing between the monistic notion that "everything is God" (called in Sanskrit *advaita* philosophy) and the *bhakti* philosophy that "nothing is different from God."

As a devotional photographer, Tomanec avoids the portrayal of divinity as an amorphous energy or abstraction of color. His decisions would have been different had that been his intention. Instead, he shows us divinity as personal, playful, and beautiful. Deities are presented as they are in temples, honored with the integrity of their individuality and unique person hood. He shows us sadhus and pilgrims warm with human emotion, eyes wide open, acknowledging us, seeing us as much as we see them. The *bhakti* view that "nothing differs from God" acknowledges God's presence in all things and within all life, without need of subsuming that life into His own being.

We as observers have an assignment when

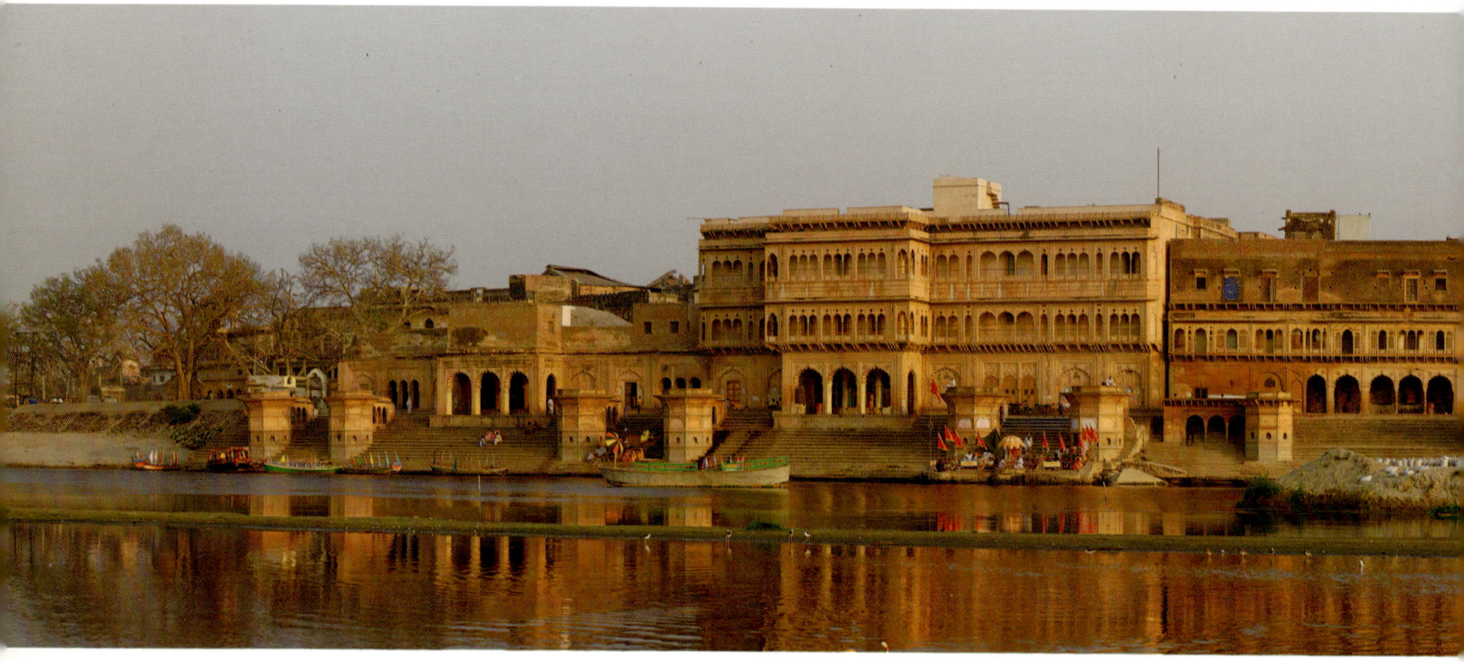

viewing such works. How well we can perceive divinity in these photographs depends on our how seriously we are committed to our spiritual practice. Neophytes appreciate phenomena on a literal level: "Here is a photograph of a tree." More advanced meditators appreciate an object's deeper symbolic meaning: "Here is a photograph of a tree and in this tree-body lives an eternal soul," or "This tree is a hair on the body of God's Universal Form." Advanced practitioners see their Beloved before them — Krishna, Govinda, Gopal are names often associated with personal divinity in India. For them, the response to inspired photography such as Tomanec's becomes "Here is not a photograph, but my beloved Krishna in His deity form, in His incarnation as mother Ganges, and in His loving devotees." On that rasik plane of pure perception, everything becomes a stimulus for love of God, whether is it *en pleine air,* on a canvas, or in a photograph. As you contemplate this exhibit,take time to breathe before each image. Meditate on each one, not as an object separate and apart from yourself but as a part of you, as an evocation of a vision you once had, but which has been subsumed beneath the temporary ephemera of material life. Let the image's deeper dimensions penetrate your heart, and watch what happens.

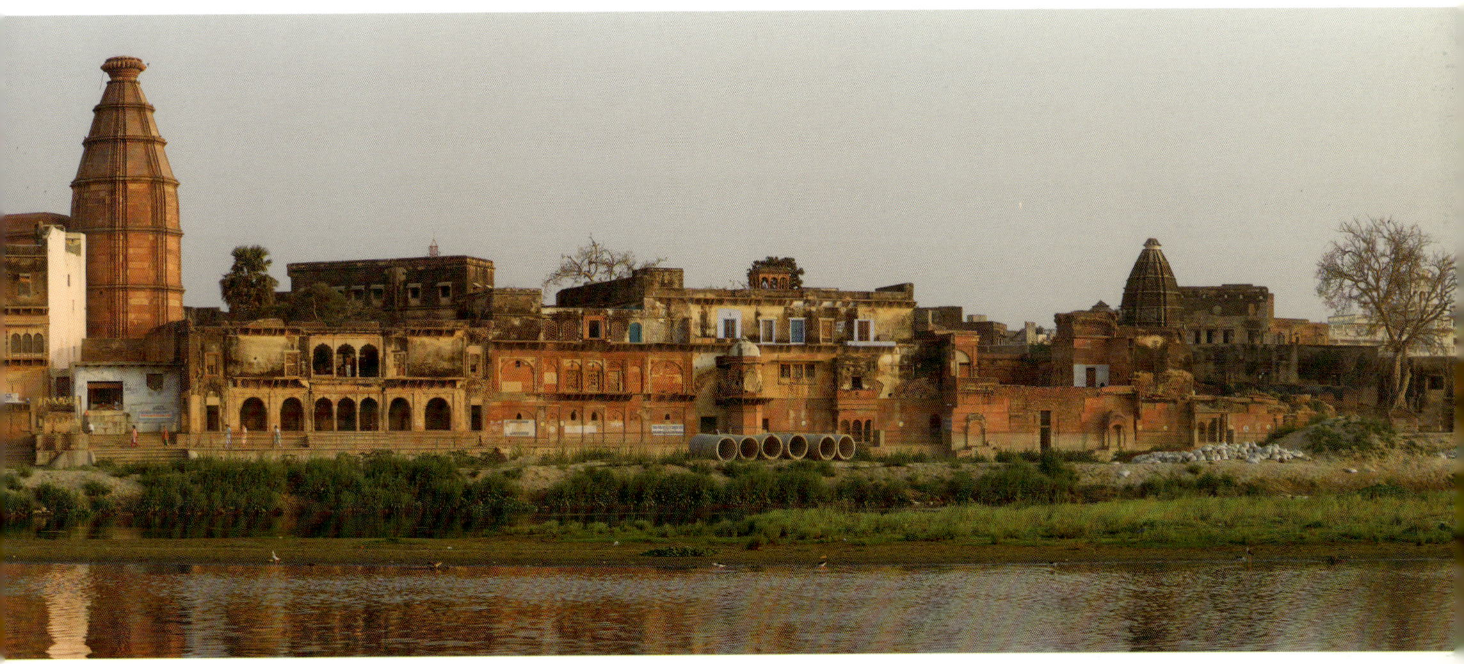

Keshi Ghat

PORTRAITS OF A SACRED PLACE

Silke Lange

When I was invited to write about Param Tomanec's photography exhibited at the Museum of Sacred Art in Belgium, I was delighted to hear that Param's photographs have been selected to be shown in a solo exhibition Rasa Yatra, focusing on Hindu tradition and the historical significance of pilgrimage. Having been familiar with Param's visual interpretations of India – its culture, landscape and people, for a number of years, the museum seems one of the most suitable places for his work to be celebrated. Param's photographs go beyond the mere representation of a place; they reflect and celebrate in themselves that which is, for him, a way of life to which he is completely devoted.

Writing about Param's photography without reference to his remarkable journey through life seems impossible for me. Born in 1977 in Czechoslovakia (now the Czech Republic), he grew up in a cultural and political environment very different from the one he has come to adopt. His experiences during his monastic life, his spiritual practice and path are continuously depicted in his still and moving images. To a large extent his photographic works of India serve as metaphors for places of hope and liberation found in his new world. At first glance the richness of the colours in the images included in Rasa Yatra is what is most striking, making the scenes depicted look distinctively surreal. On closer consideration, it seems as though the spiritual atmosphere of the locations captured by Param has enhanced the appealing aesthetic created.

Looking at the image Gauri Kund Yatra, for example, taken during a short pilgrimage from Krishna Ashram to Gauri Kund. The colours, shapes and textures of the experience of the place are emphasised through a carefully considered photographic approach, attempting to show the history of this place as well as traces of natural phenomena. As Param comments: "One can only imagine the power of Ganga's flow here in ancient times when her waters were reaching to the top of the rocks."

'The power of flow' may also be a pertinent expression to describe how Param has photographed the devotees and pilgrims in divine celebration at the Balarama temple in the Vrindavana area in the image Dauji Yatra. The combination of movement, colour and light in this image has created a visual reflection of the ecstatic, spiritual experience lived out by pilgrims on their journey.

In addition to inviting the viewer to imagine the experience of pilgrimage, Param shares some profoundly personal moments through his image making. Dwaraka Yatra, for example, shows the temple of Krishna, which, according to Param, "has a special place in my heart". The temple was built in the 6th century on the shore of the Arabian Sea on the most western part of India, Gujarat. Param created the photograph on his third visit to the temple. He recalls, "The nights are so pleasant that I used to sleep on a roof of the guesthouse and operate the camera from there. My ears would listen to the distant sounds of mantra chants throughout the night, permeating into my dream and back into waking state."

For me, in Dwaraka Yatra (Krishna Temple), Param has captured the temple in a light as if it were center stage of a theatre, waiting for a performance to begin; a performance such as the Rasa Lila dance, as seen in Param's photograph Holi Yatra, Crescendo.

Contemplating Param's photography of India, I get the sense of viewing the country through a lens that reveals its culture and traditions, its ancient history and holy places, along with people who have embraced these traditions and chosen to follow a spiritual path throughout their lives. Param's images convey his respect for the India he has explored during his own photographic pilgrimage, and the people he has encountered on this journey. However, perusing some of his written descriptions of the places visited and experiences gained on his journeys, another picture emerges. In this he shares his concerns about the impact of certain developments on the immediate environment of some of the sacred places captured in his photographs.

With the early morning view of Badrinath Valley, Garhwal Himalaya, for example, Param describes that '50 years ago there were no cement buildings here. The majority of the change in the landscape took place in the early 1980's. In the foreground of the photograph one can see that large parts of the land have already been prepared for a construction'. He then continues to look at other details of the area, namely Gangotri Yatra, Garhwal Himalaya. The photograph shows the three majestic Gangotri peaks and a place of pilgrimage which is known for worship of the river Ganga.

Param tells that inexperienced travellers and business interests have affected this area and now an active scholar, Dr. Harshvanti Bisht, is working in the area with the aim of protecting this holy site. Param is proposing to use his photography to support such initiatives in the future. Talking about the image Yogini Yatra, for example, he explains that the Yogini Waterfall, Kullu Himalaya is a sacred place for the people of the Kullu Valley. According to legend, 16 out of 64 female devotees of Lord Shiva are living here. The waterfall serves as the natural veil to cover their ethereal bodies during their bathing ceremony. Scriptures call them yoginis.

Since 2003 this holy site has been subject to the demands of the hydroelectric industry, which has shown a keen interest in taking water in the name of progress and convenience. The companies want to transform the water flow into electrical energy with commercial gain in mind. The Acharya family, a lineage of teachers and servants at the Sita Rama temple, the main temple in Vashishta, have been in contact with Param to document the location photographically and support their initiative to stop the construction works of the hydro station. Any monies generated through the sales of photographs during the exhibition Rasa Yatra in the Museum of Sacred Art will go towards a fund allowing Param to travel to the location sometime in the future.

I am an ardent believer in the persuasive potential of photography as a catalyst for change as well as representing the natural and spiritual beauty of a place. I hope viewers of Rasa Yatra are encouraged to consider the versatility of the medium and its ability to open up a world of experiences beyond mere technological knowledge. Photography has the potential to enable people to grow, understand themselves and others, and supports the development of new ways of seeing through understanding connections with culture and society. I am pleased to have been able to offer my support by writing about Param's work and his future ventures employing his mesmerizing photographic style to convey his concerns. Hopefully he will be able to actively contribute to the initiative of raising awareness of current developments in the spiritual heart of India and to protect its environment from destructions driven by values very different from the ones held by the communities themselves.

HIMALAYAS

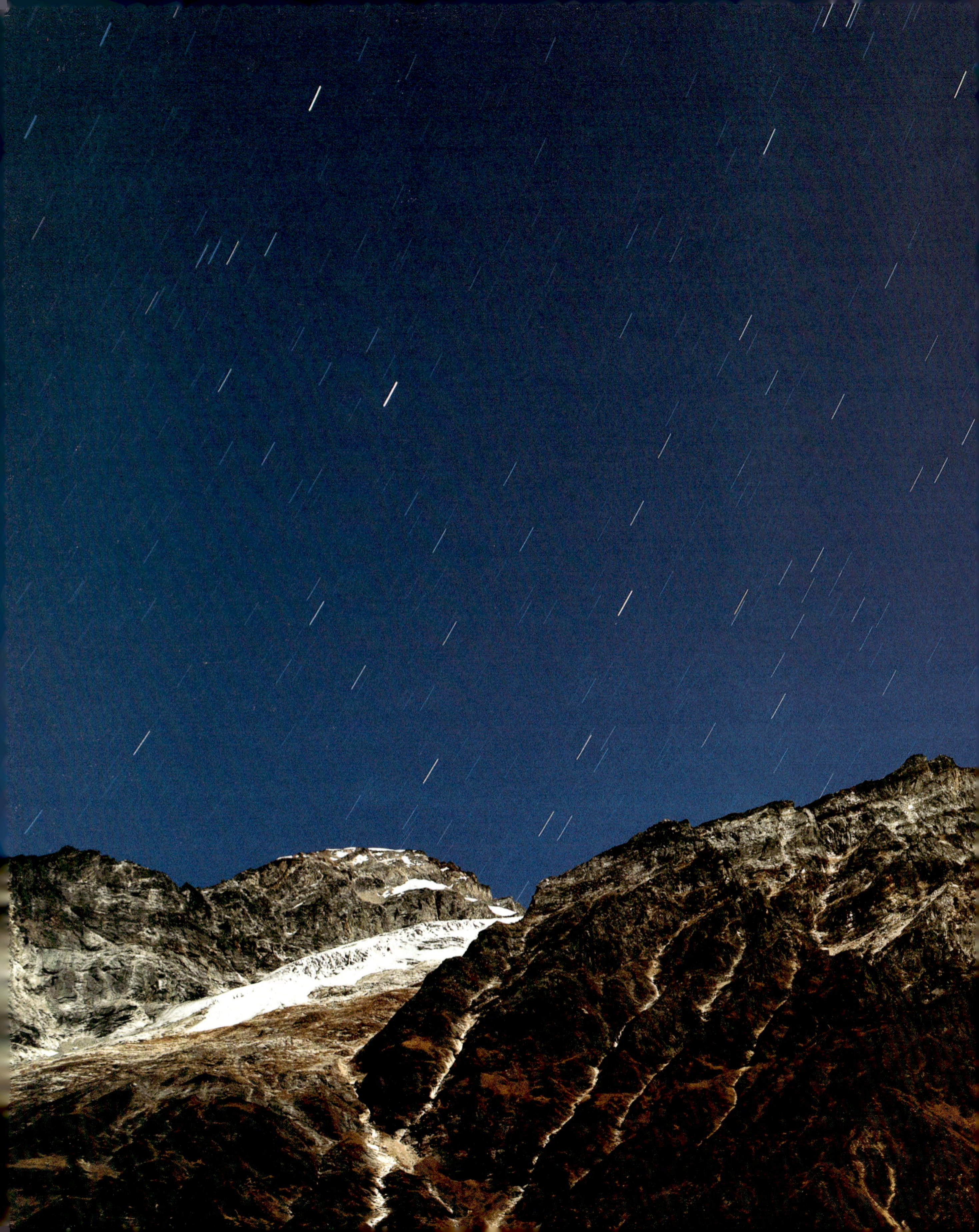

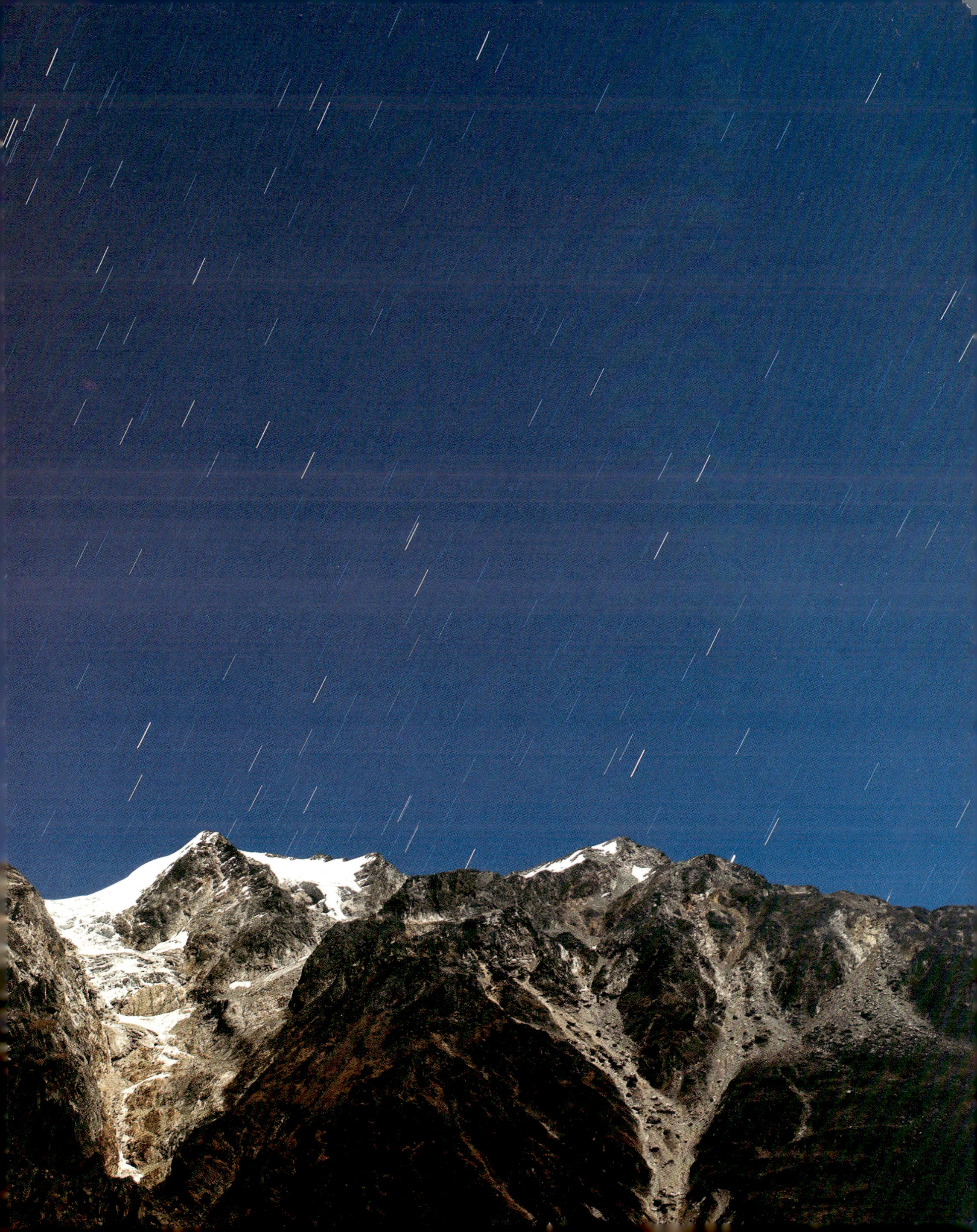

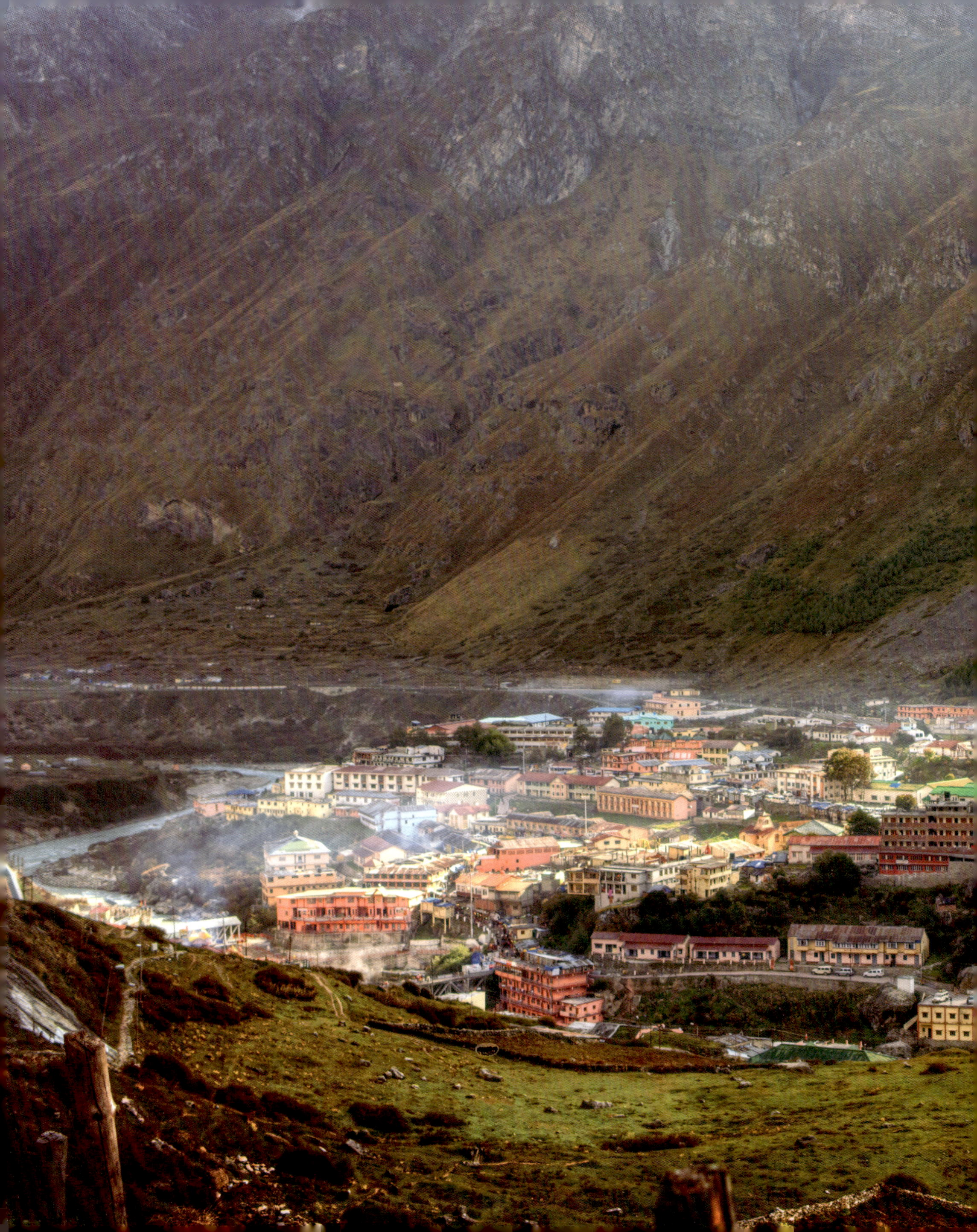

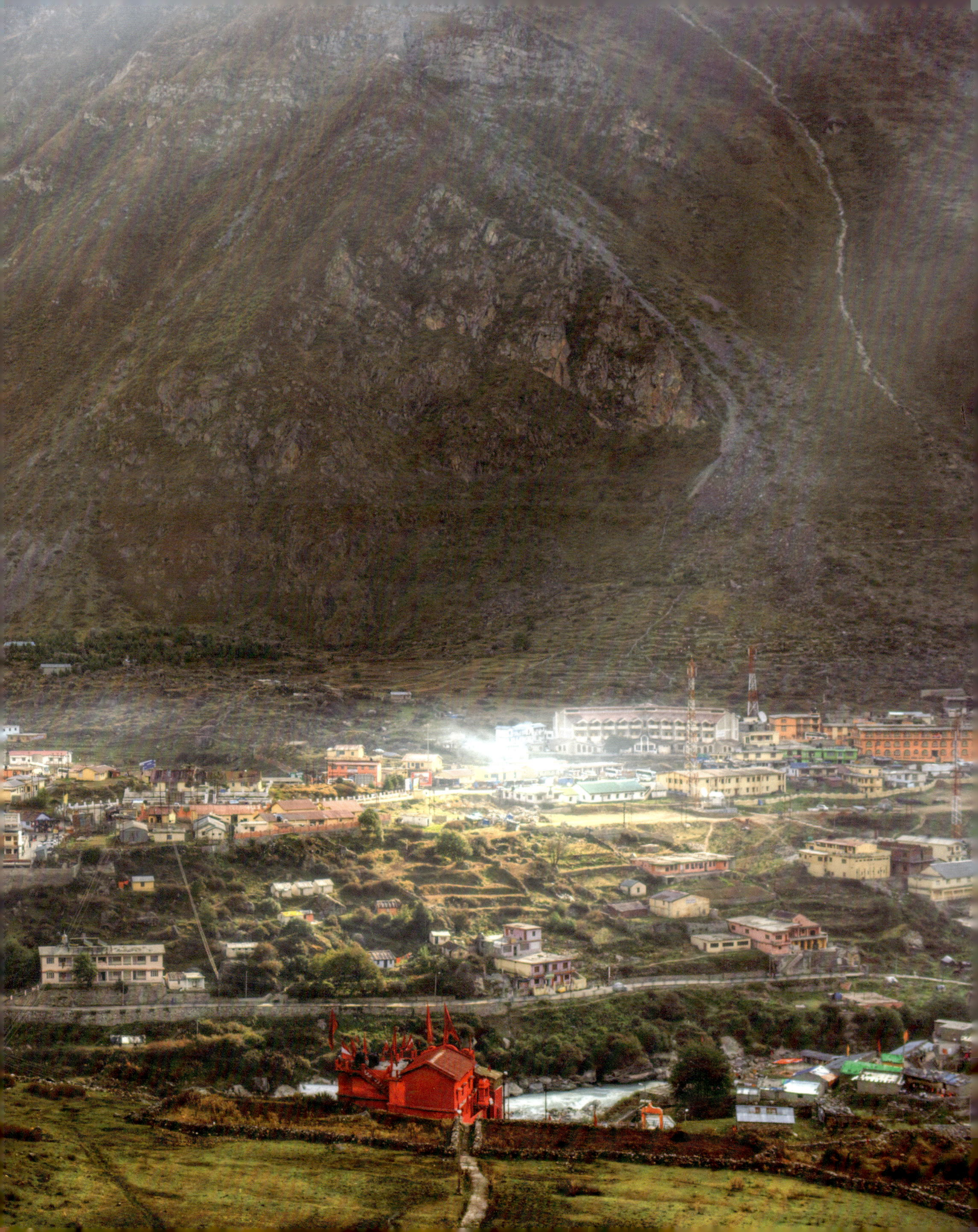

<< Karttika Yatra (Stars Rain)
< A Morning View of Badrinath Valley

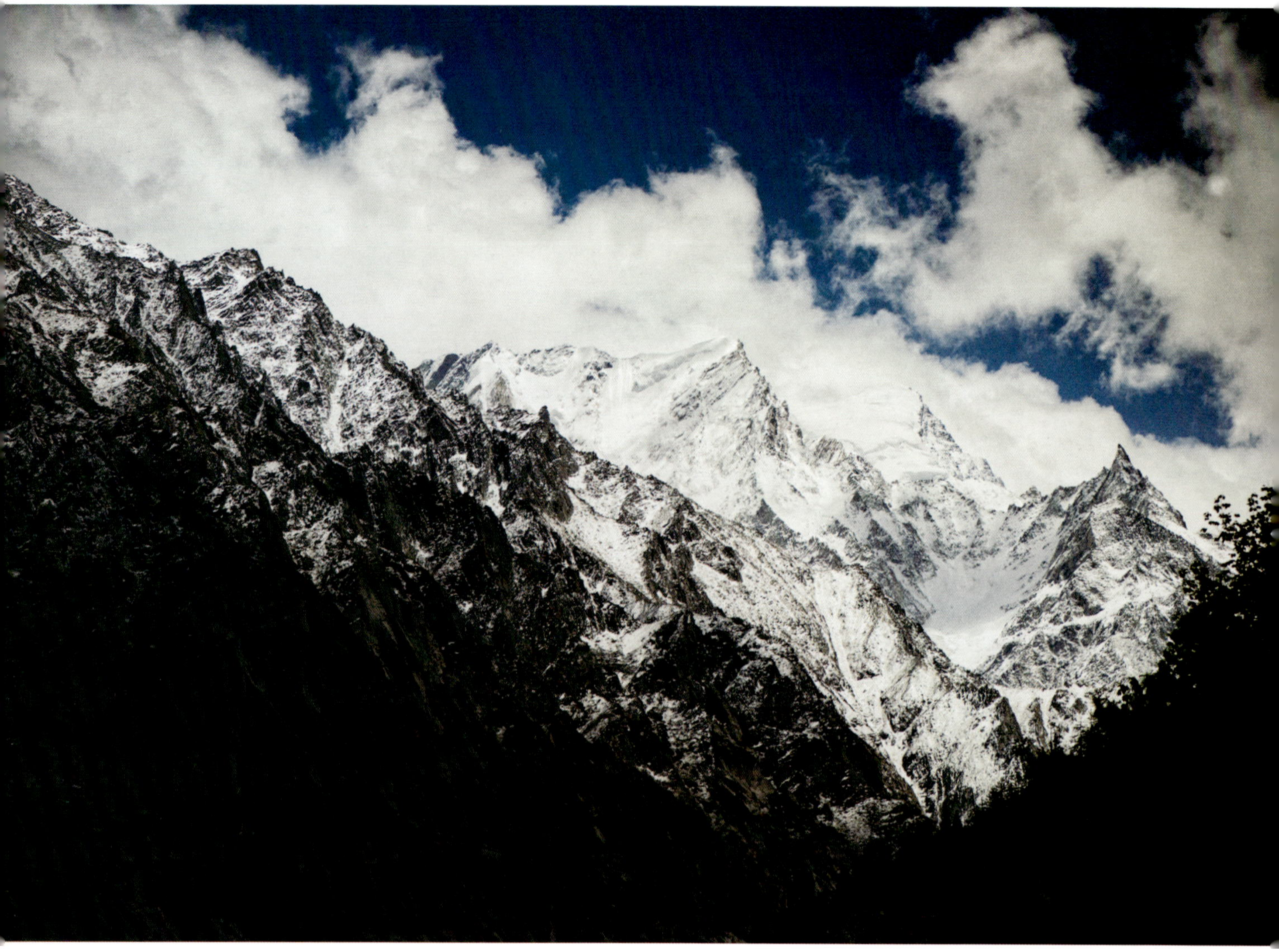

Gangotri Peaks

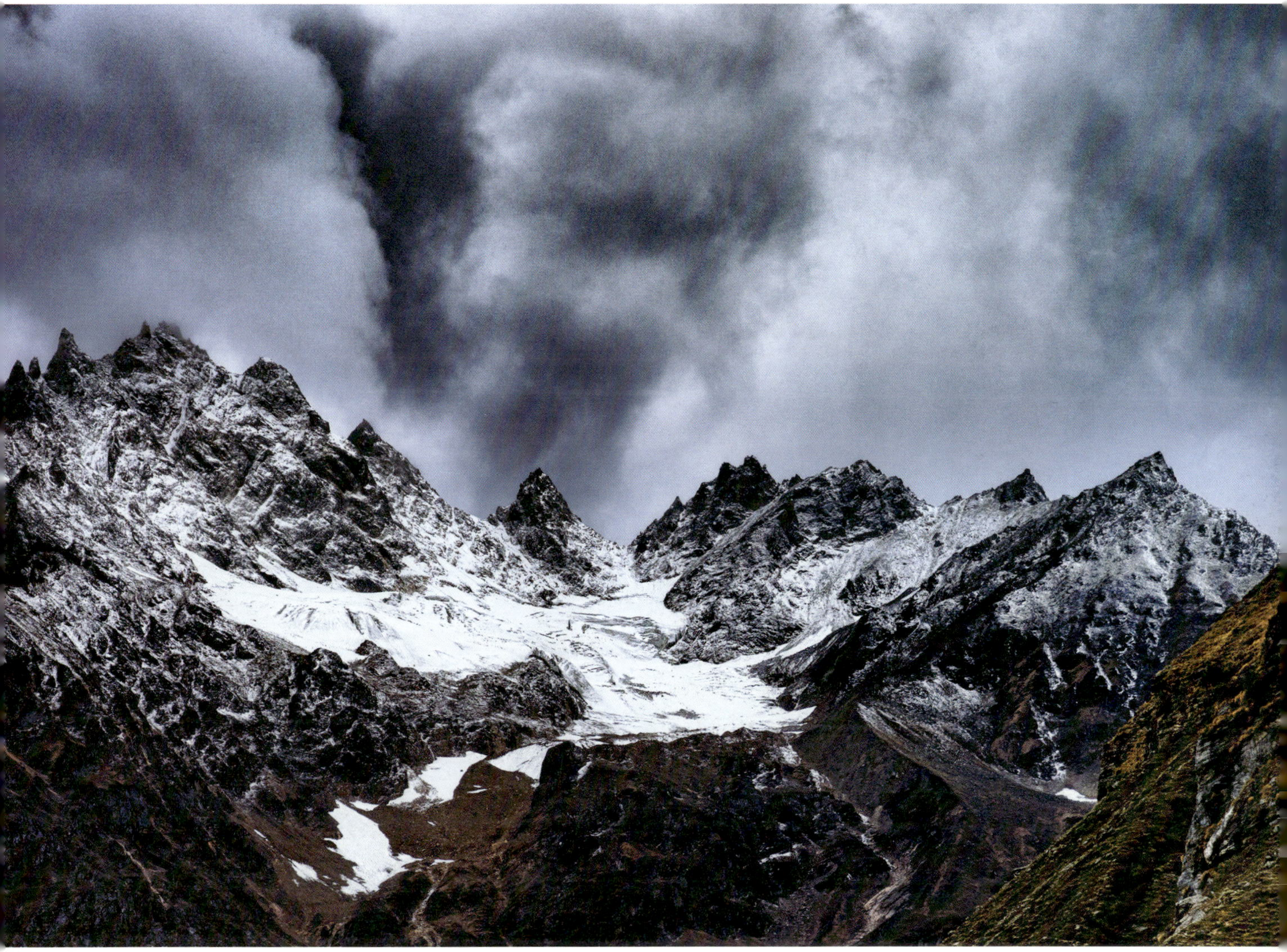

Crown of Narayana

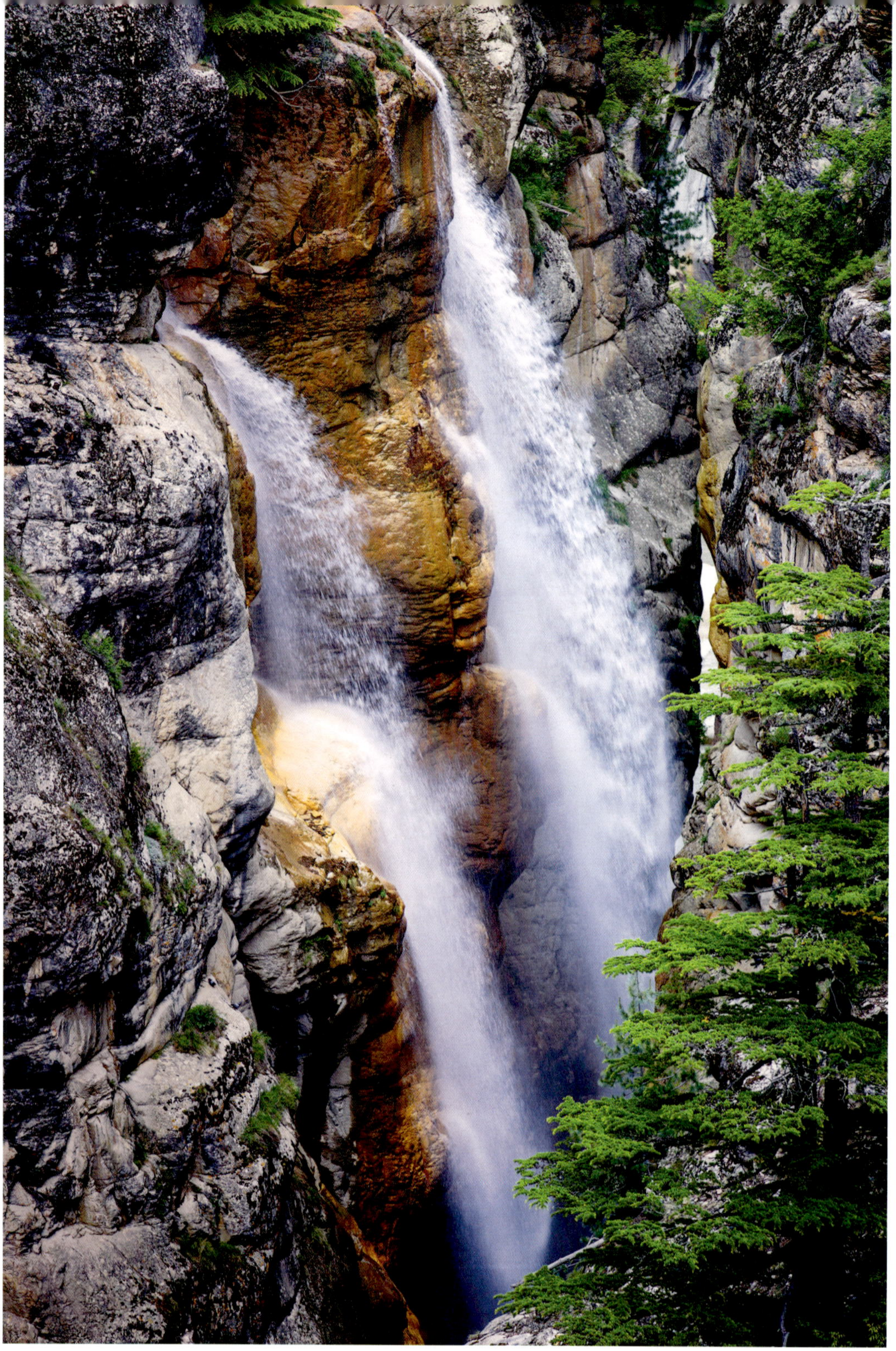

Rudra Ganga Falls

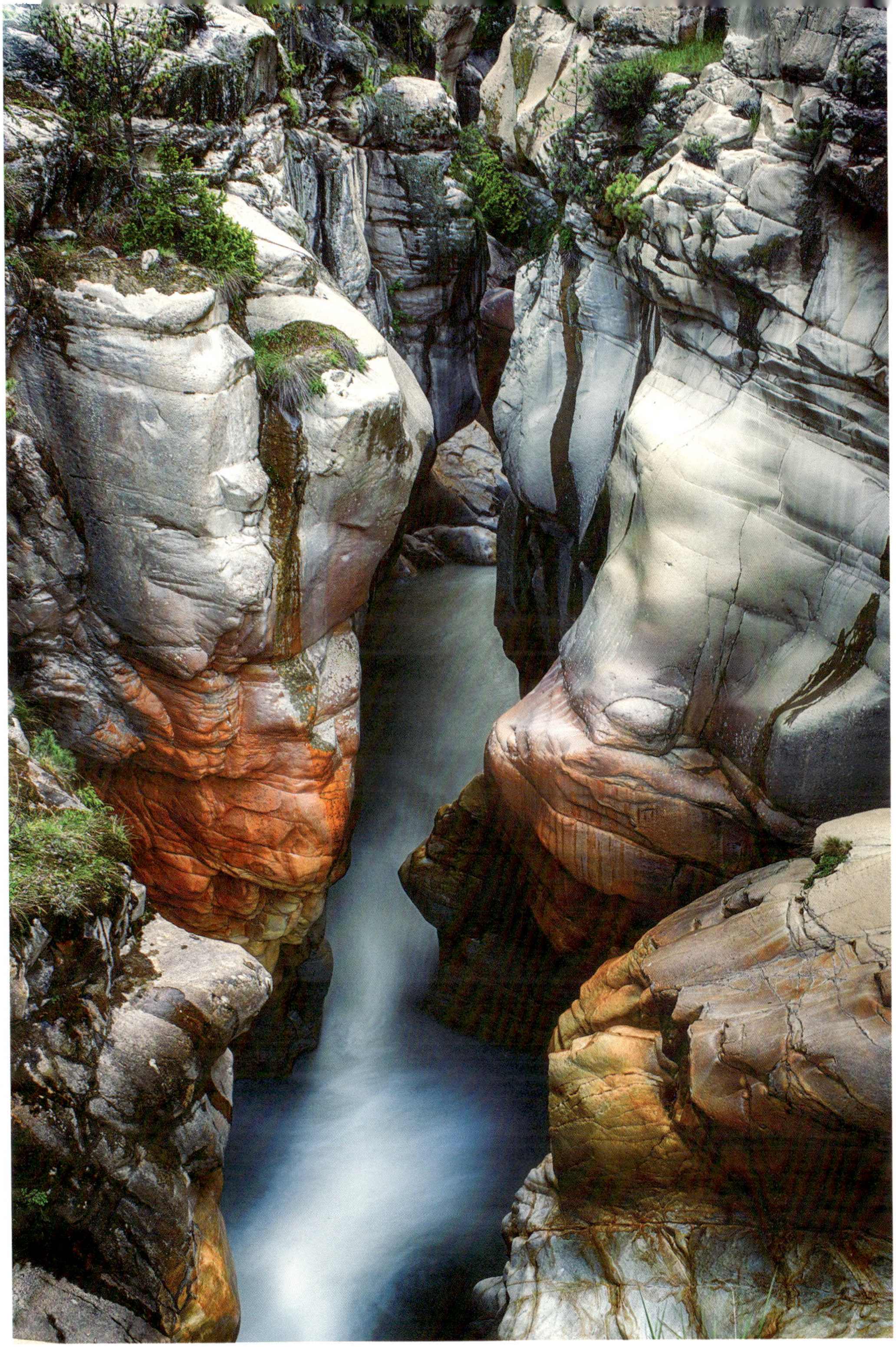

Sages of Lake Gauri

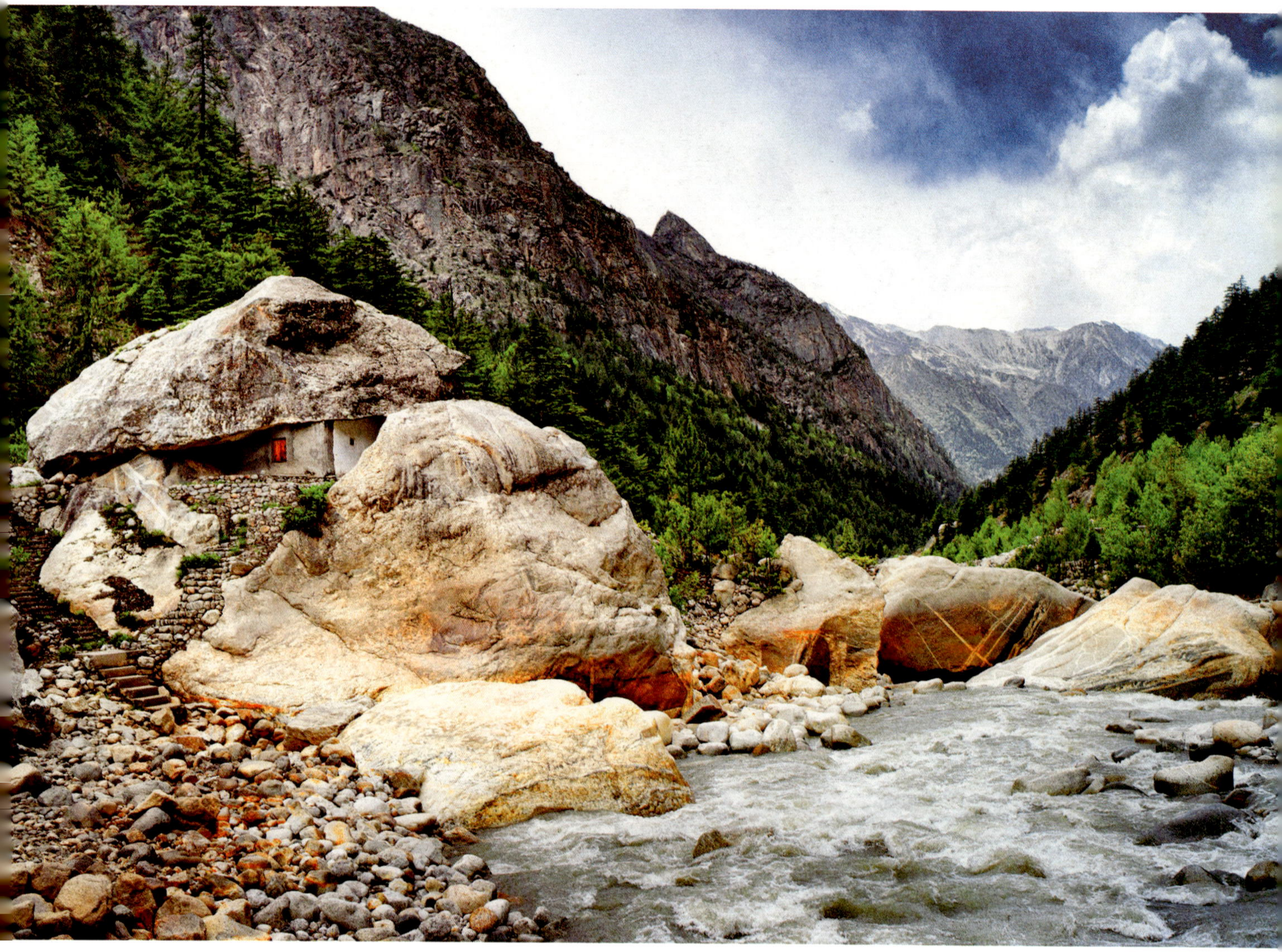

Gangotri Valley

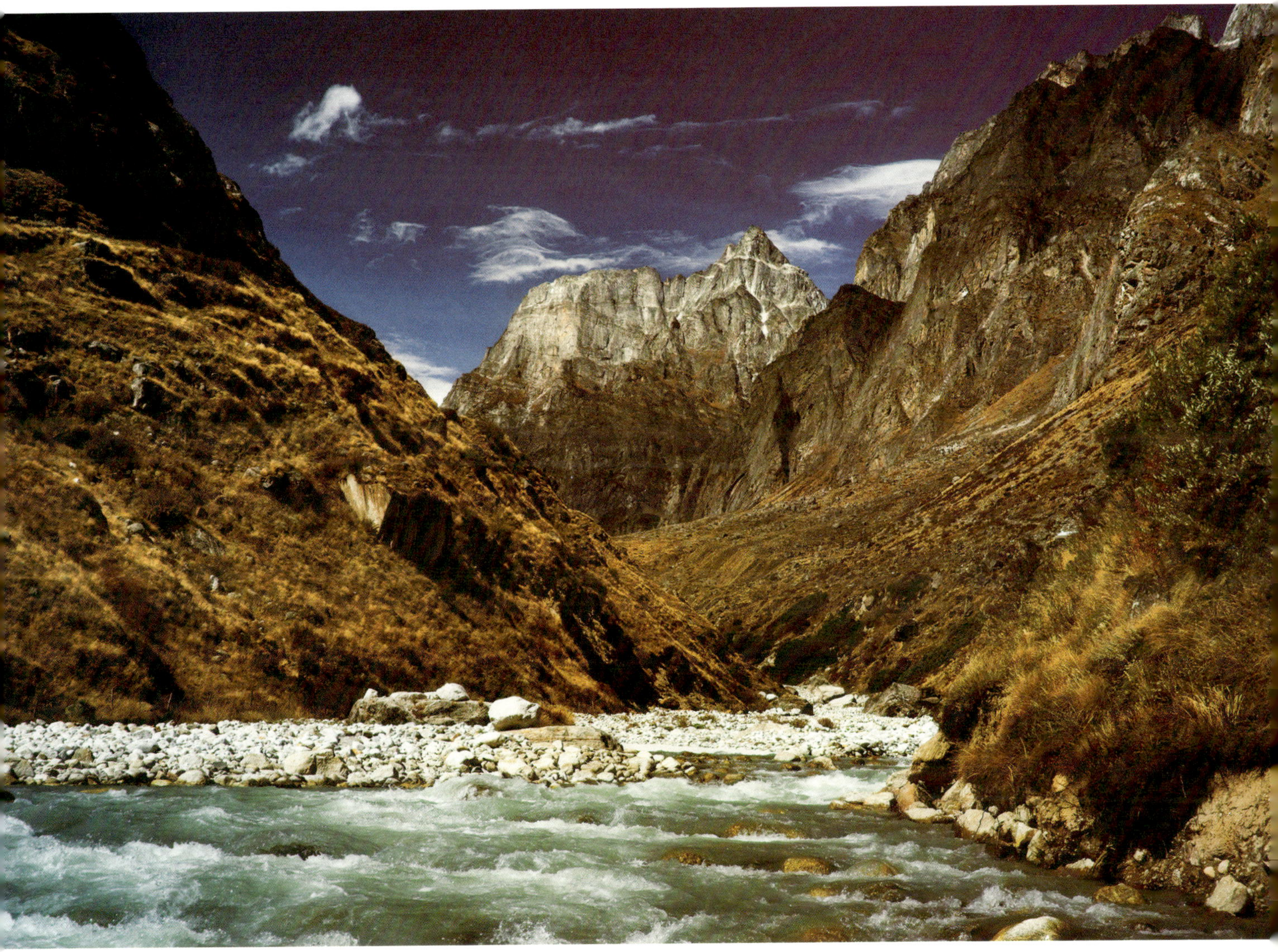

Alakananda Valley

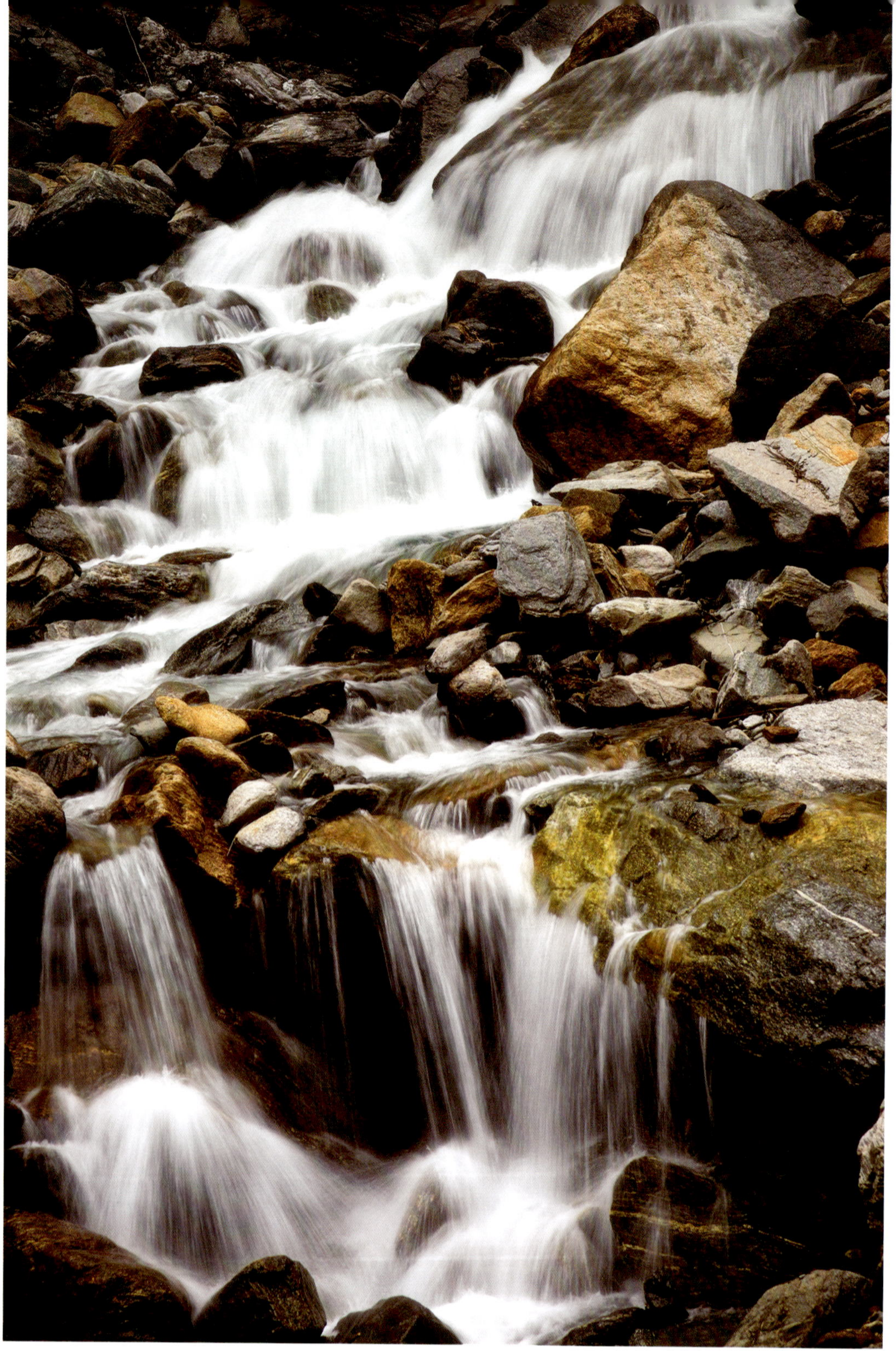

Dancing River

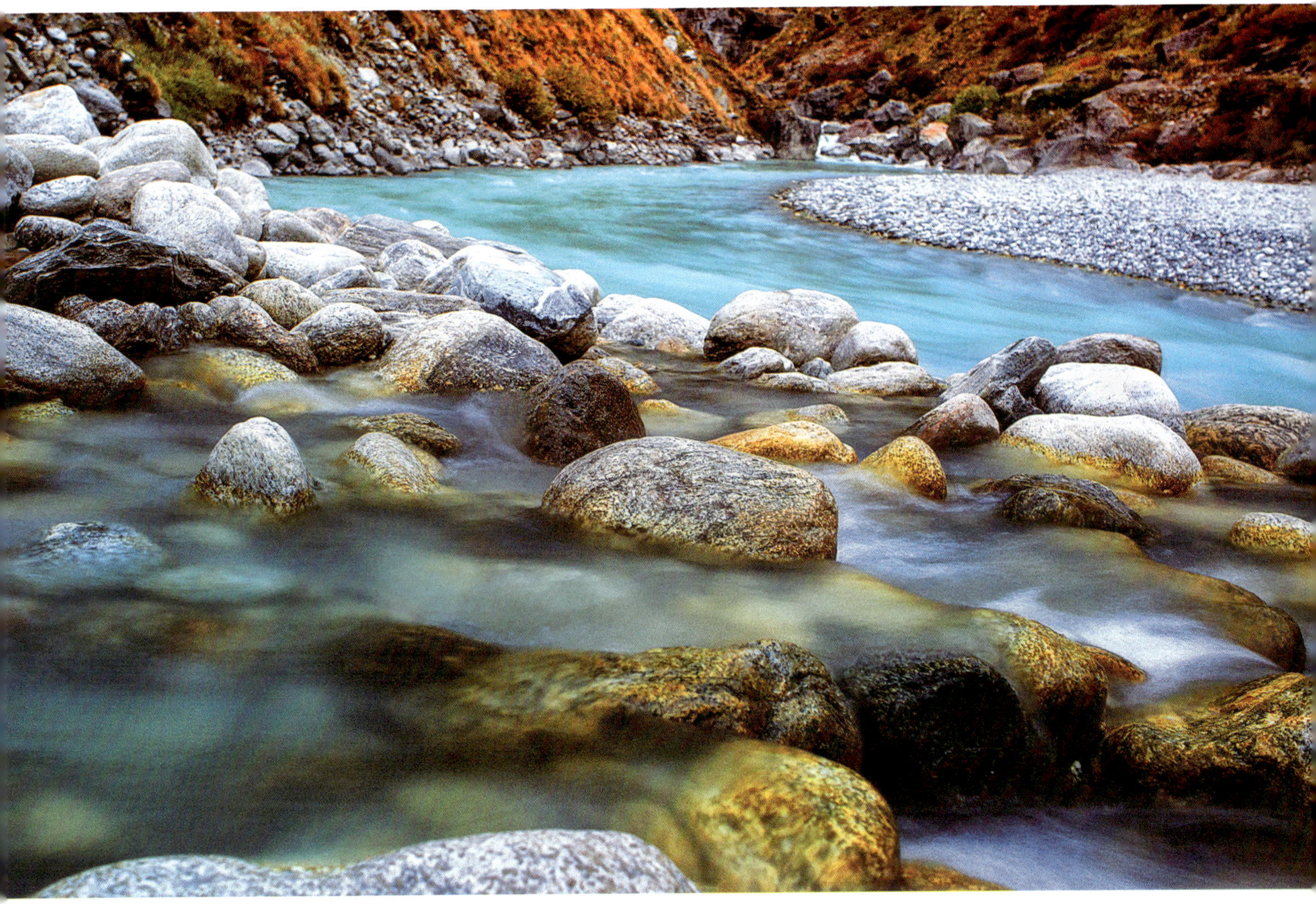

Keshava Confluence

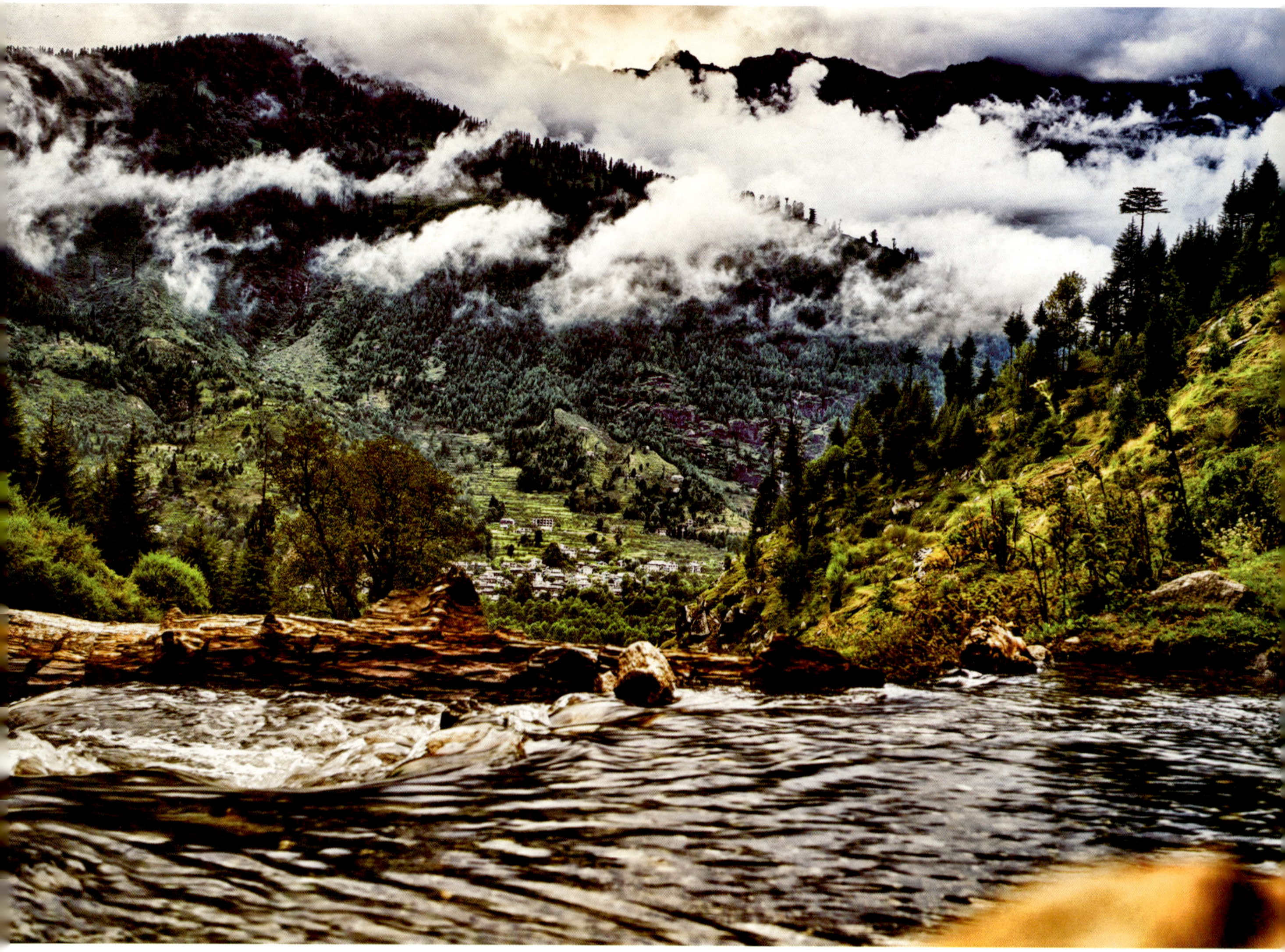

Yogini Forest

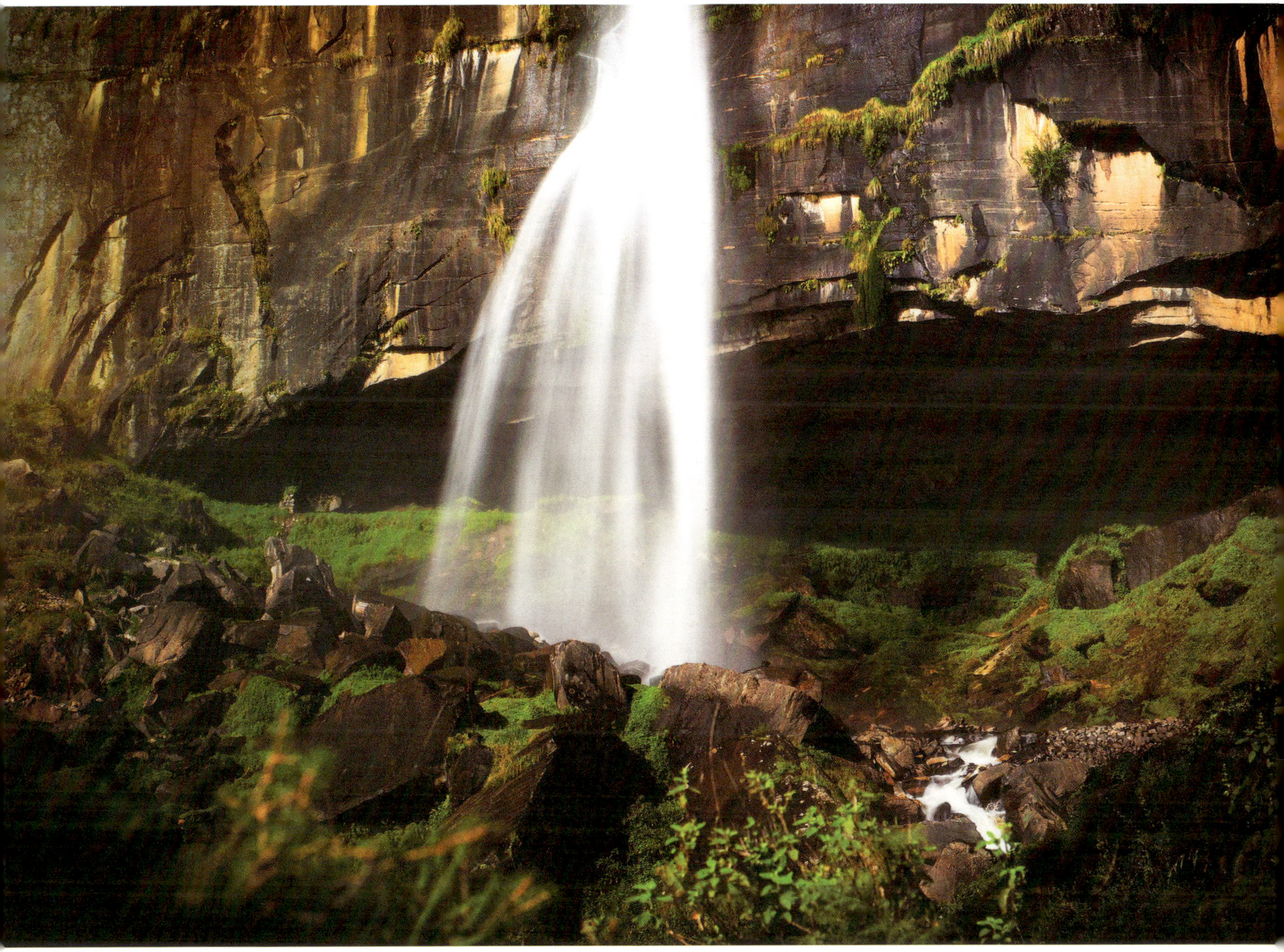

Yogini Waterfall

Nila Kantha Valley >

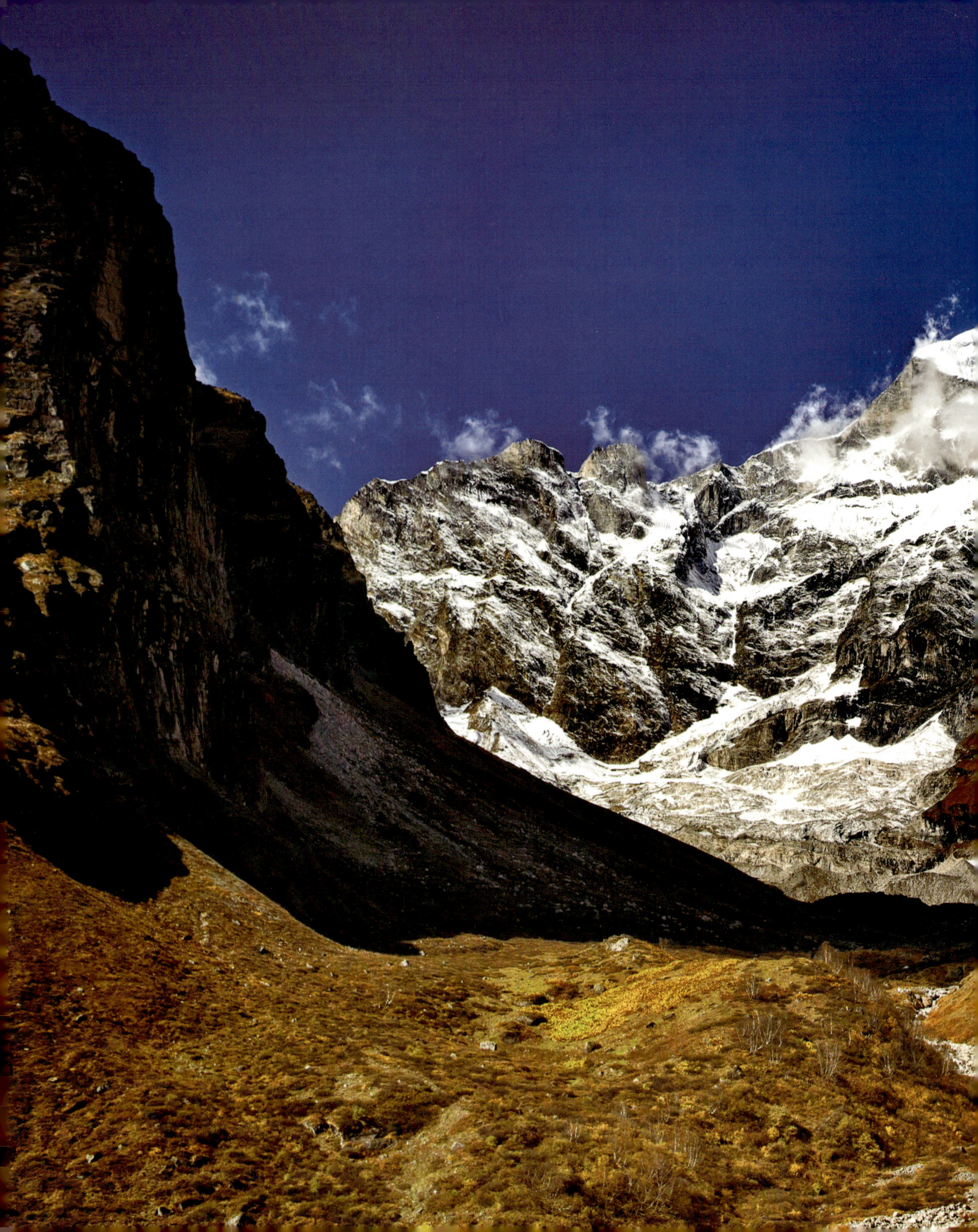

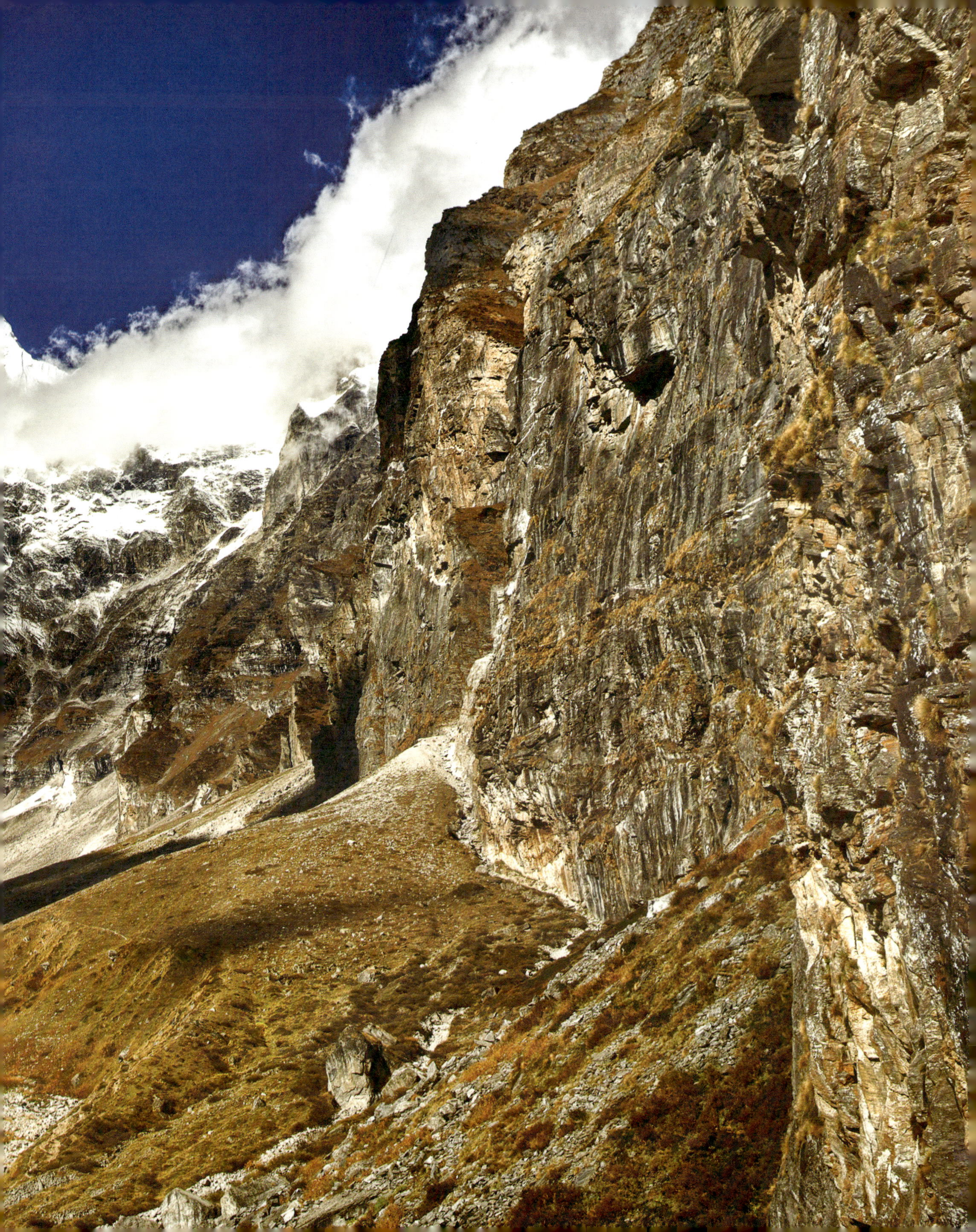

SACRED PLACES

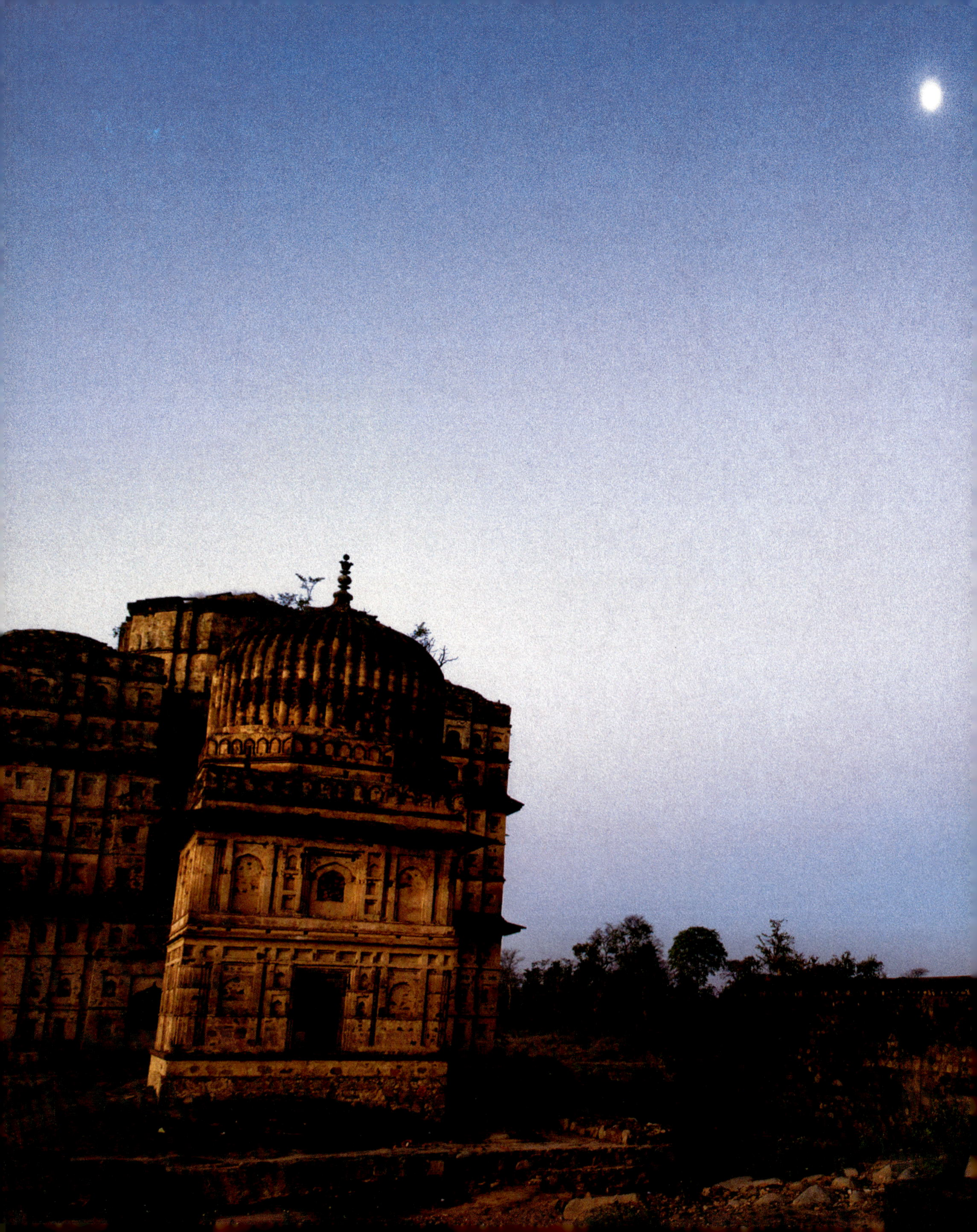

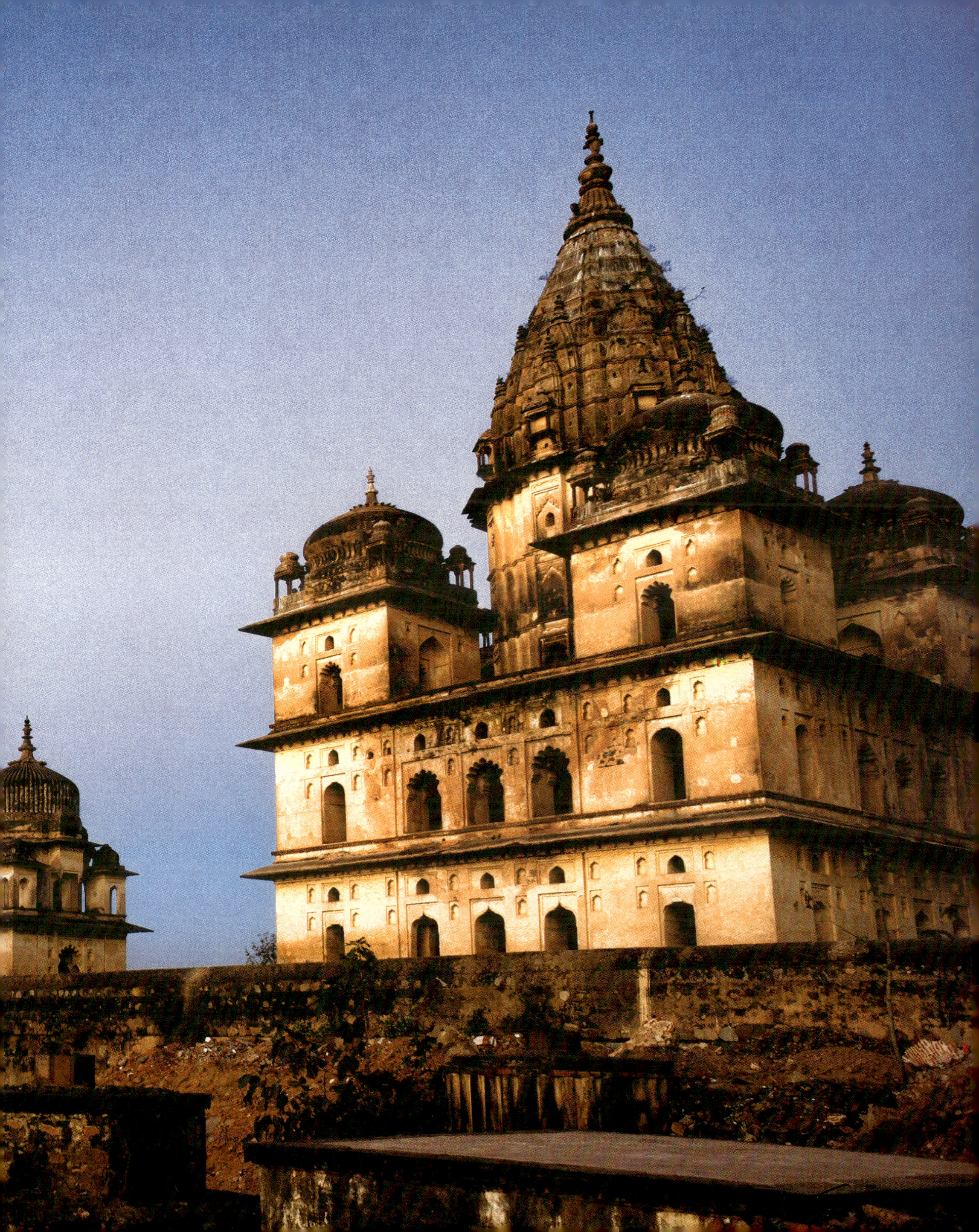

< Moon over Orchha

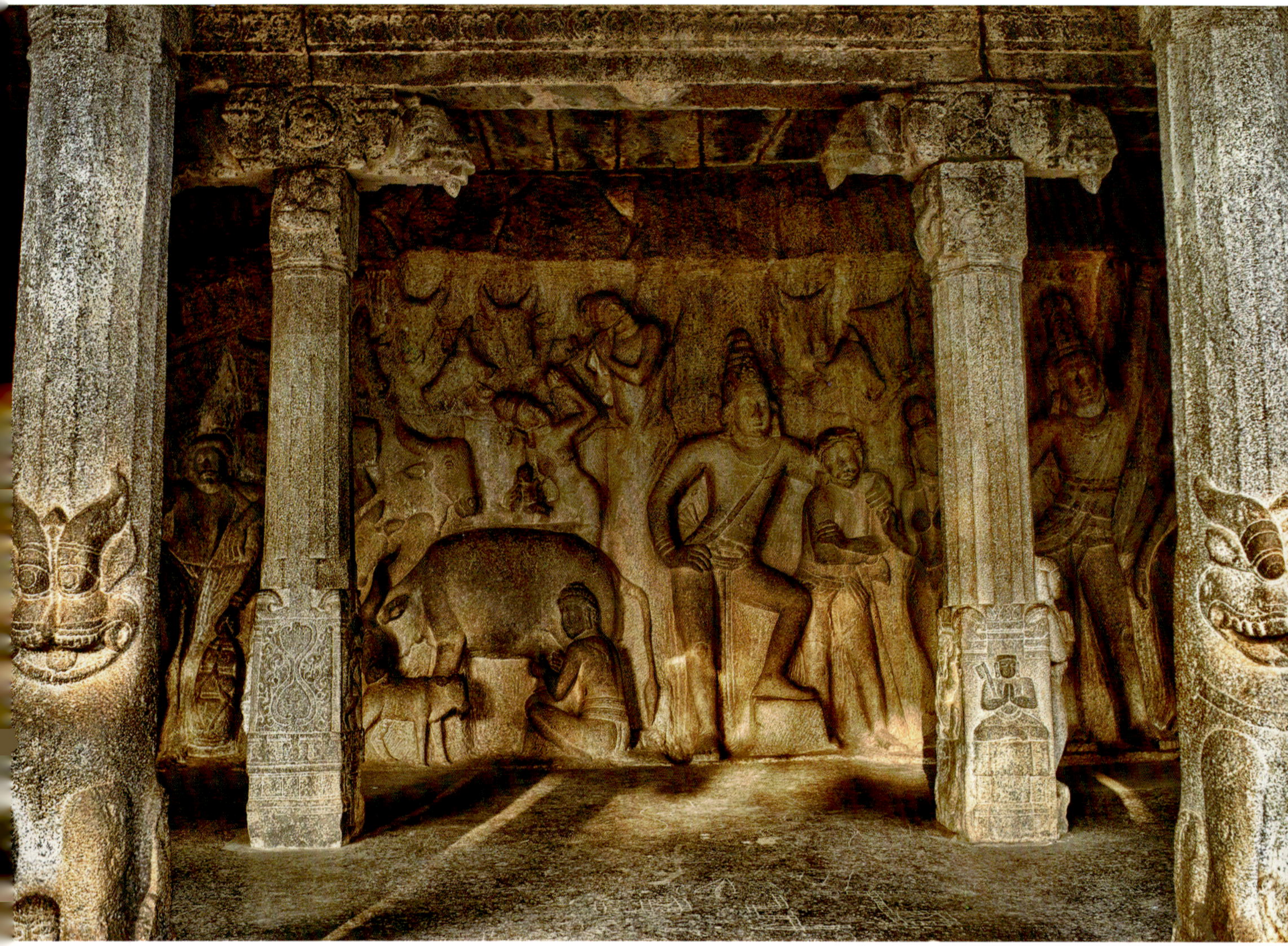

Krishna Mandapam

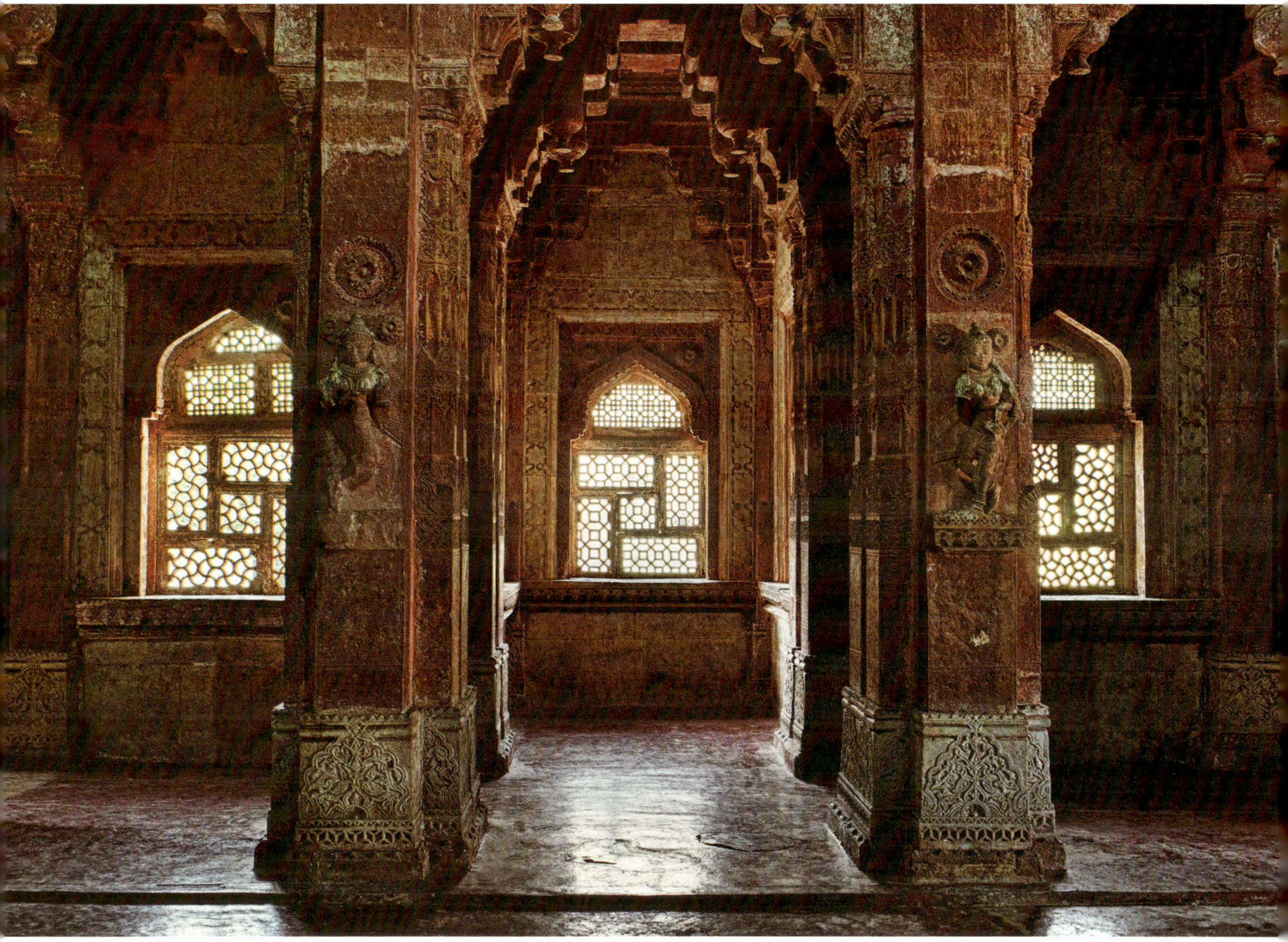

Jagat Shiromani Temple

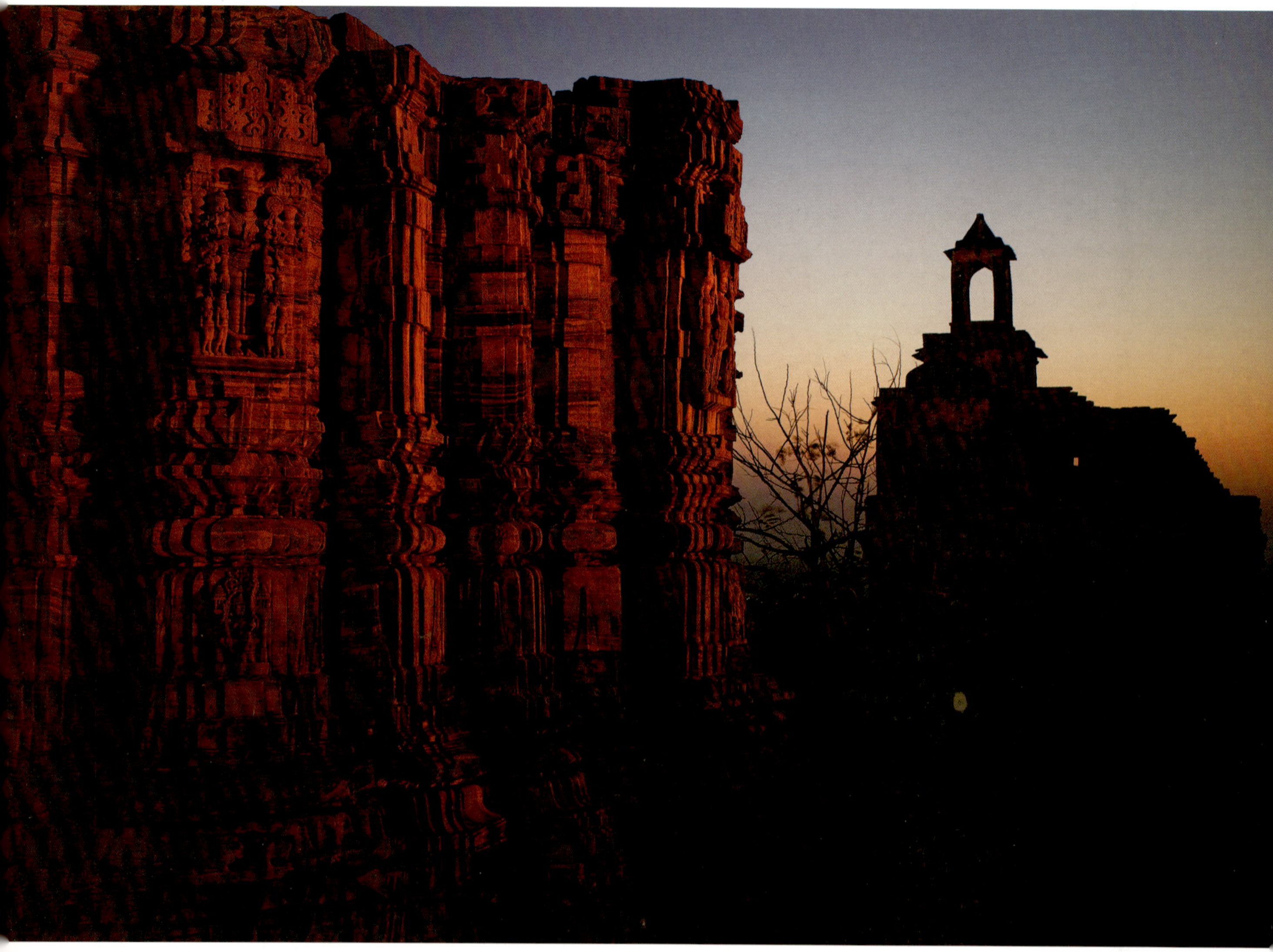

The Chittorgarh Ruins

The Tower of Victory >

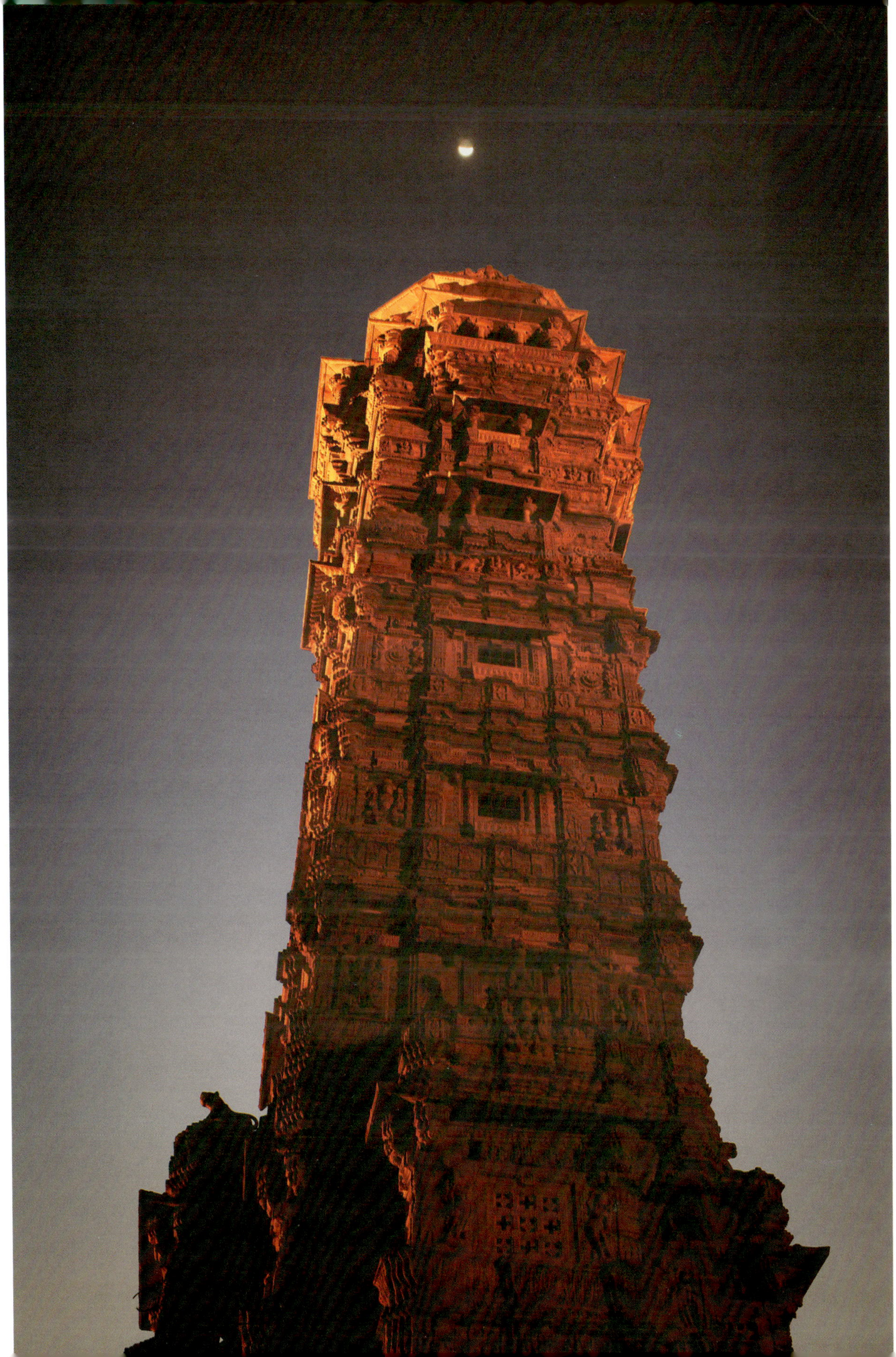

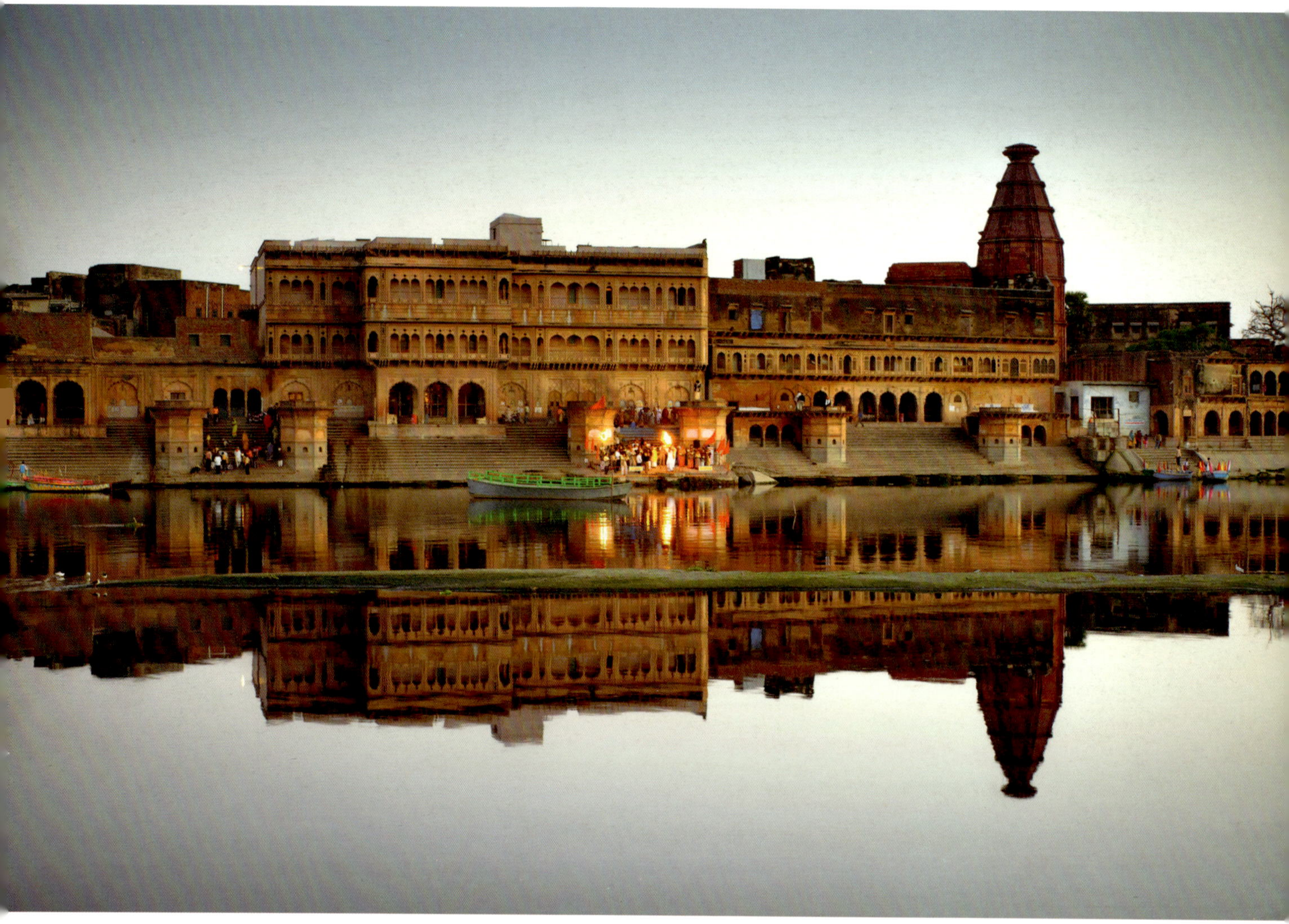

Keshi Ghat meditation

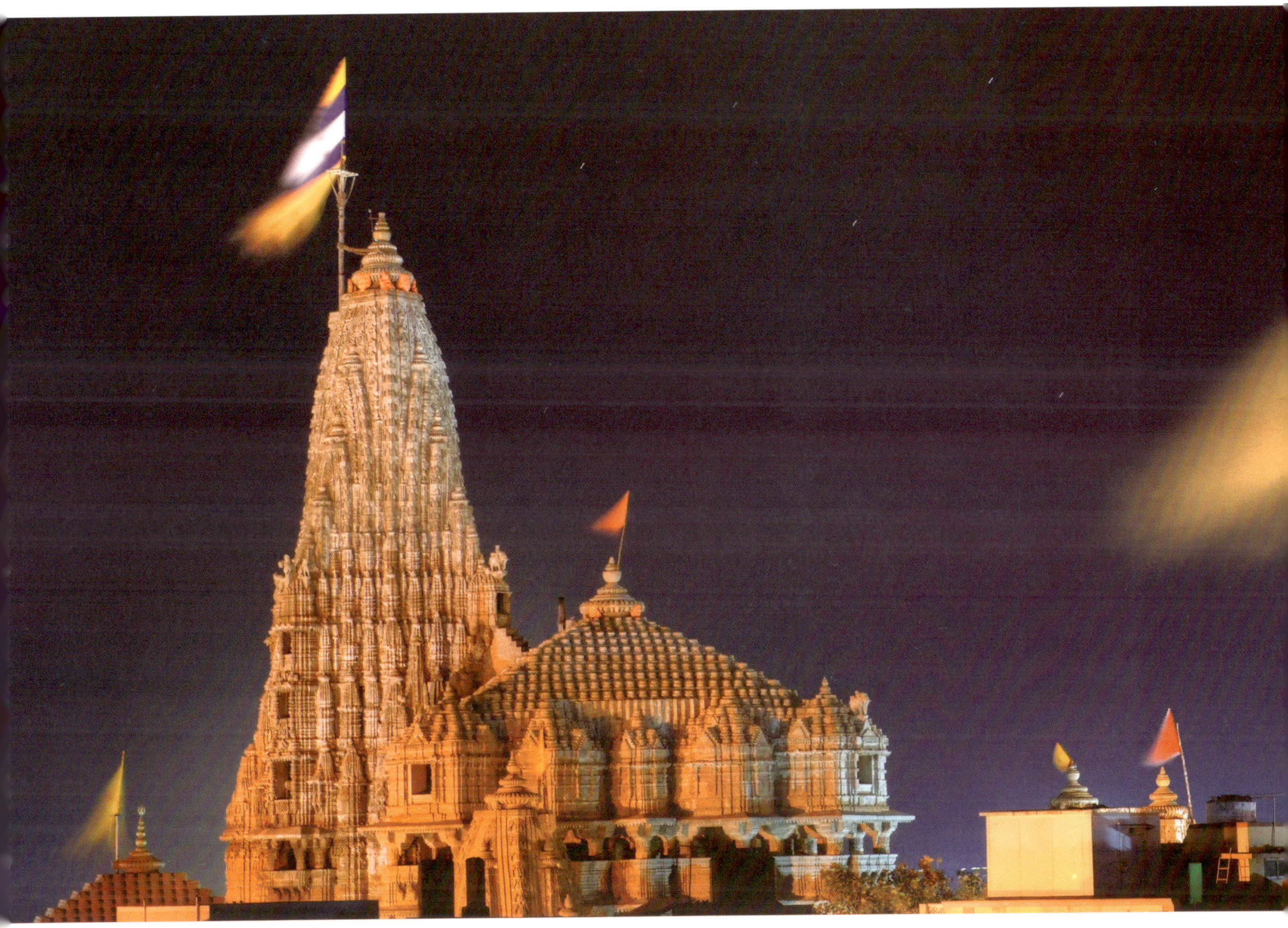

Dwaraka Yatra (Krishna Temple)

Manikarnika Ghat >

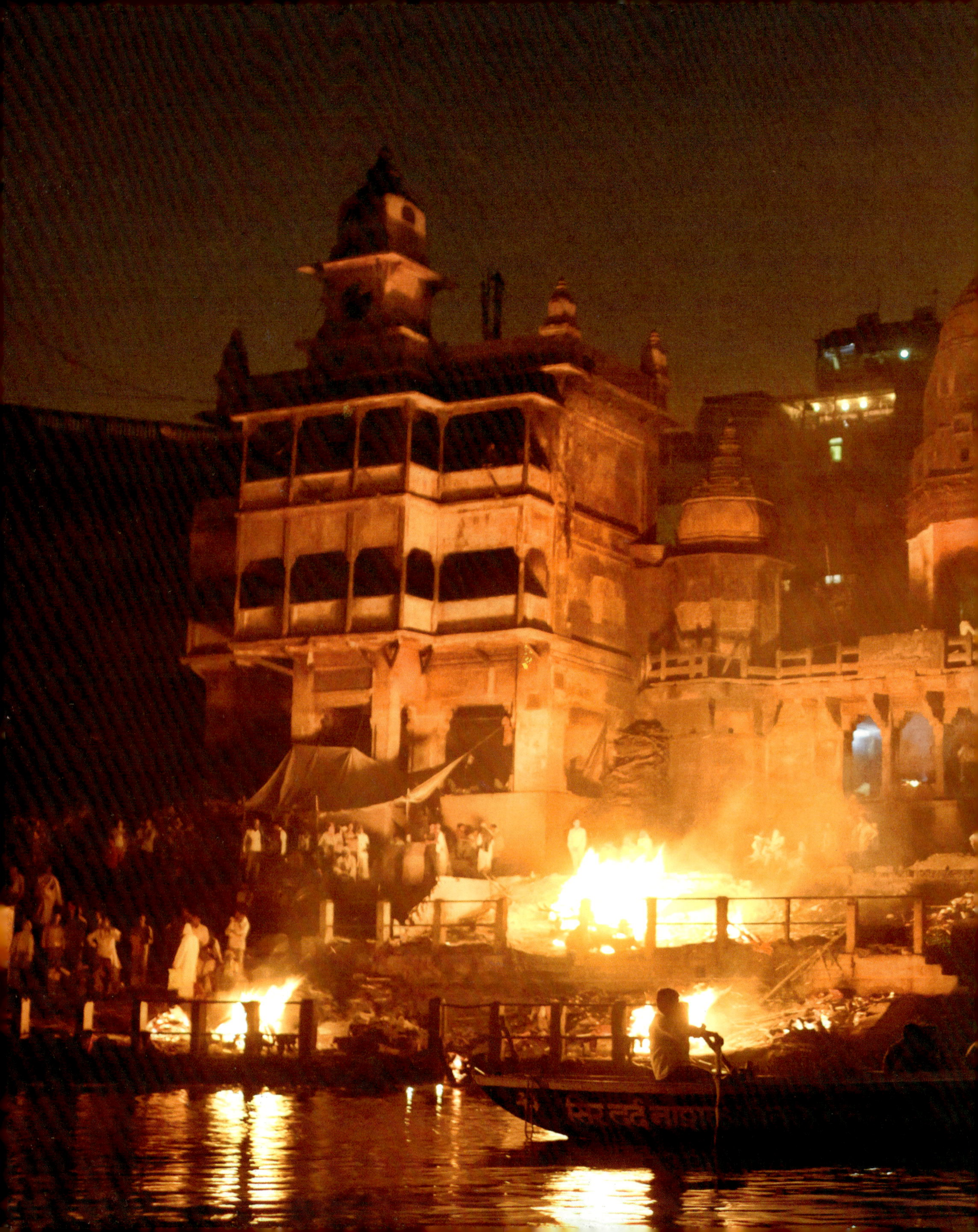

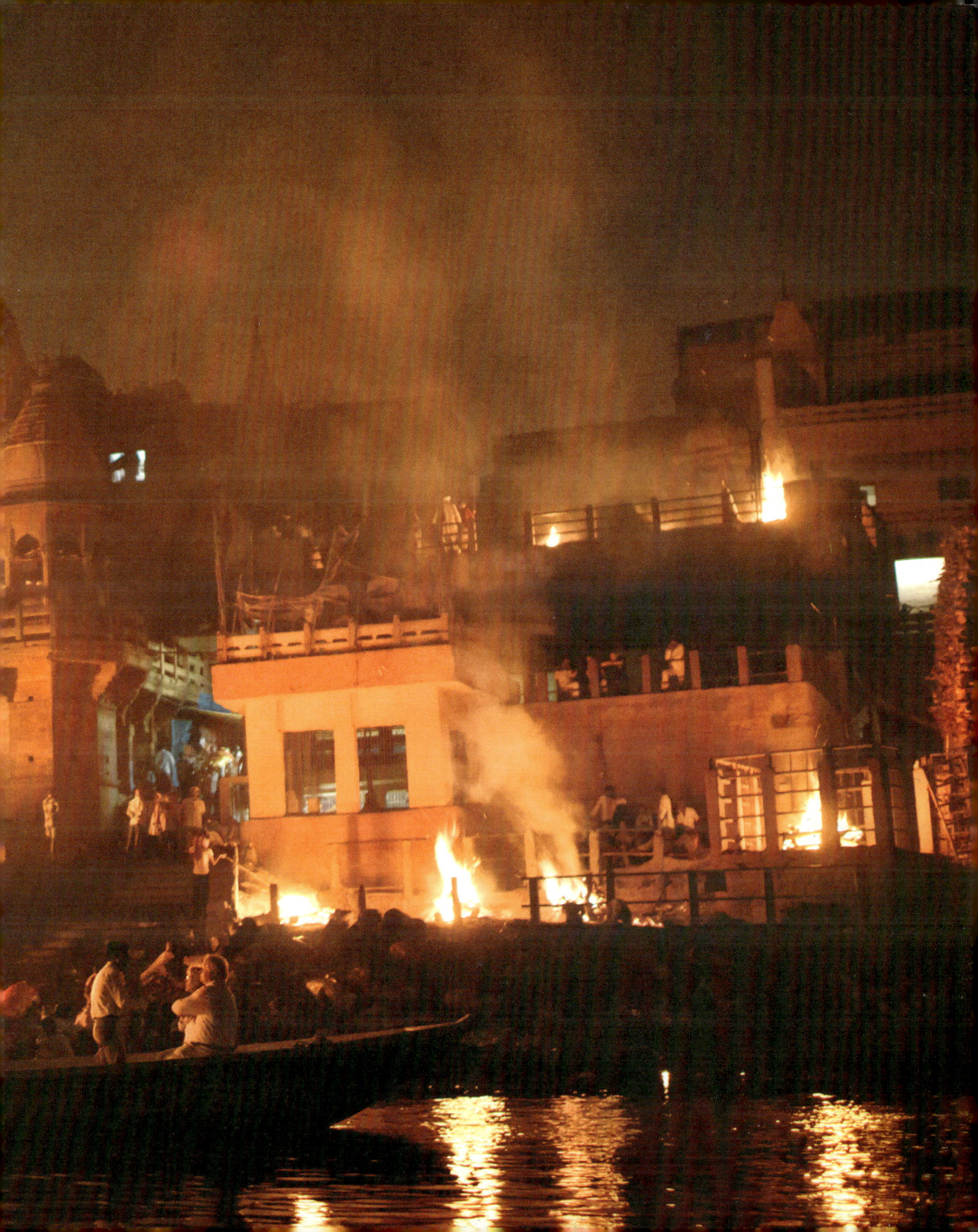

PORTRAITS

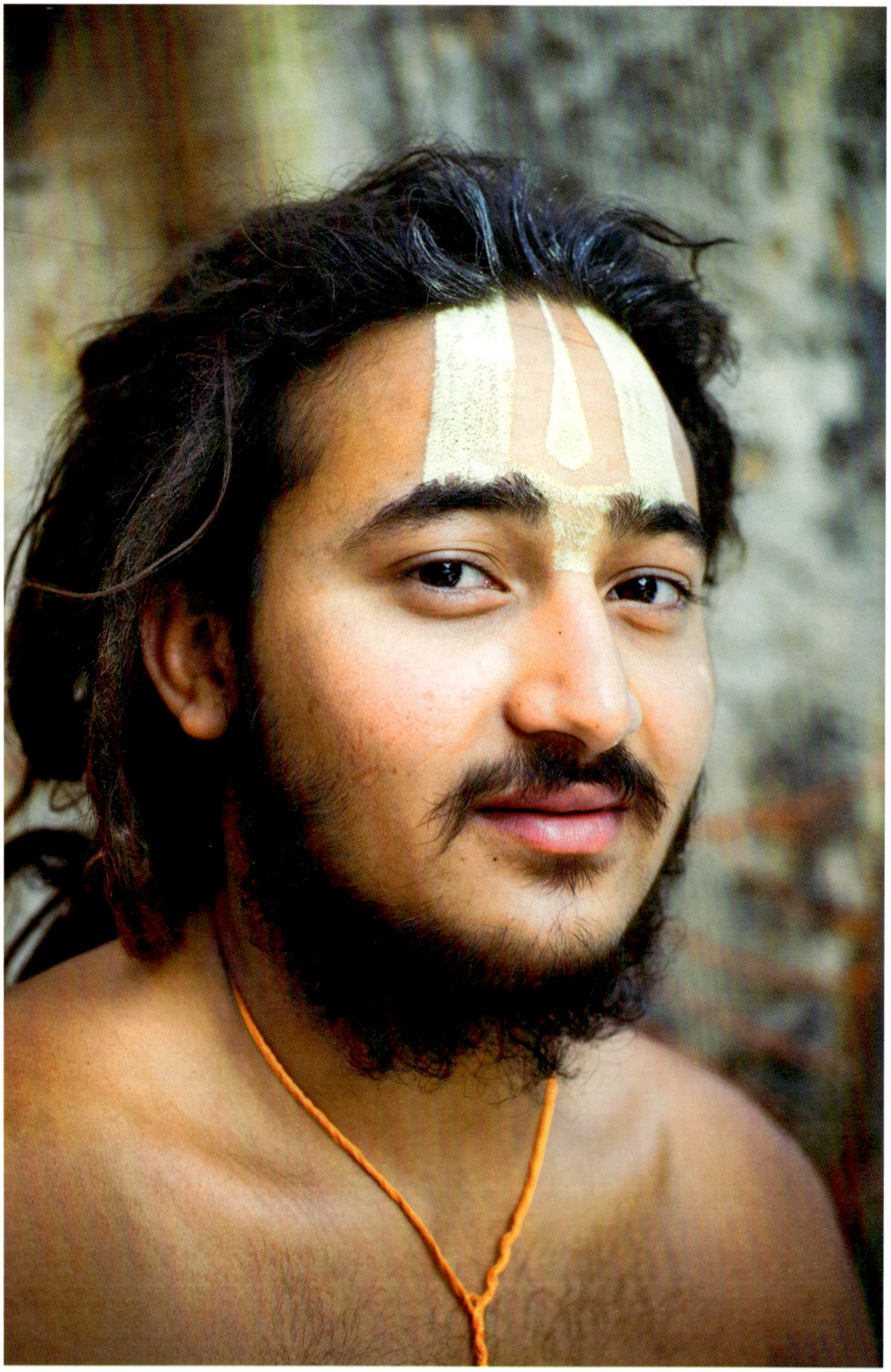

Sita Rama Dasa

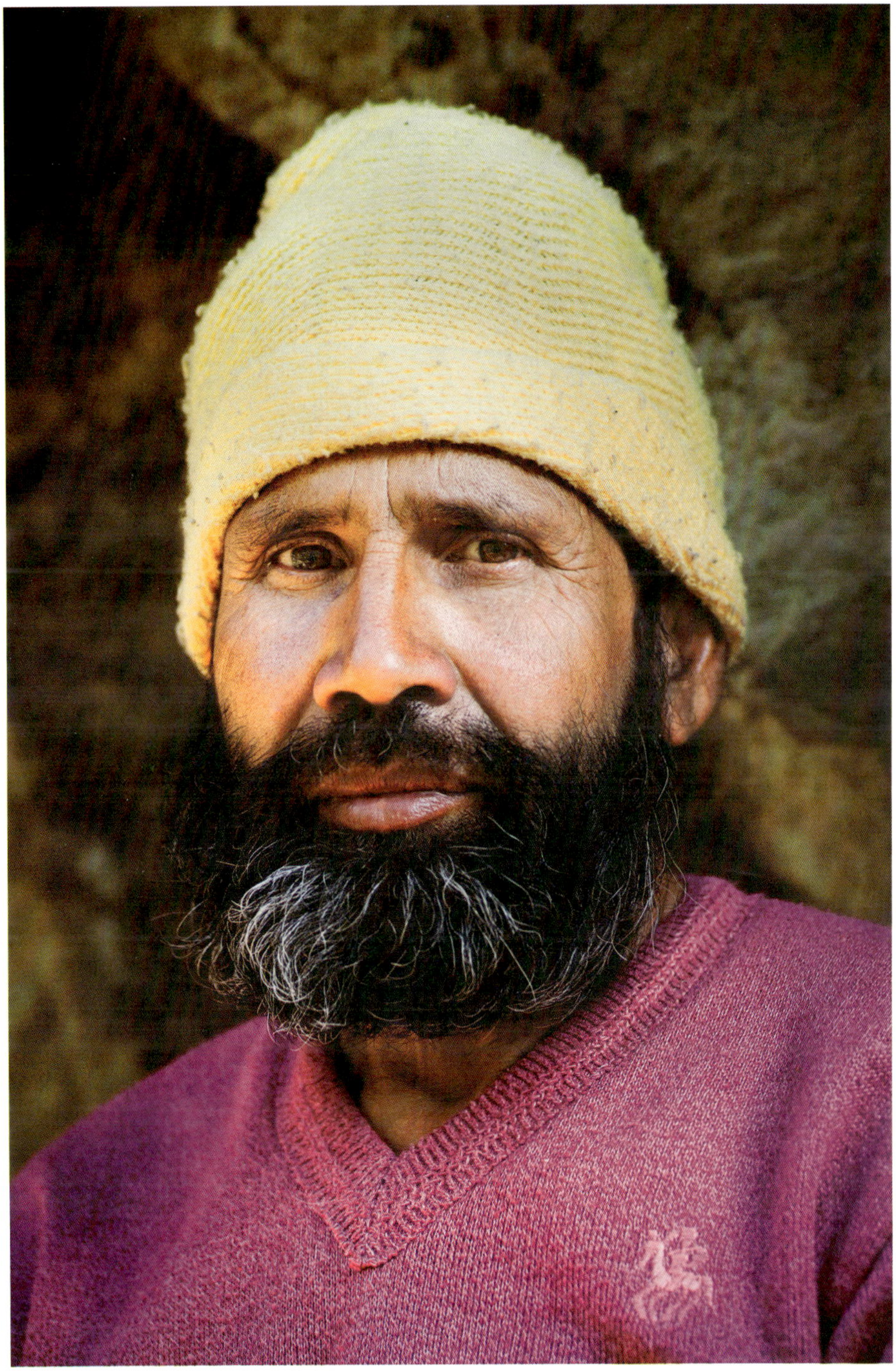

Sadhu Ramesh

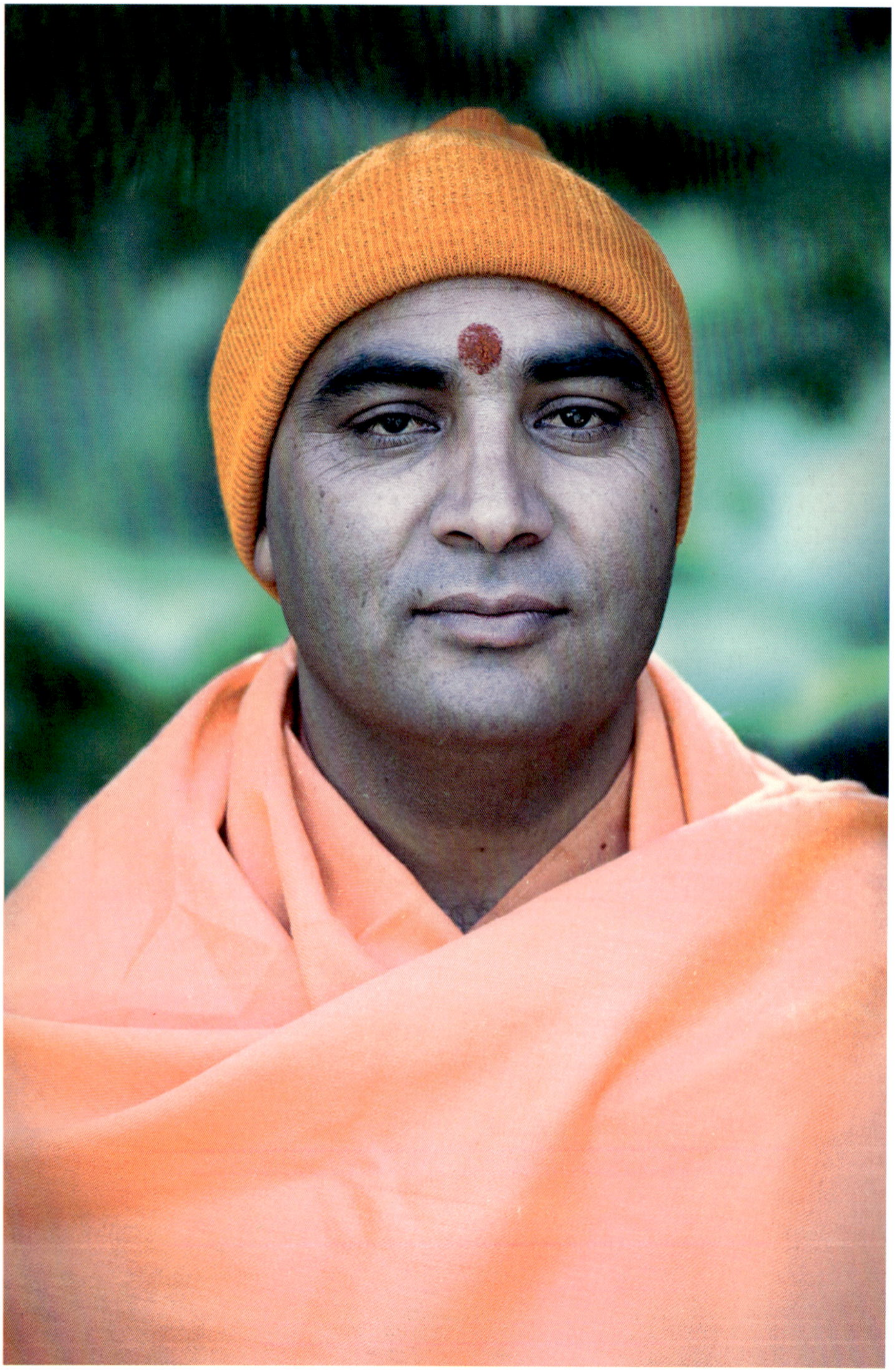

Raghavendra Swami

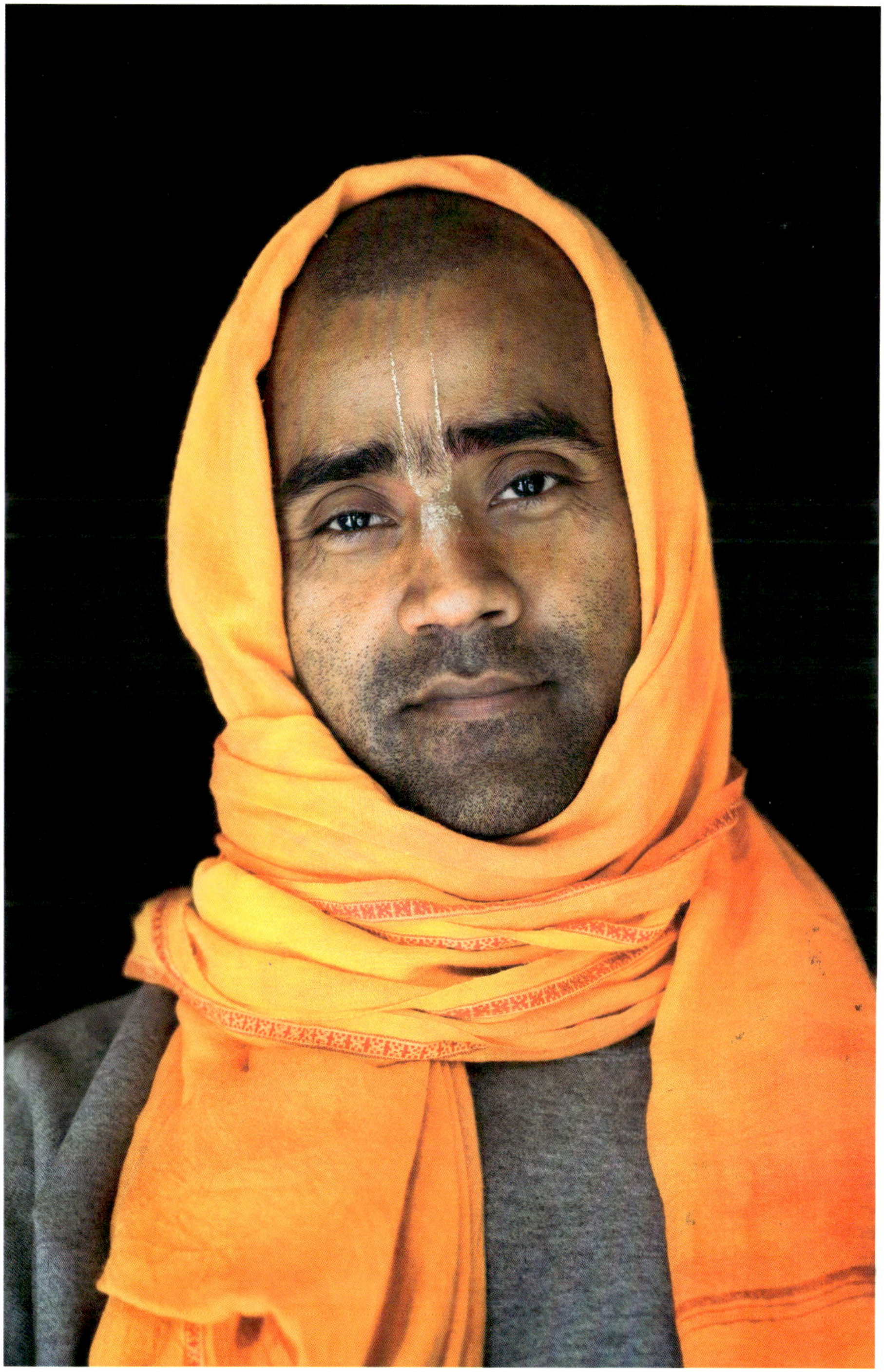

Krishnananda Dasa

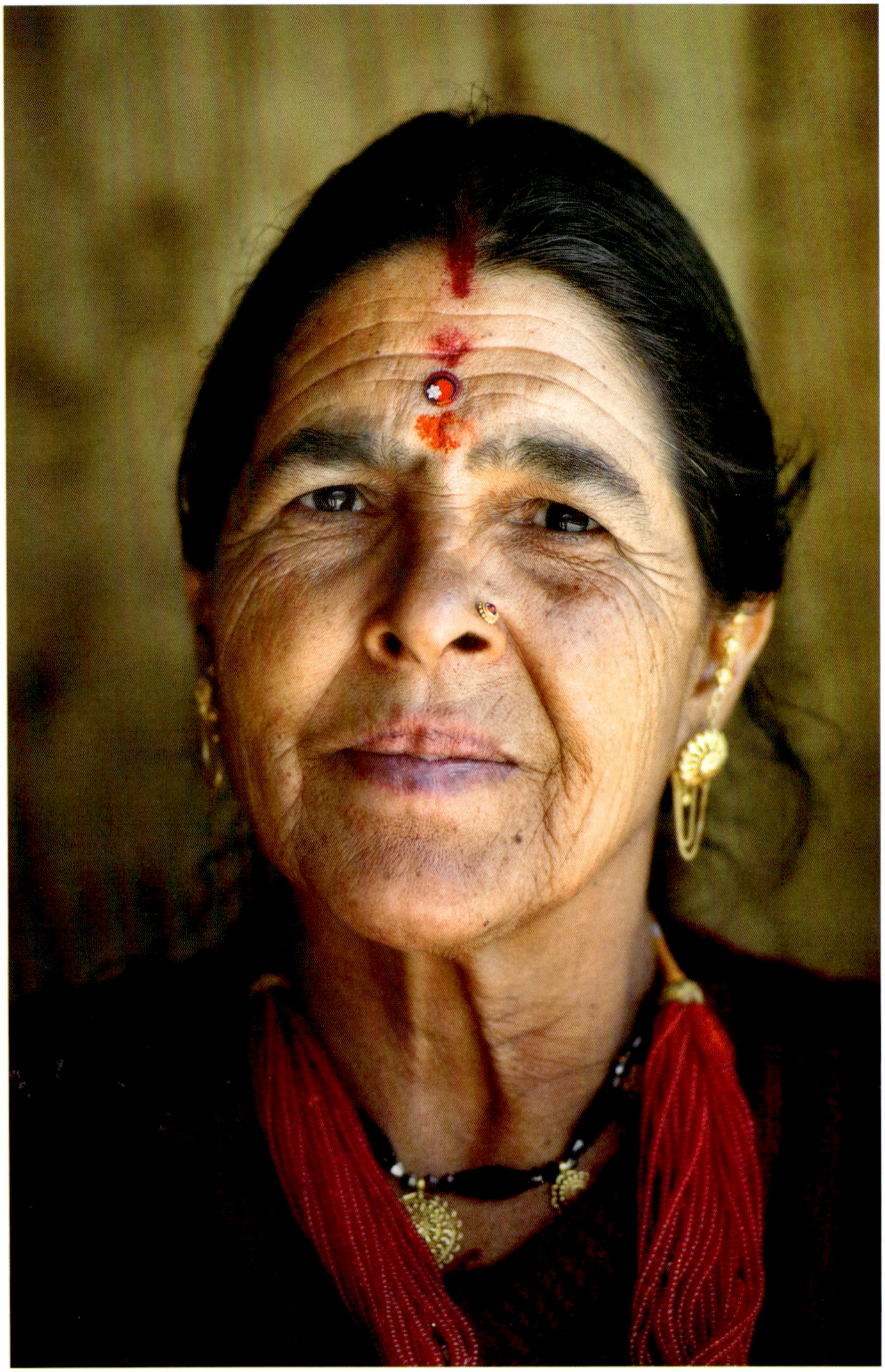

Subhadra Devi

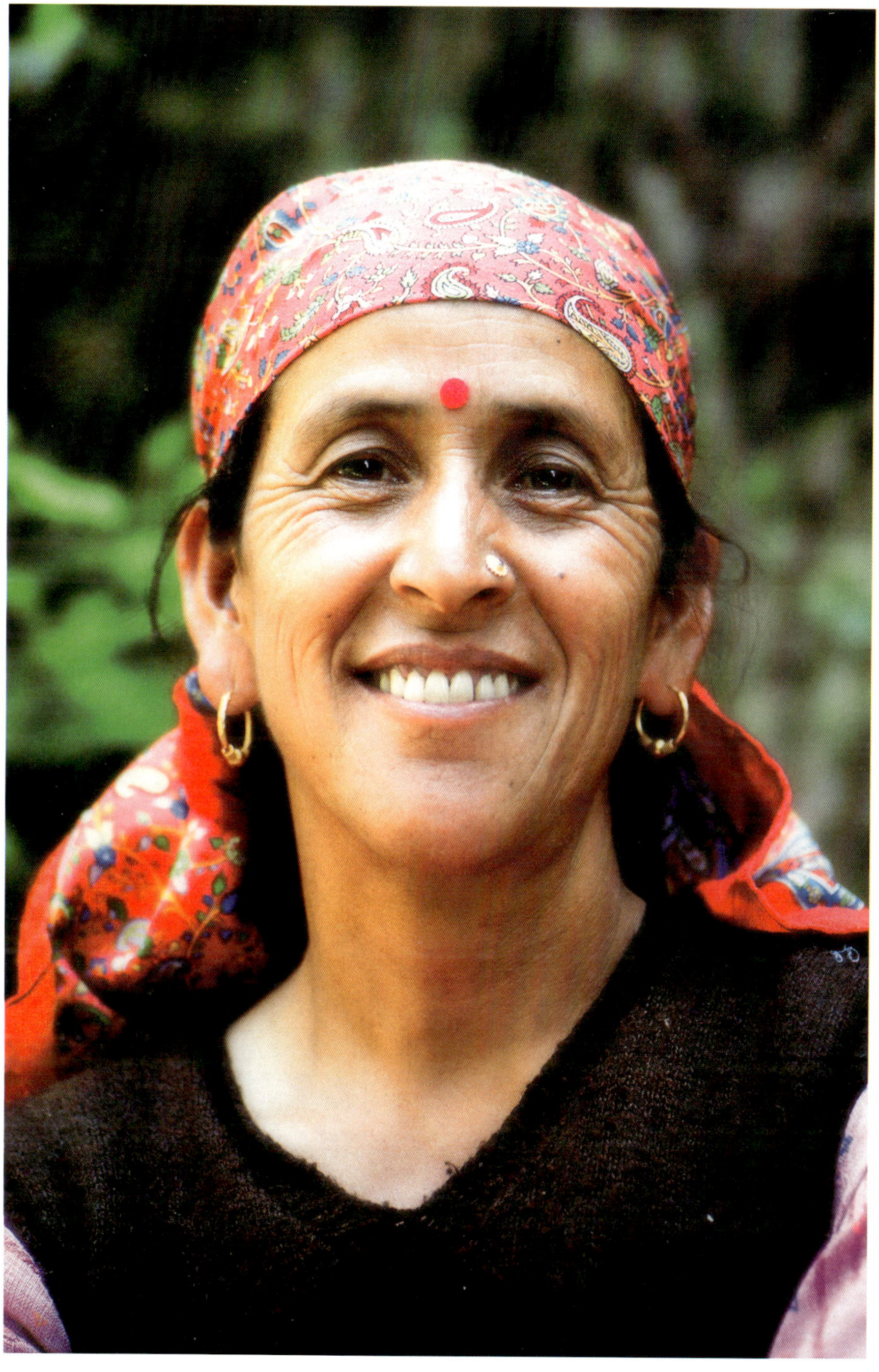

Rishi Ma

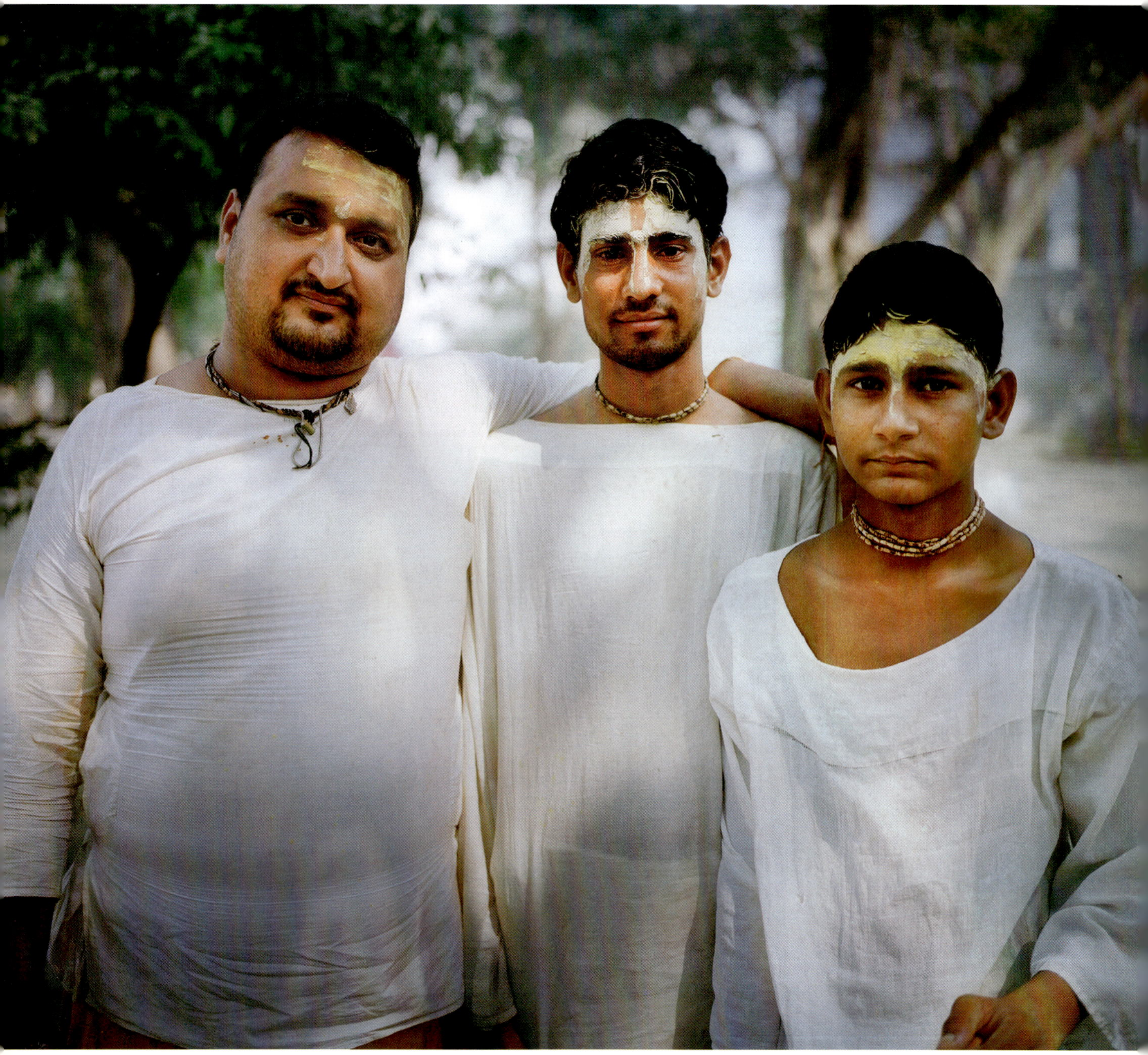

Janardan, Keshava and Kiran

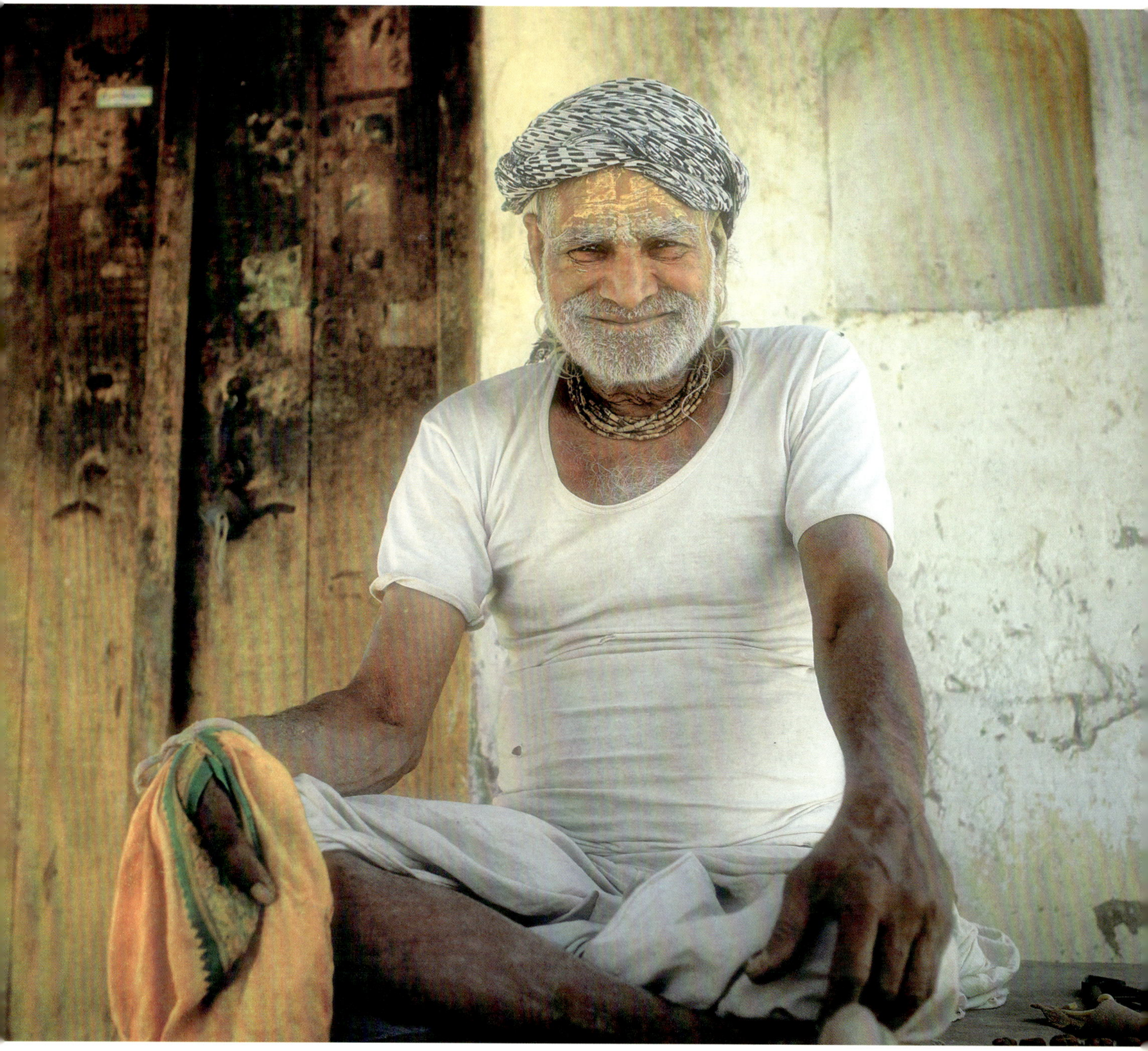

Meditating Sadhu

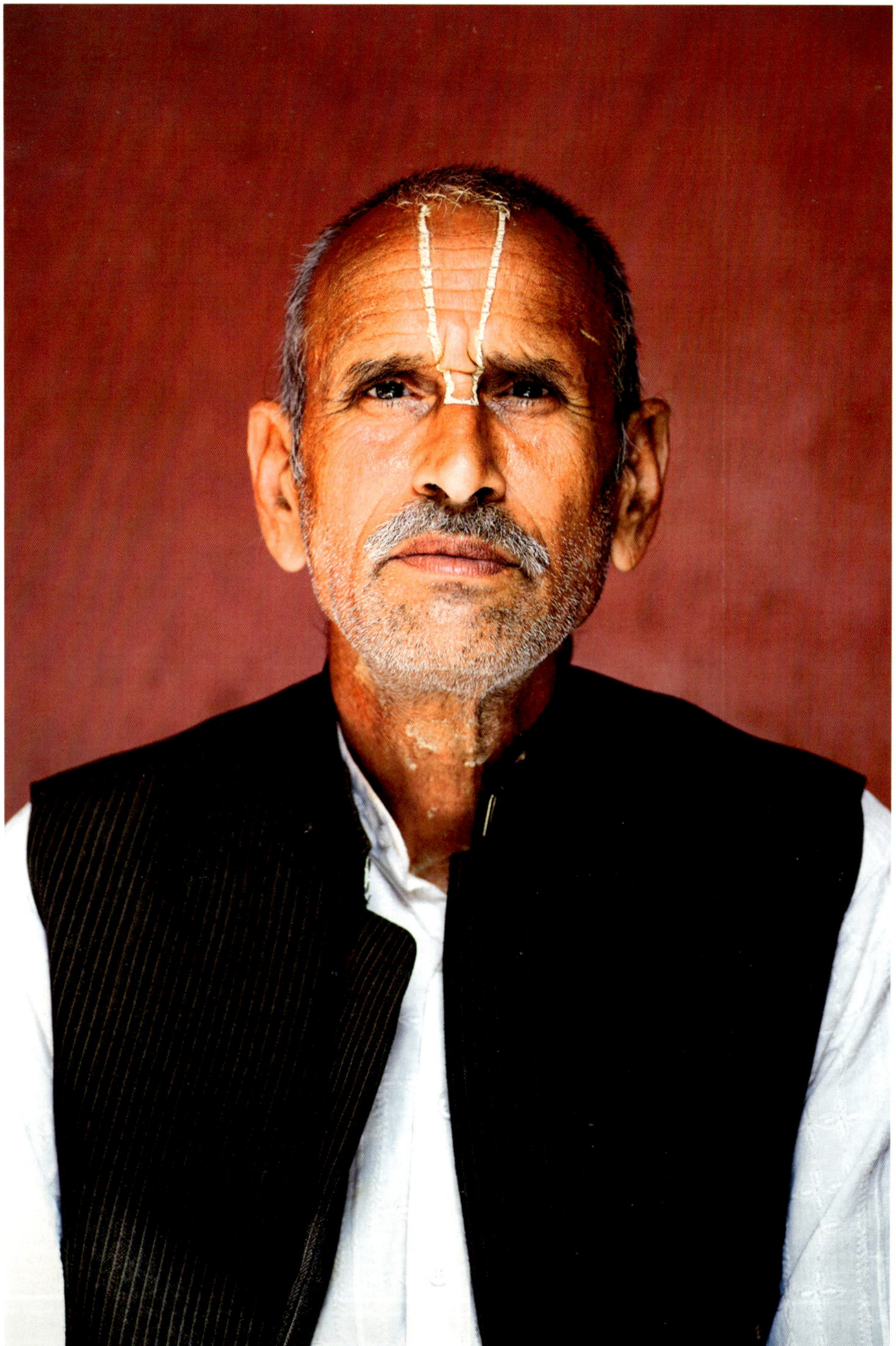

Manohar Caturvedi

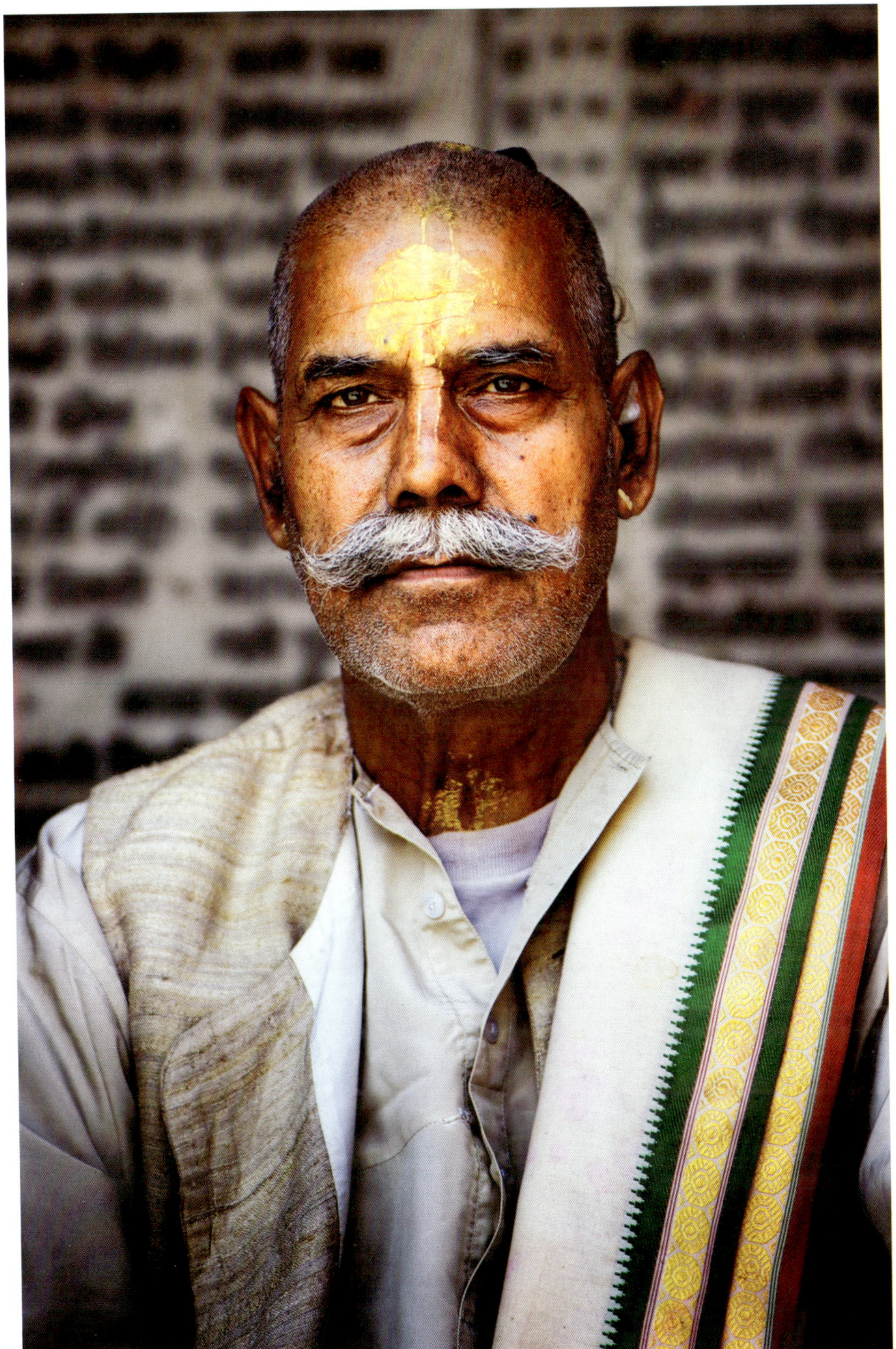

Murlidhar Caturvedi

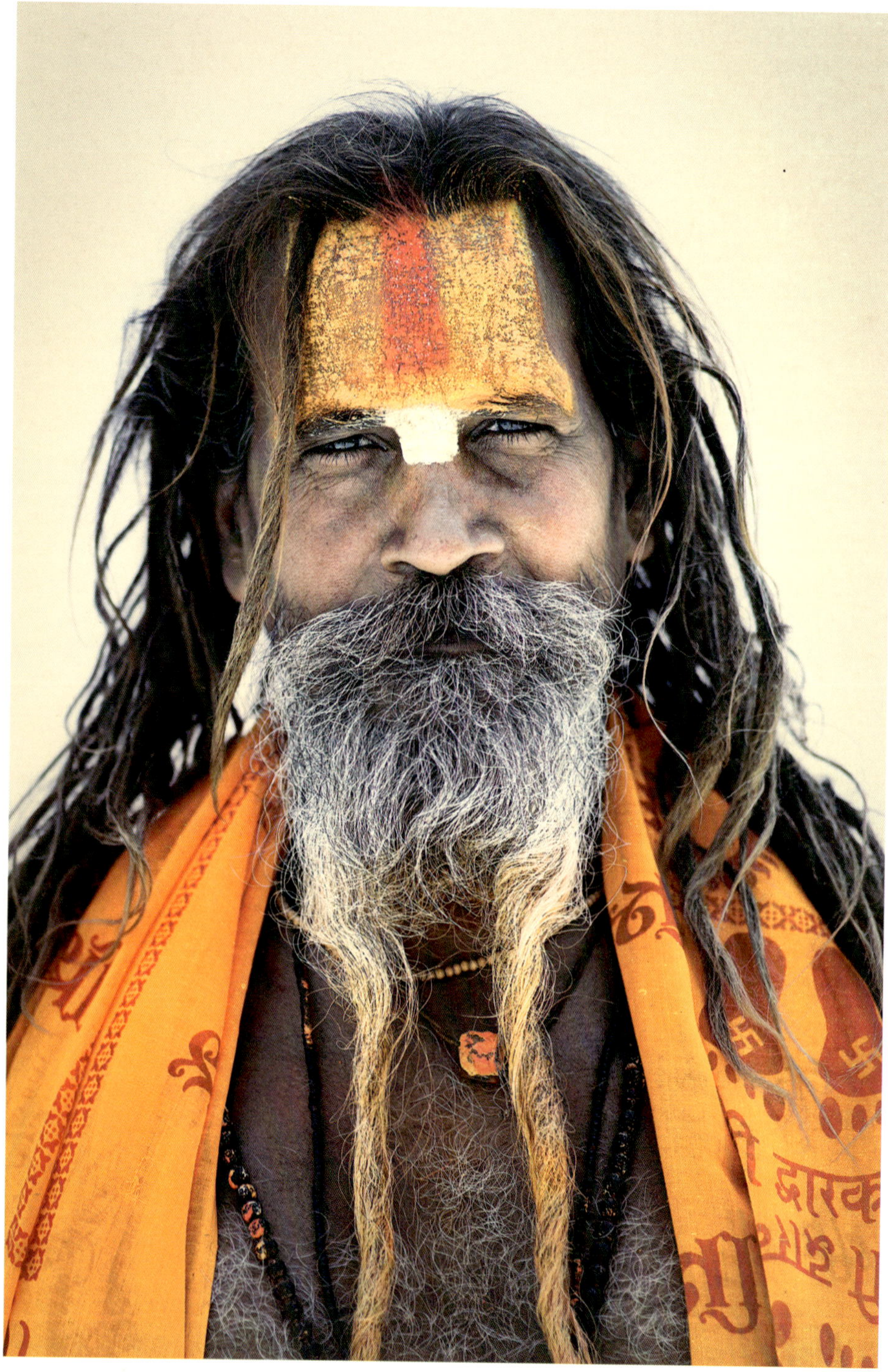

Pujan Swami

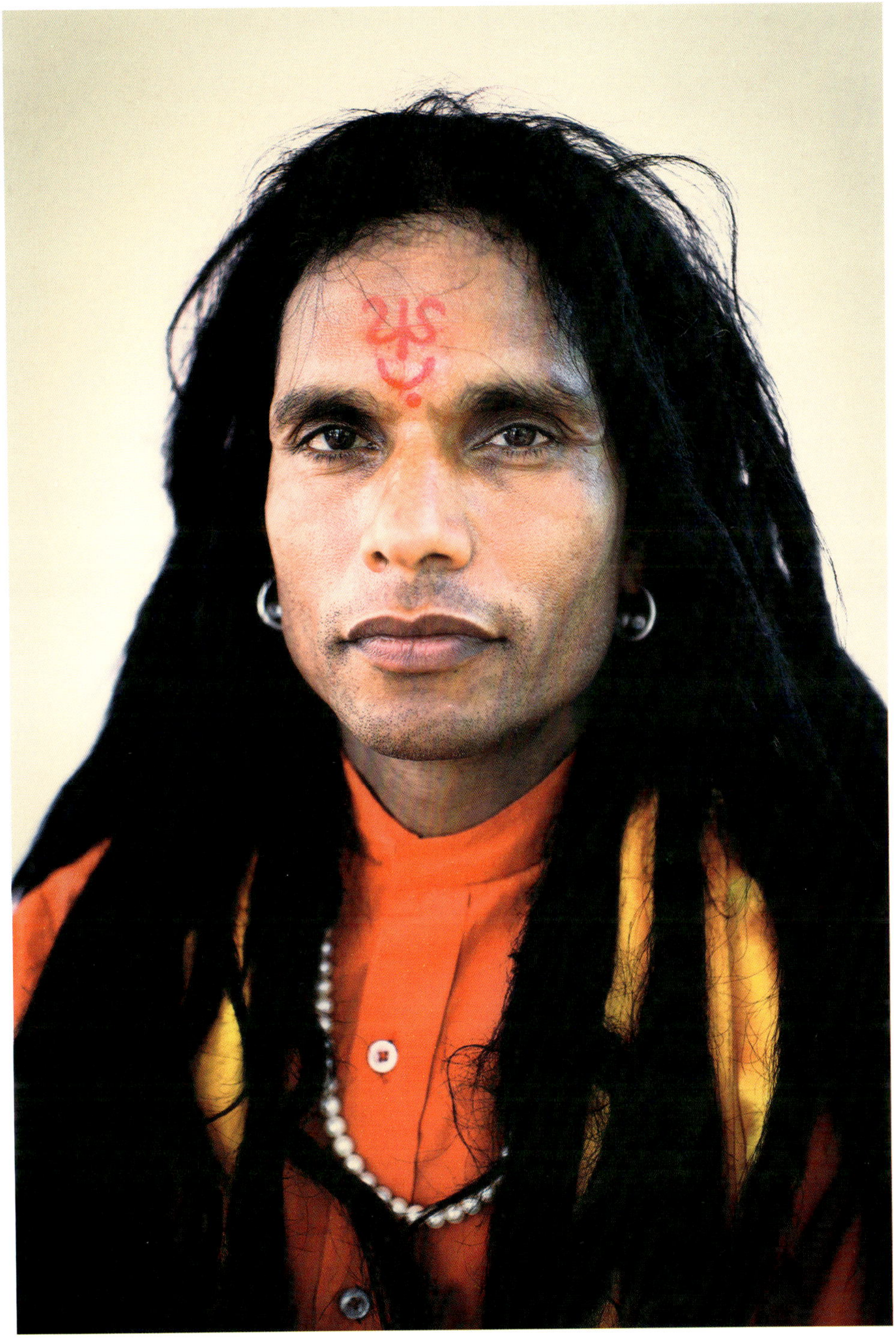

Uma Shankar Goswami

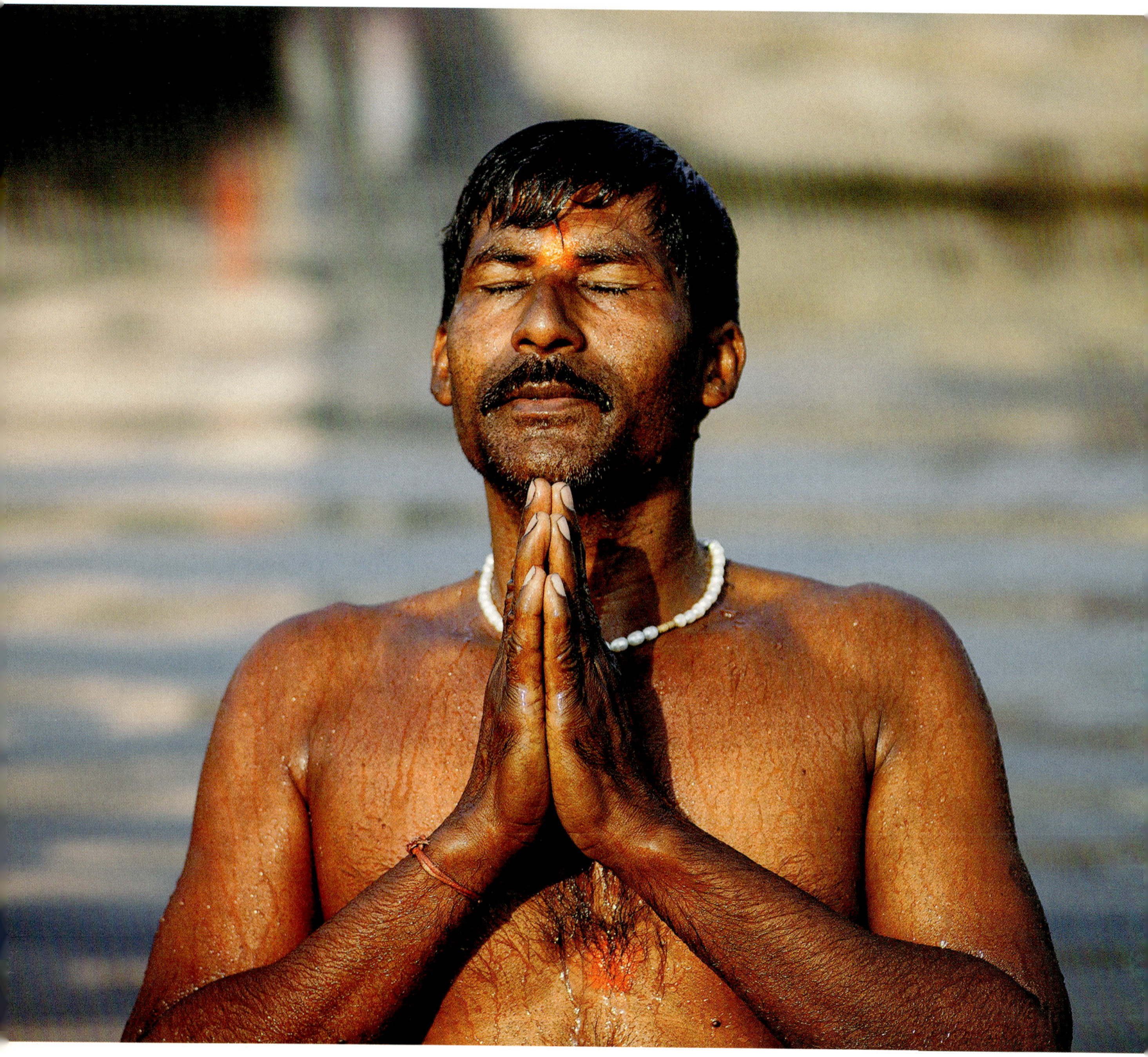

Jitendra Dasa (A Prayer to the Sun)

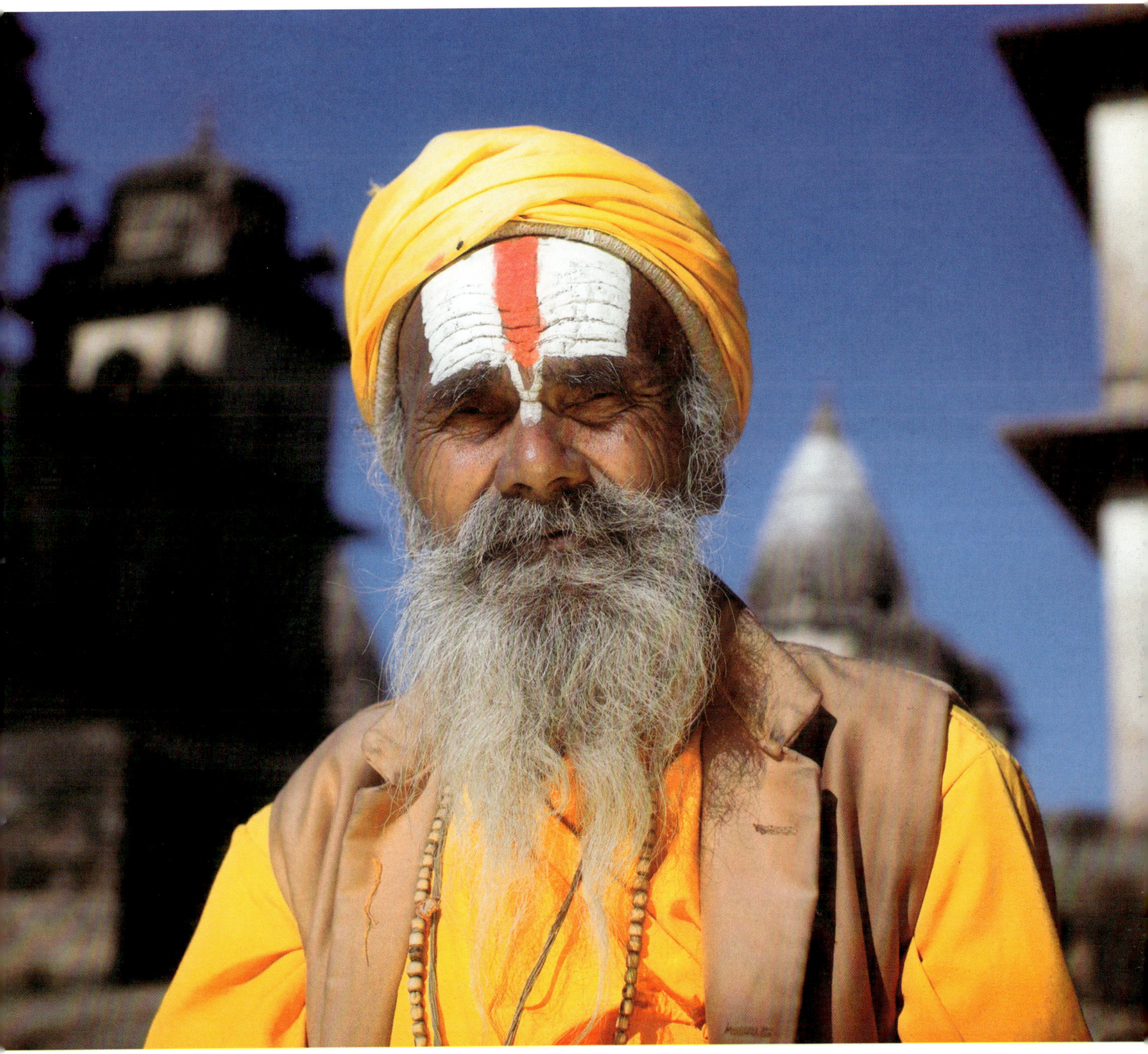

Sadhu Param Das

DEITIES

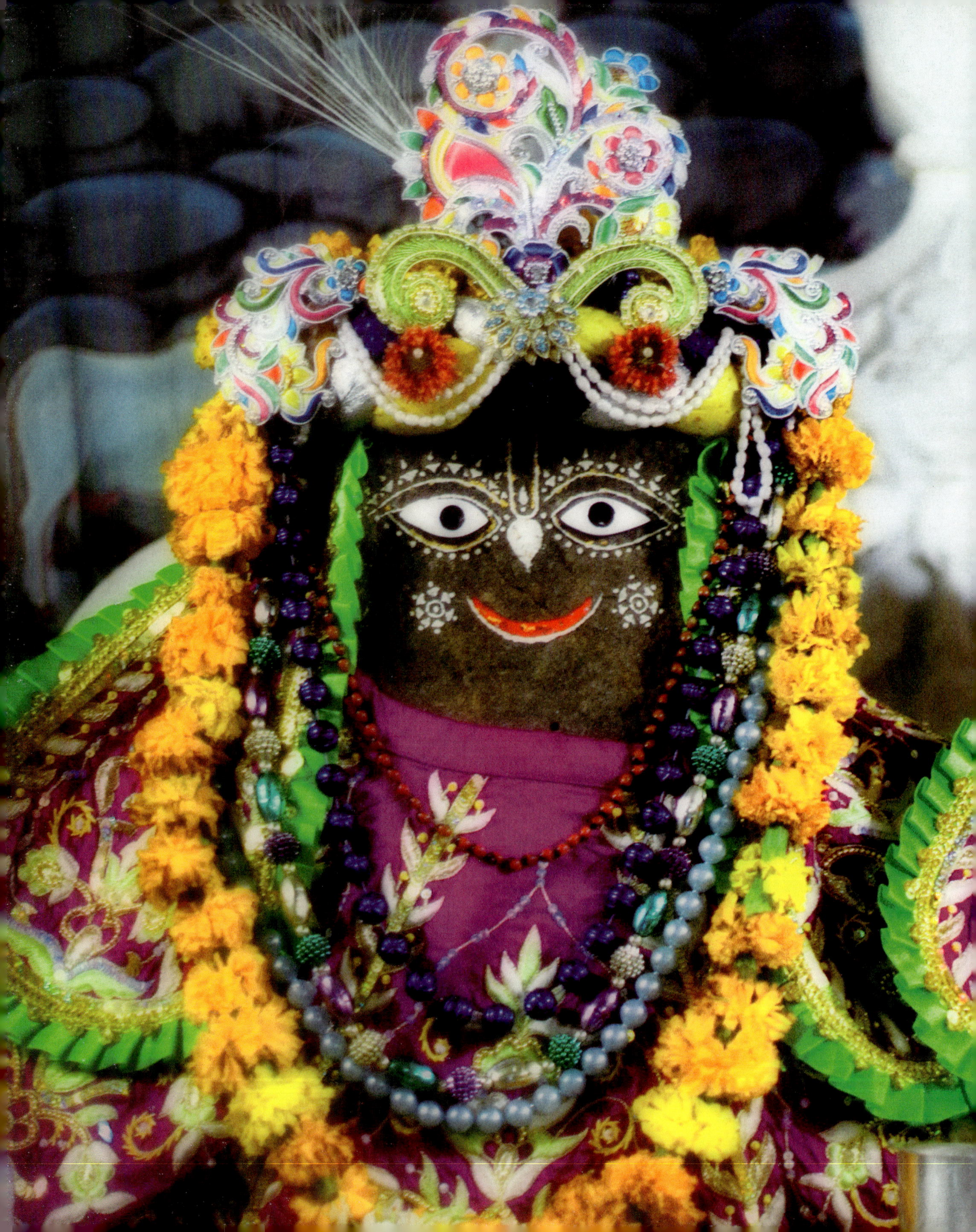

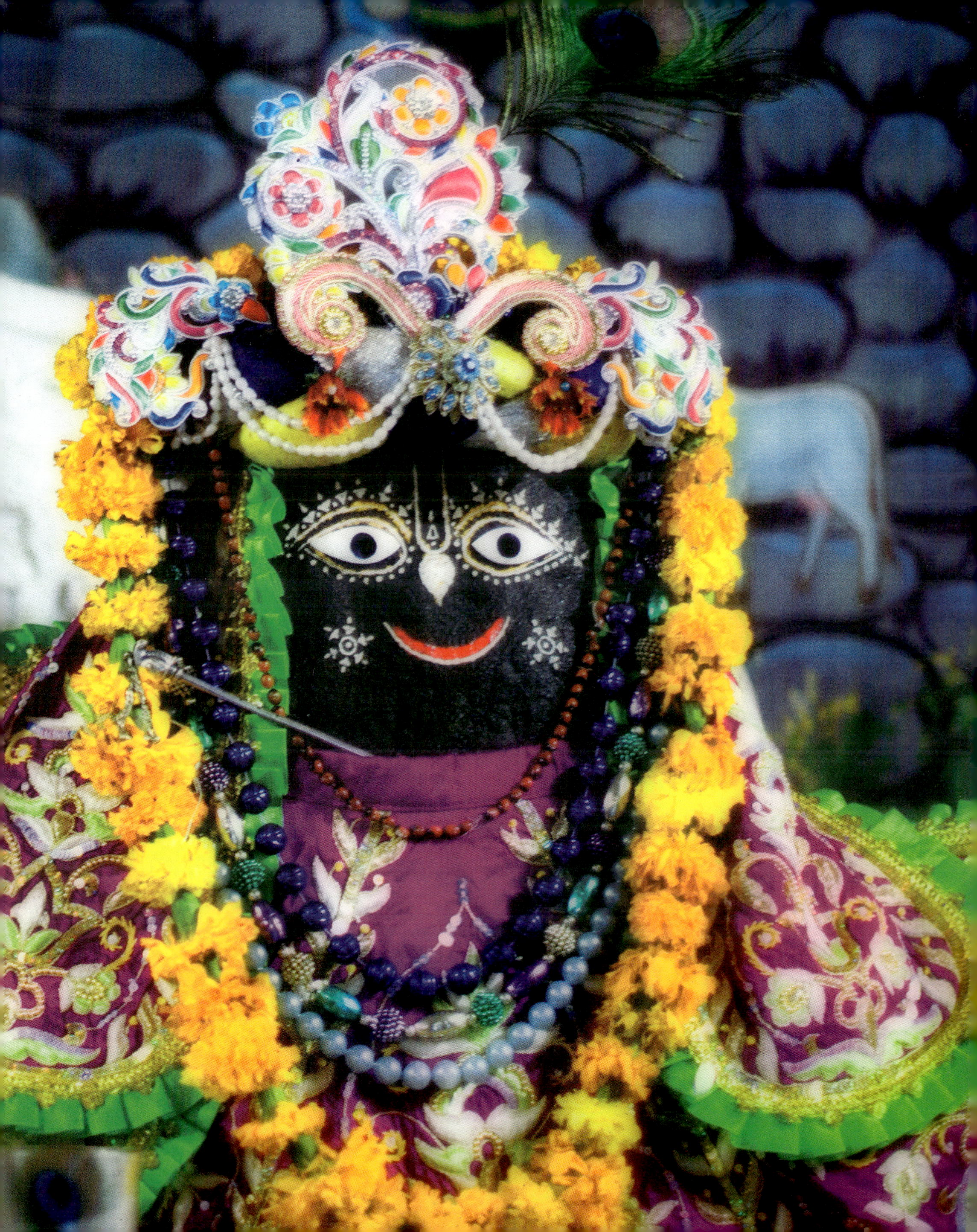

< Krishna Balarama

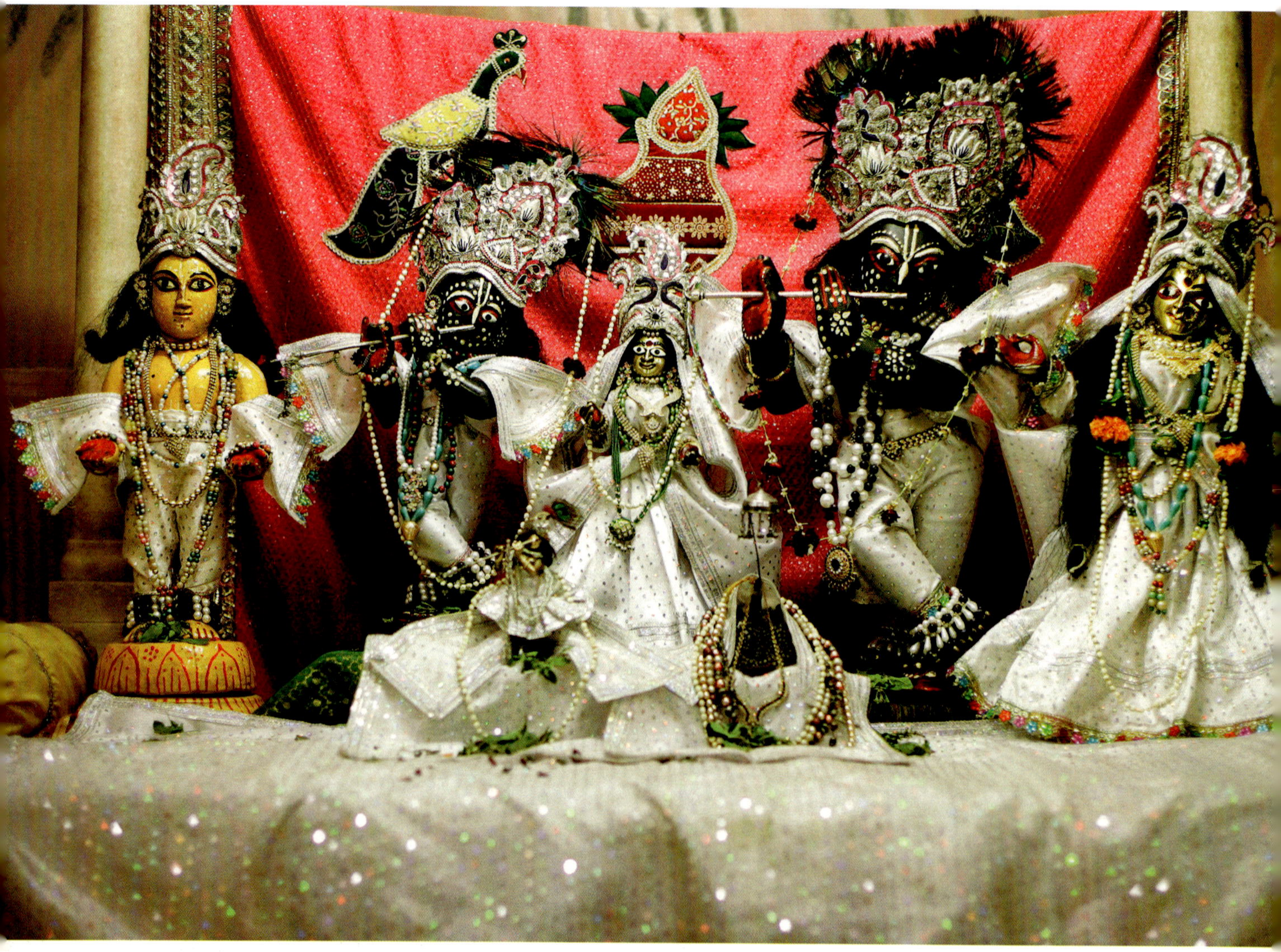

Radha Gokulananda

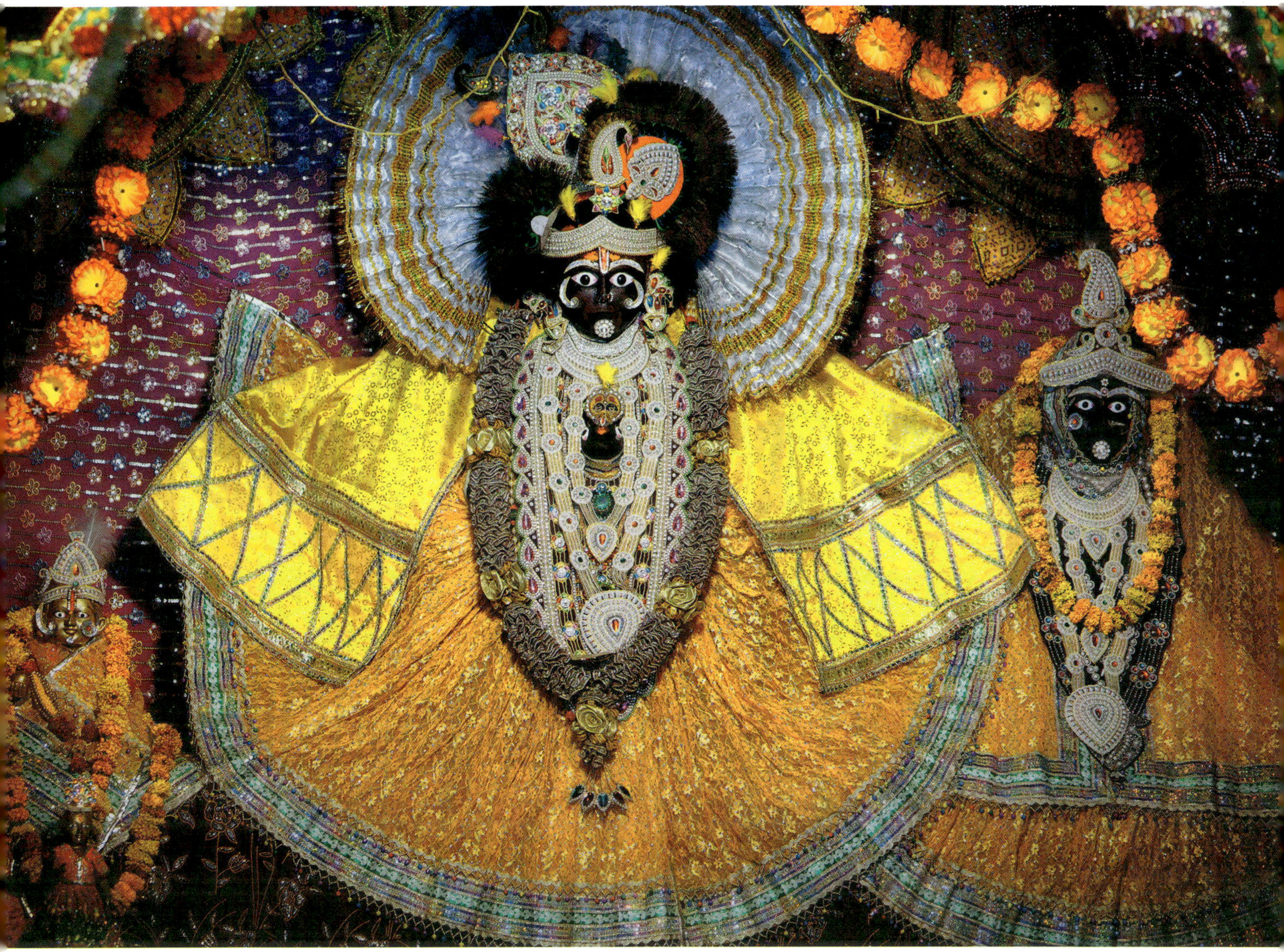

Garuda Govinda

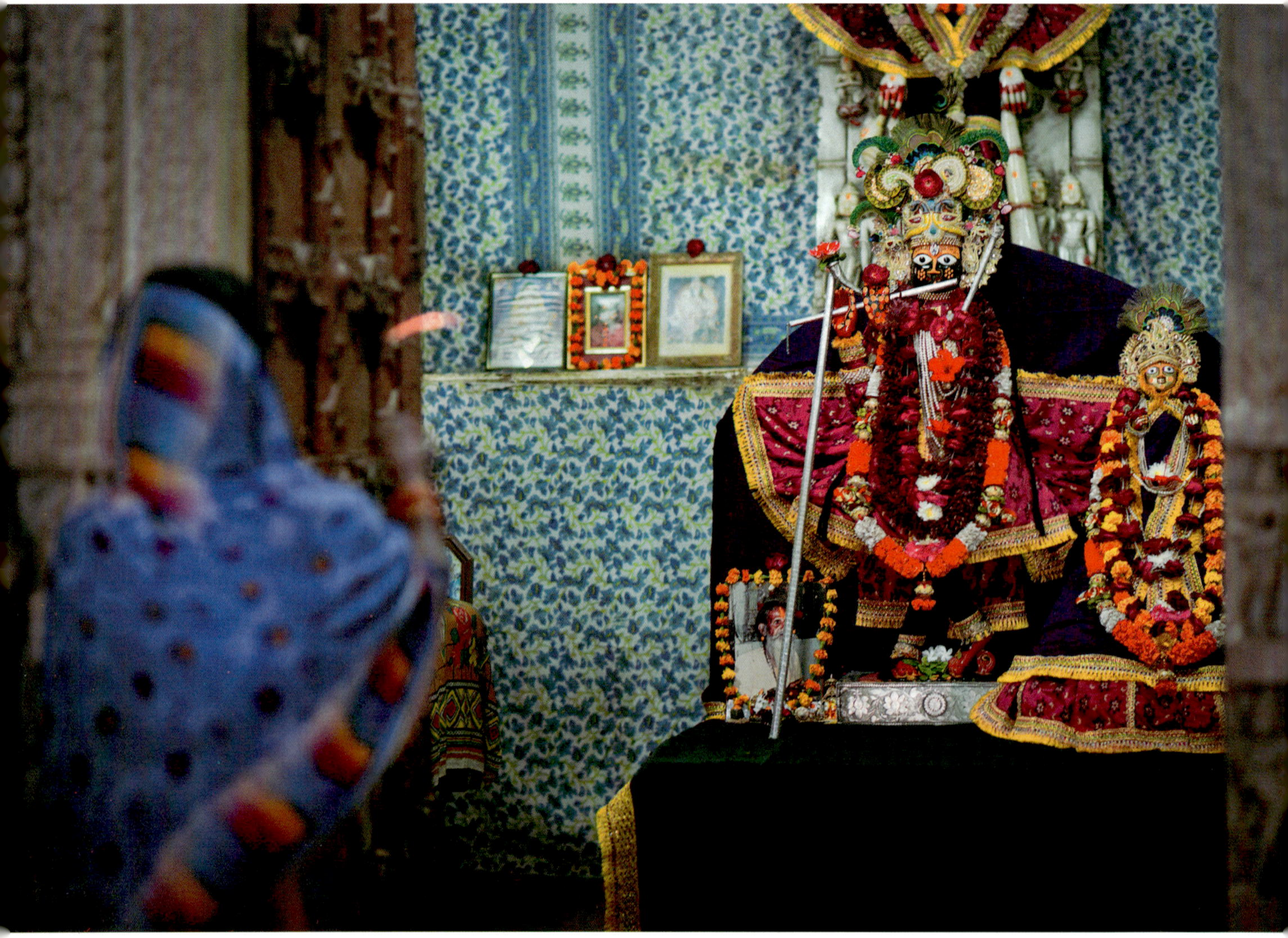

Krishna and Mira Bai Shrine

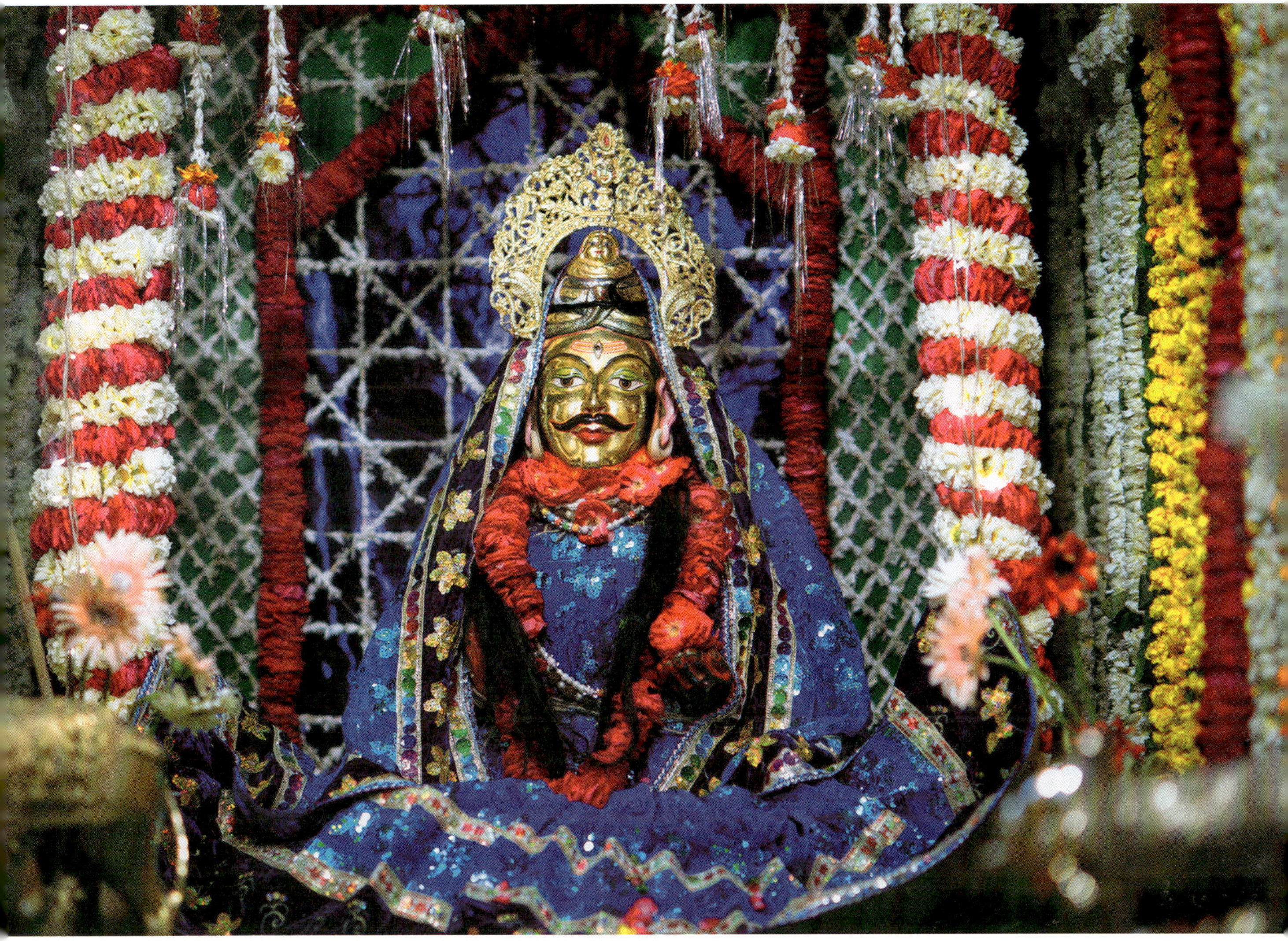

Shiva Mahadeva

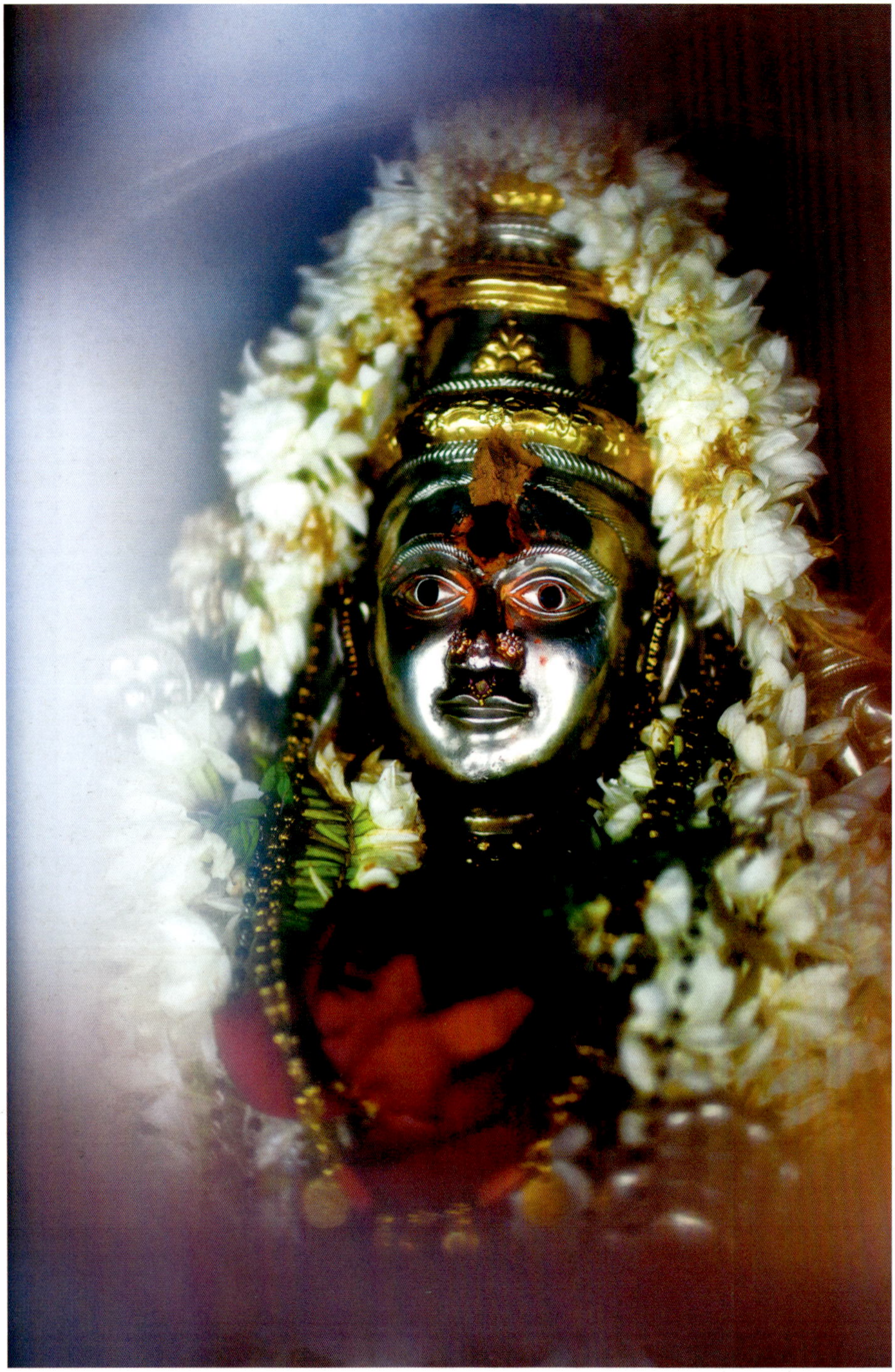

Bhagirati Devi

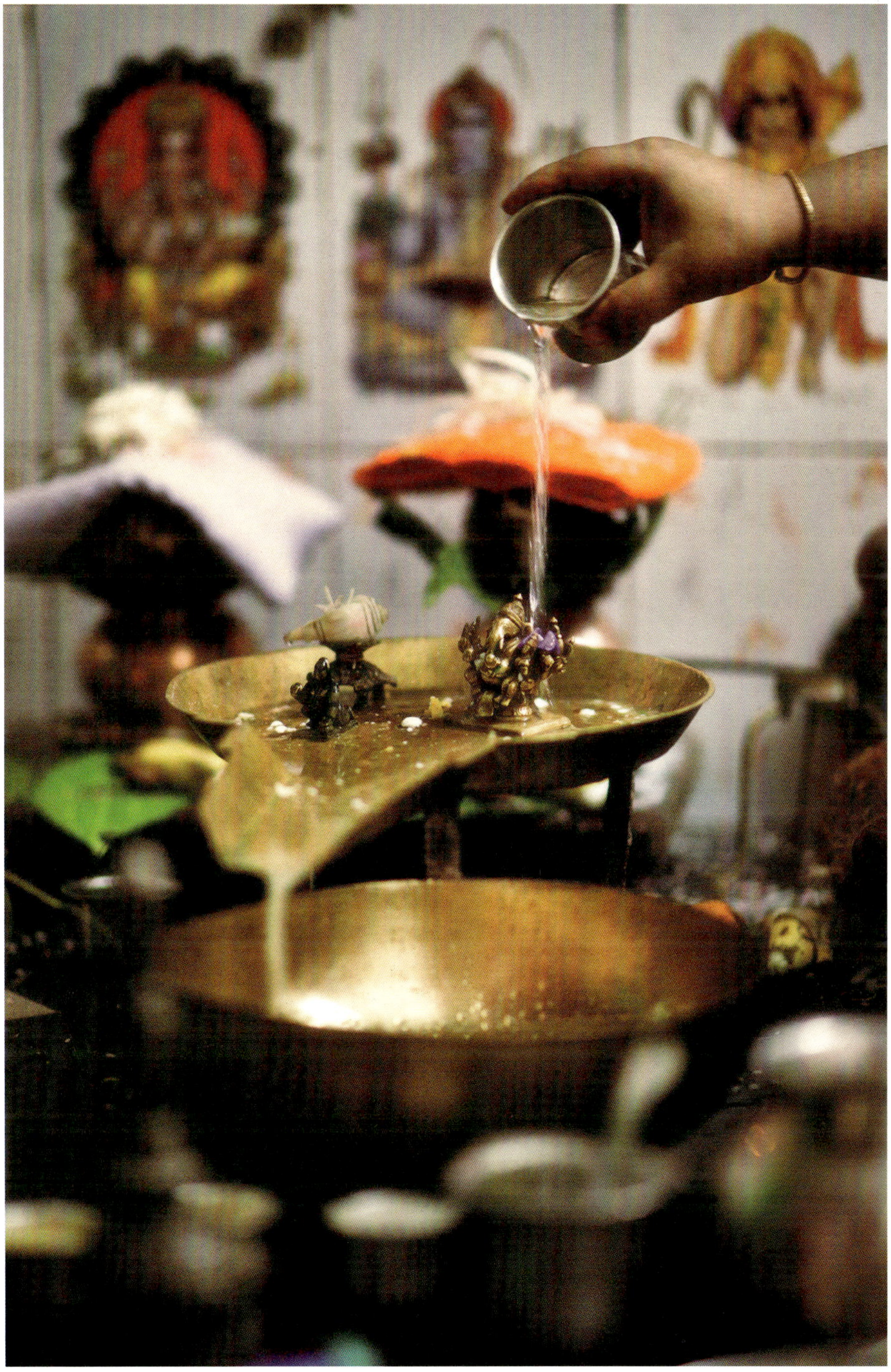

Ganesha Puja

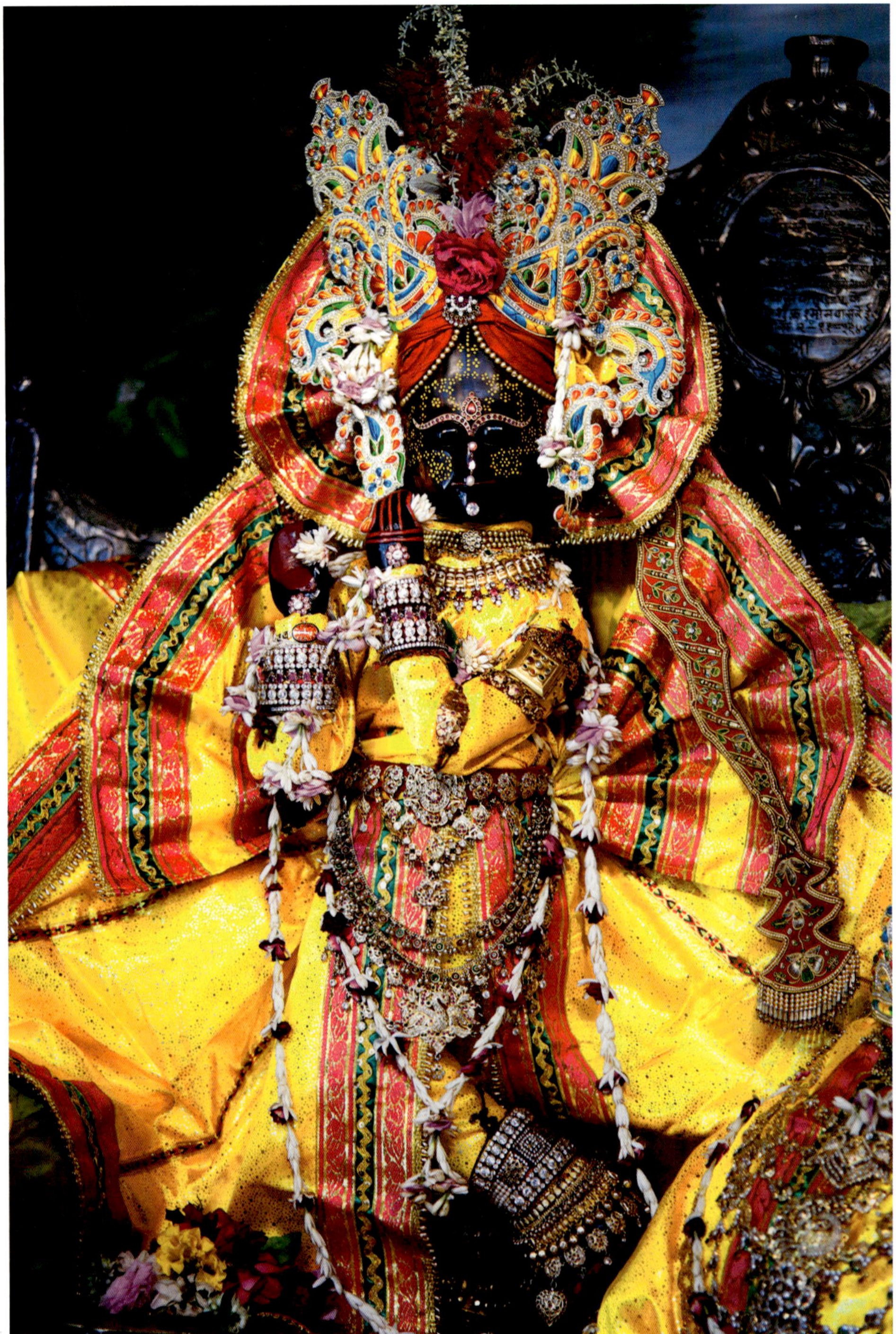

Radha Vallabha

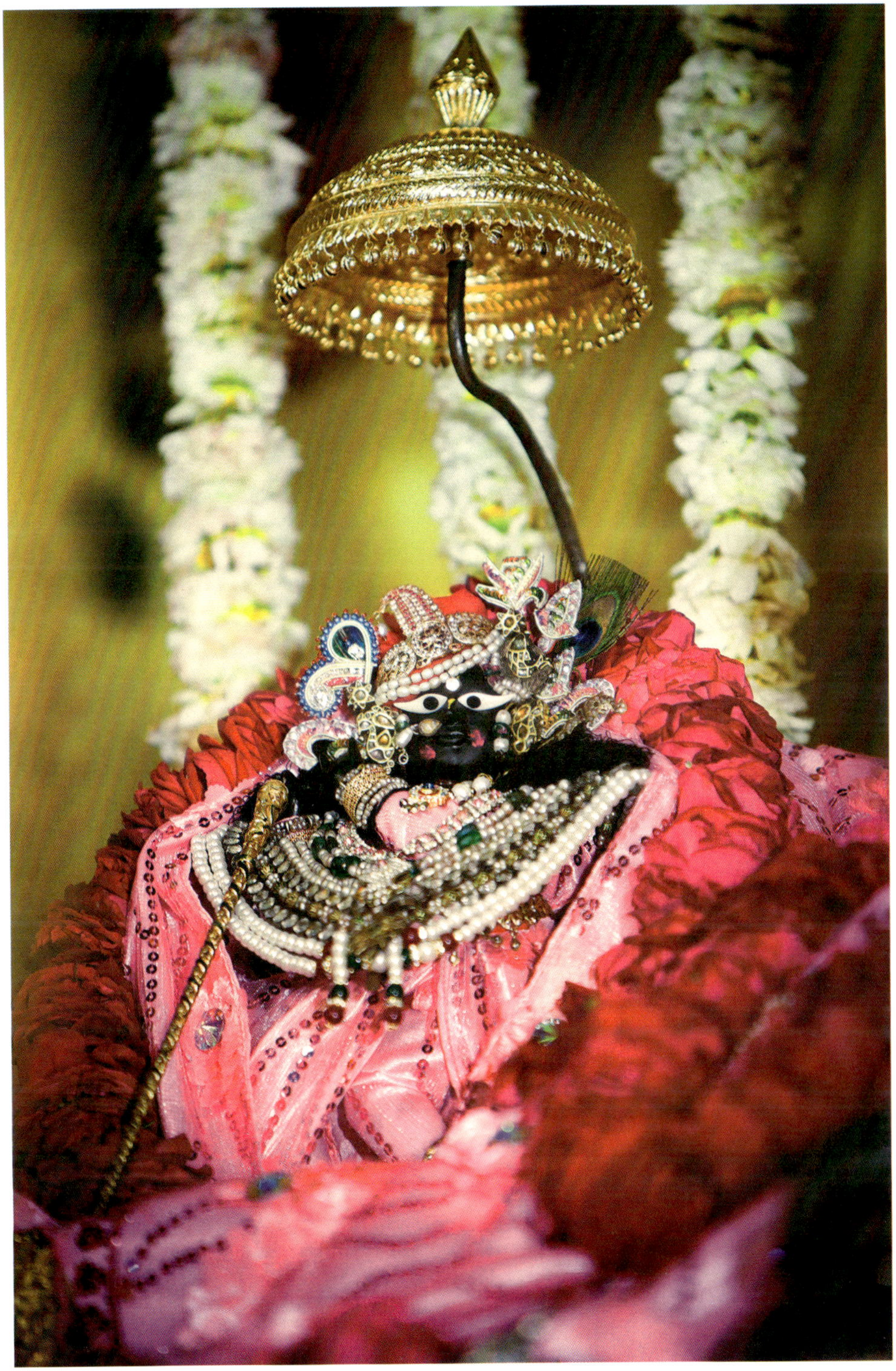

Radha Ramana

KUMBHA MELA

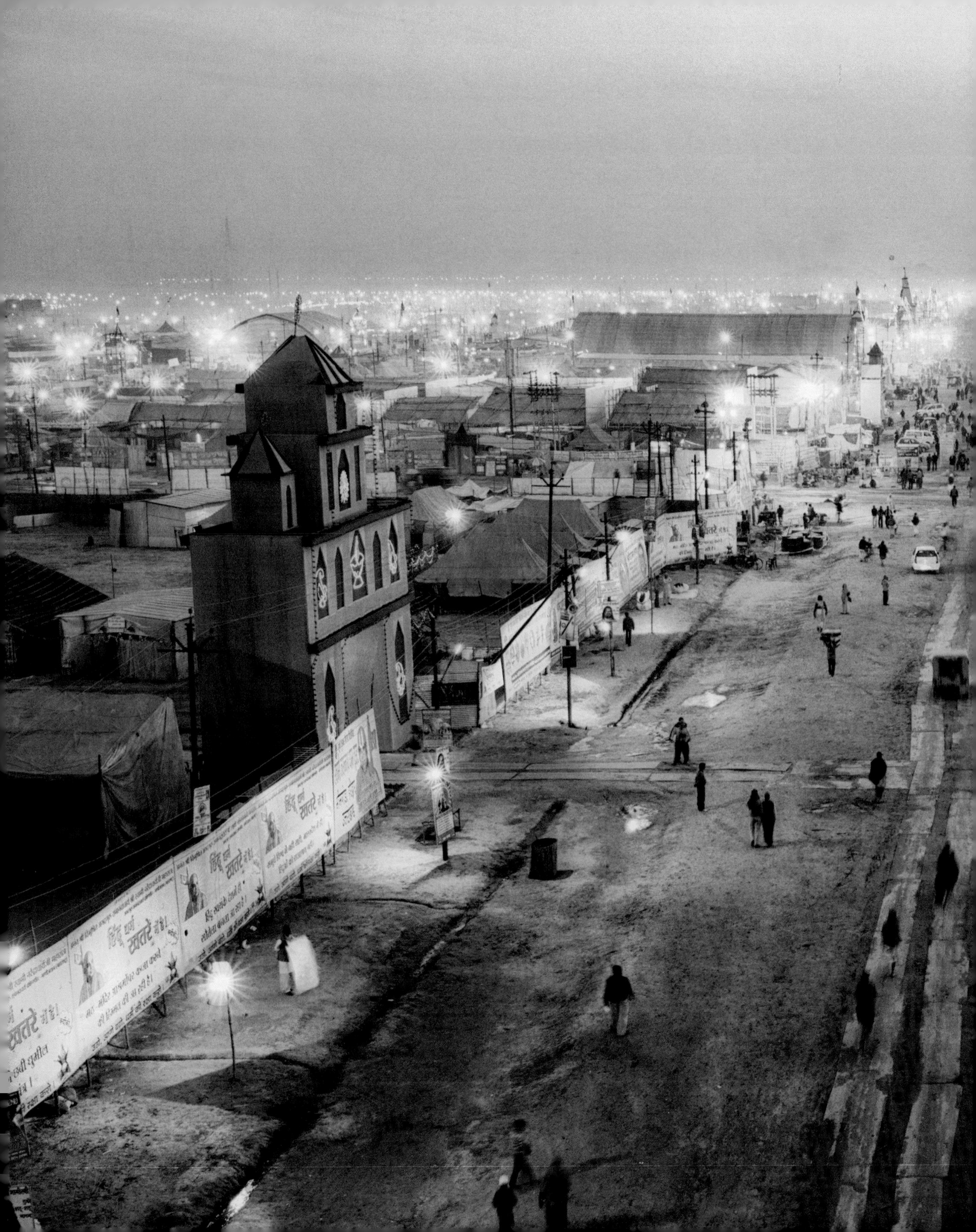

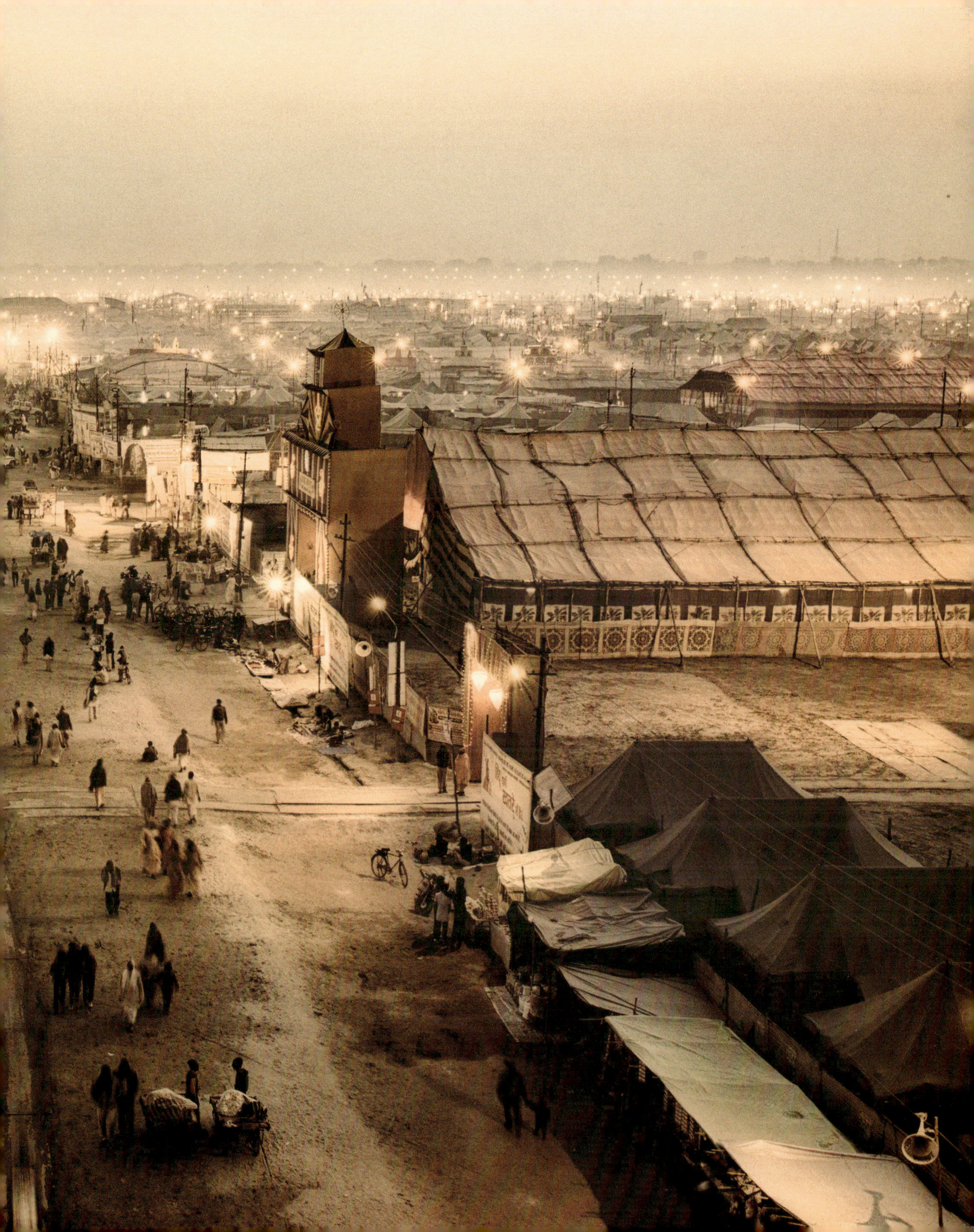

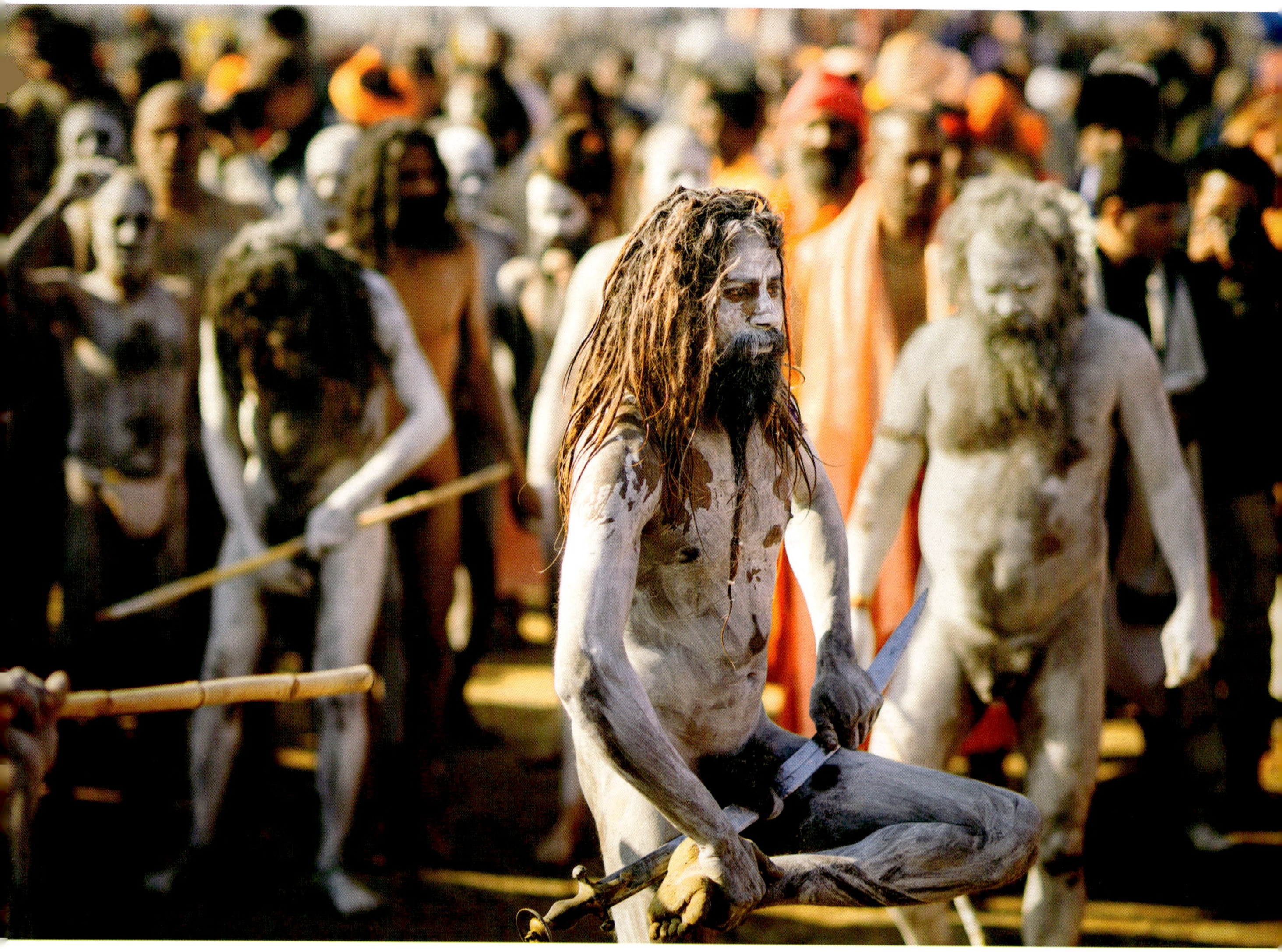

Sadhus' Feats

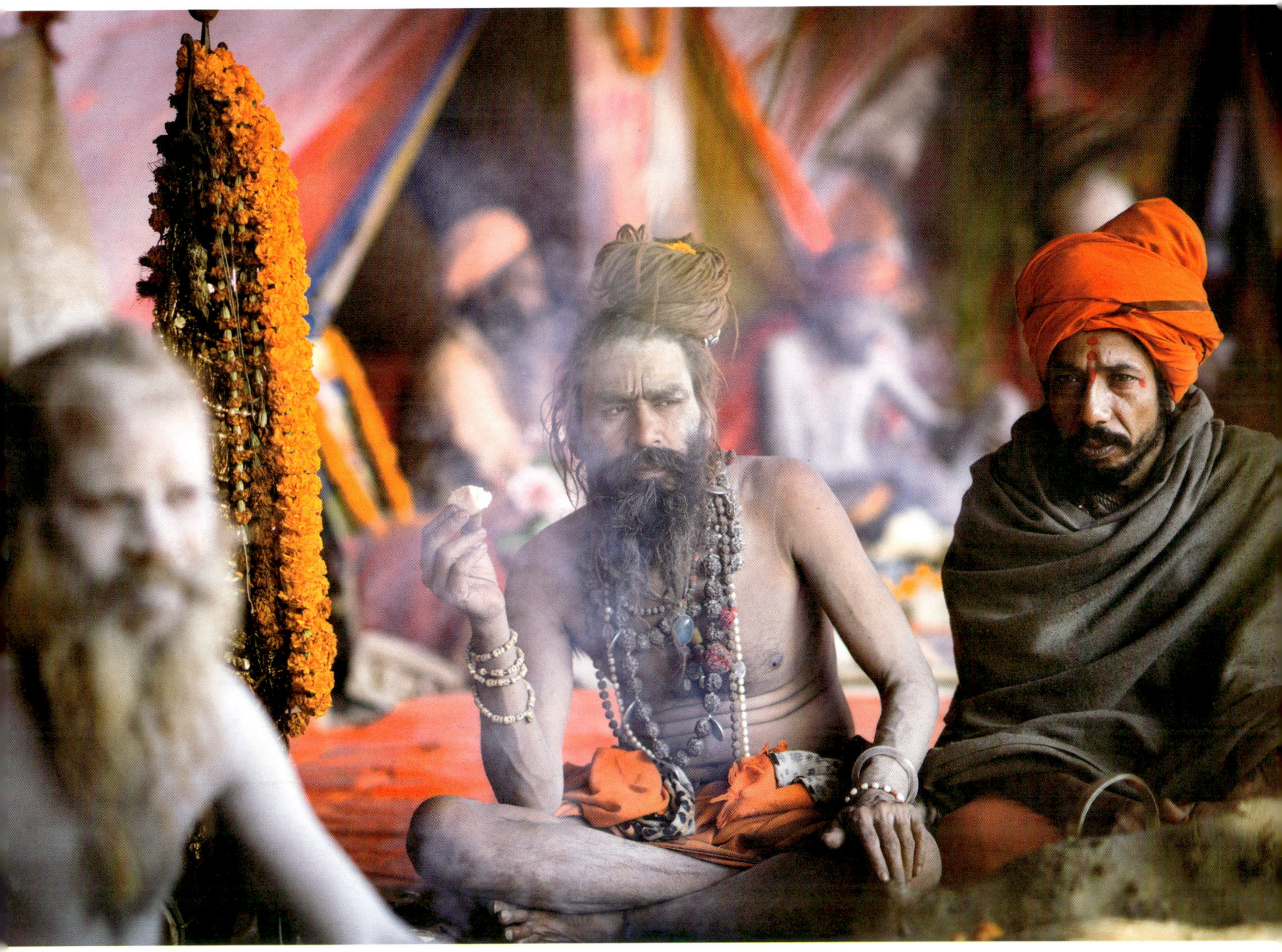

Sadhus' Camp

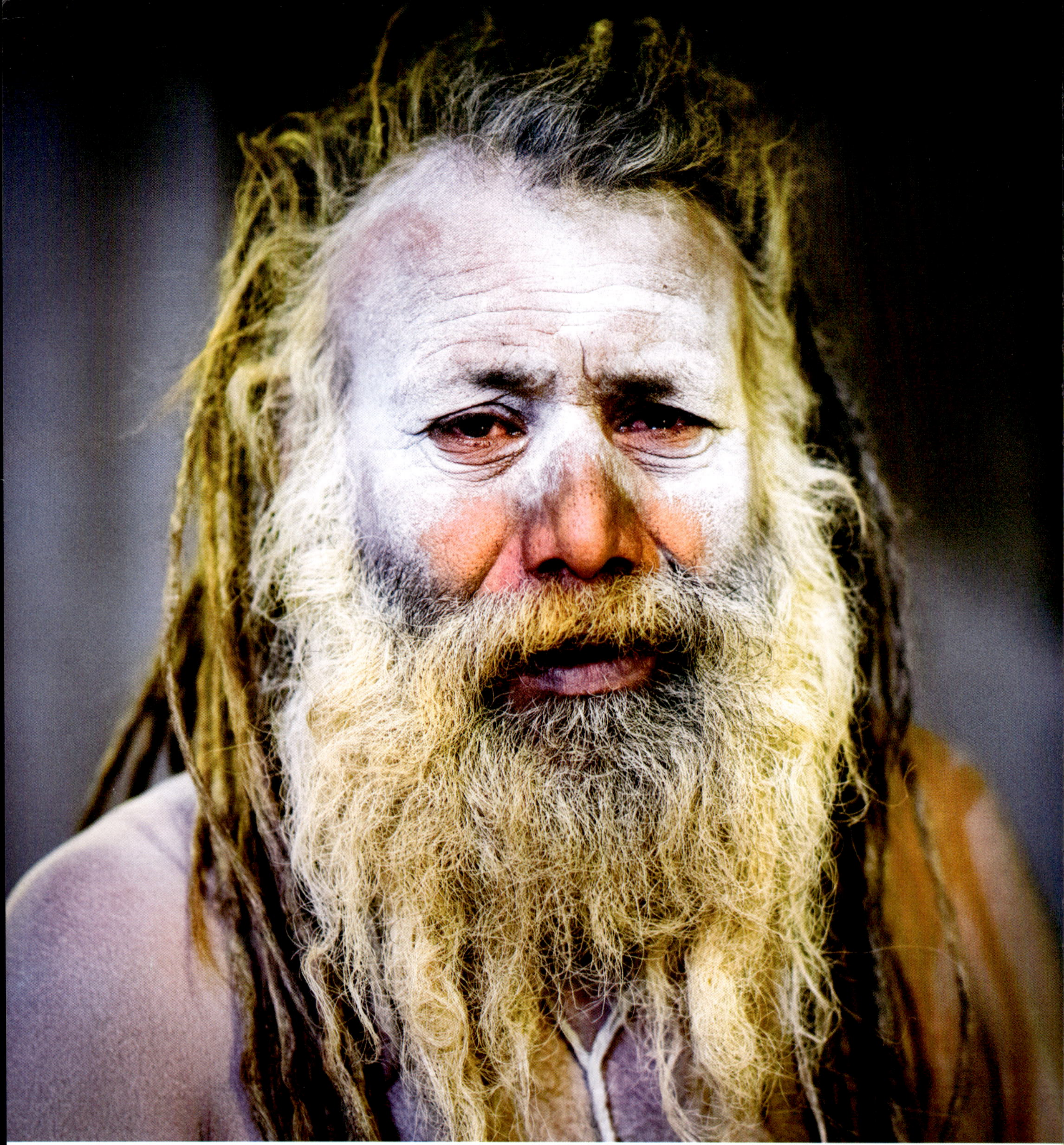

Sadhu Naga Giri

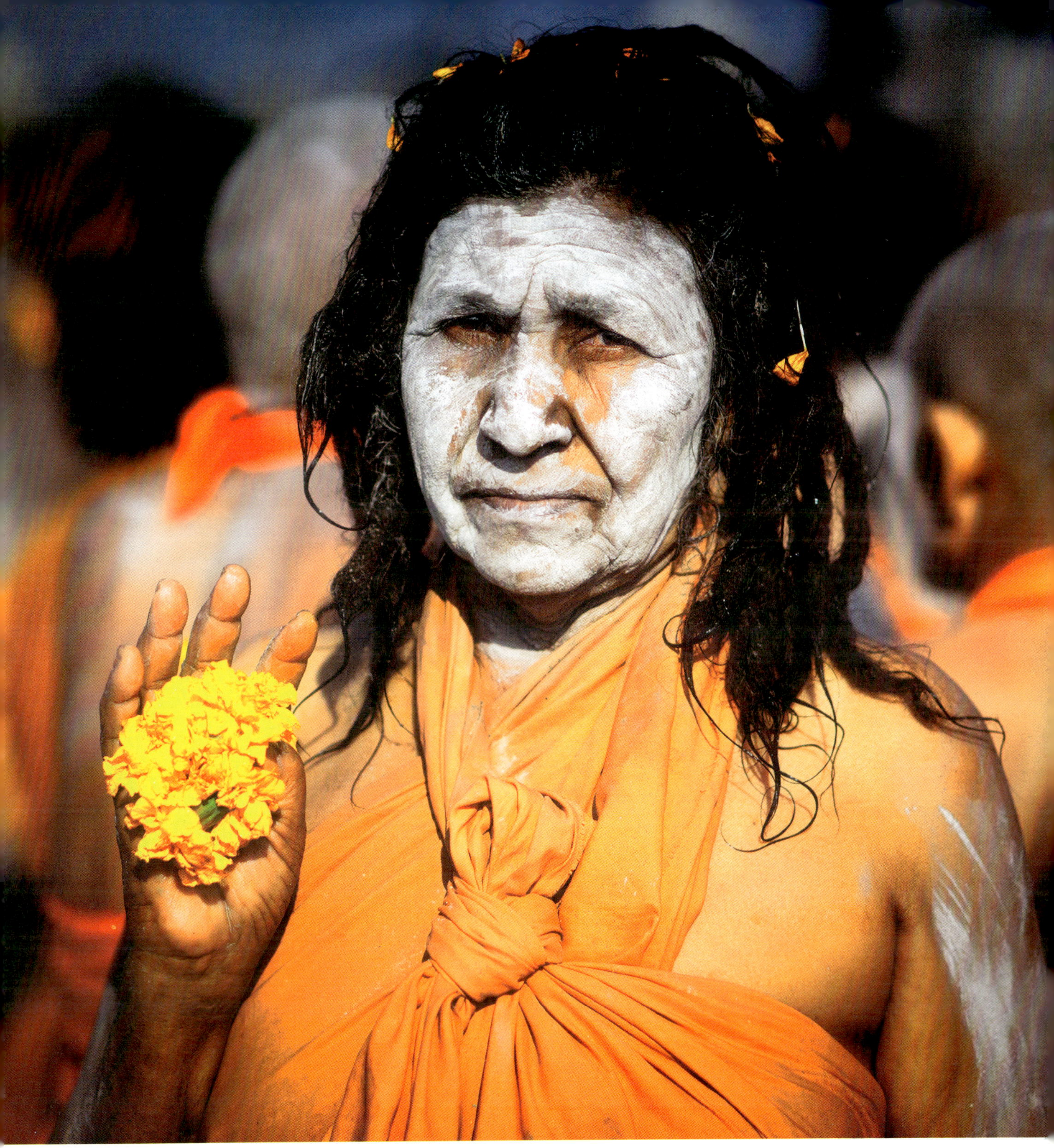

Sadhvi Narayani

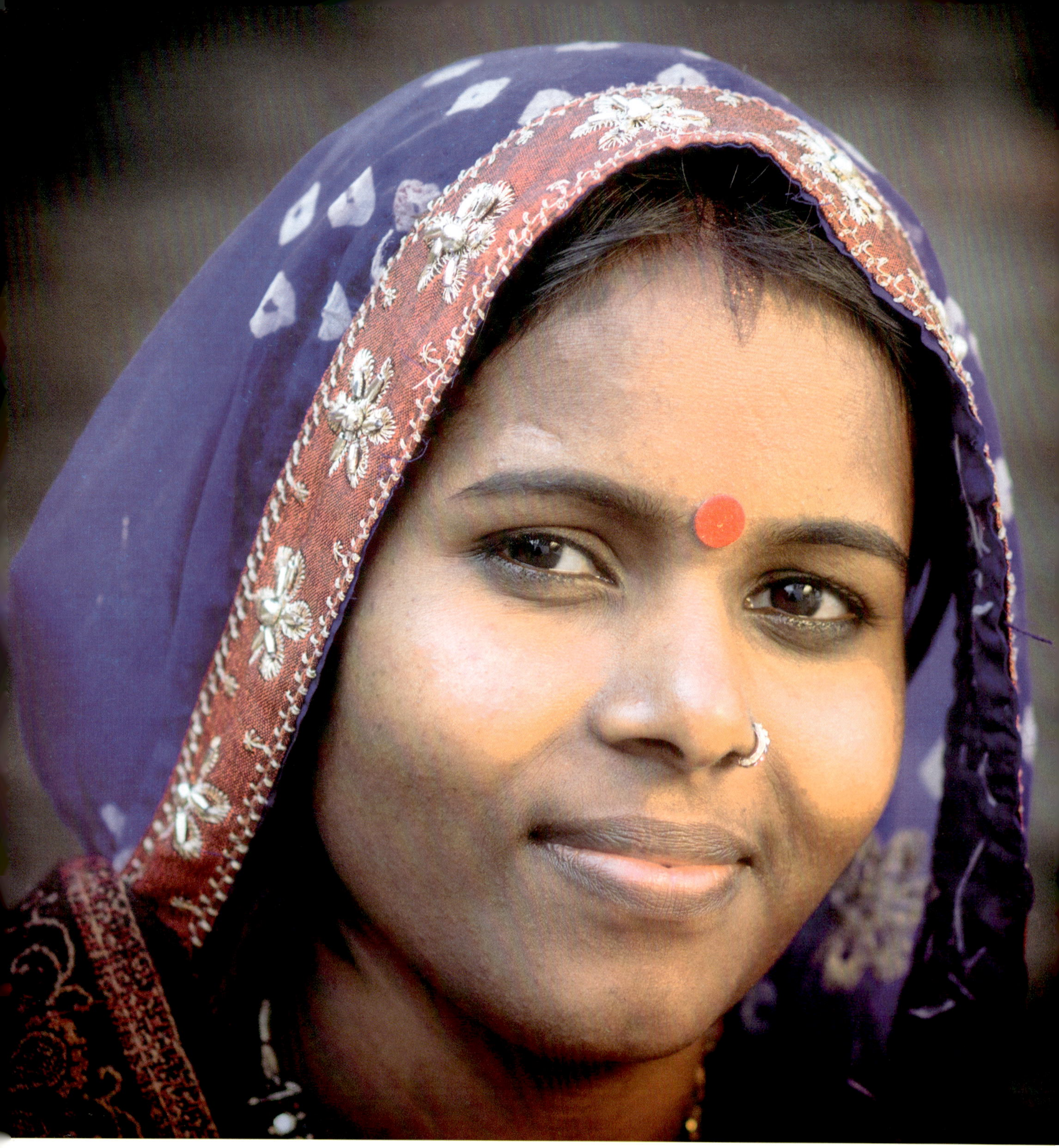

Vandana Devi

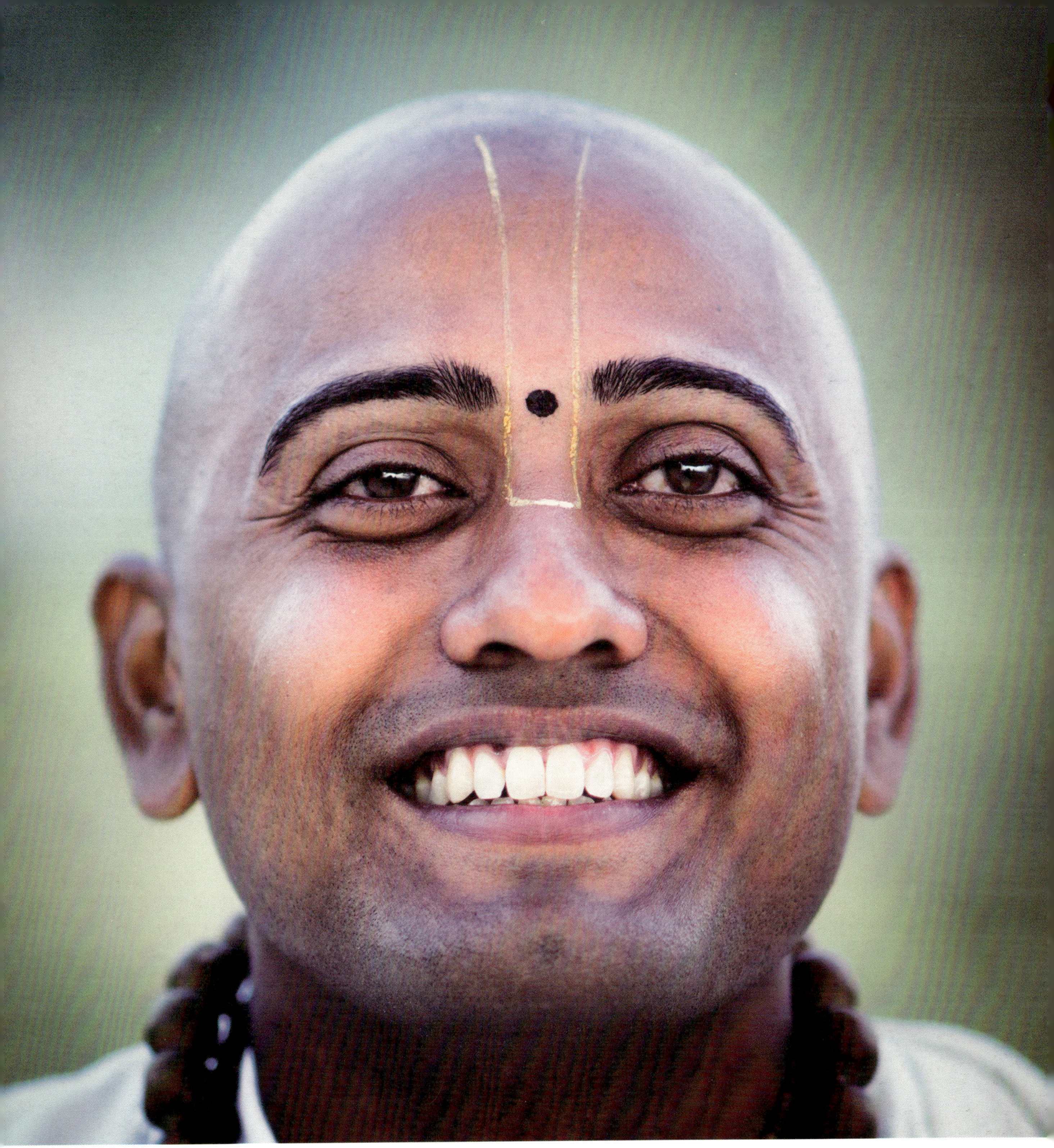

Syama Bihari

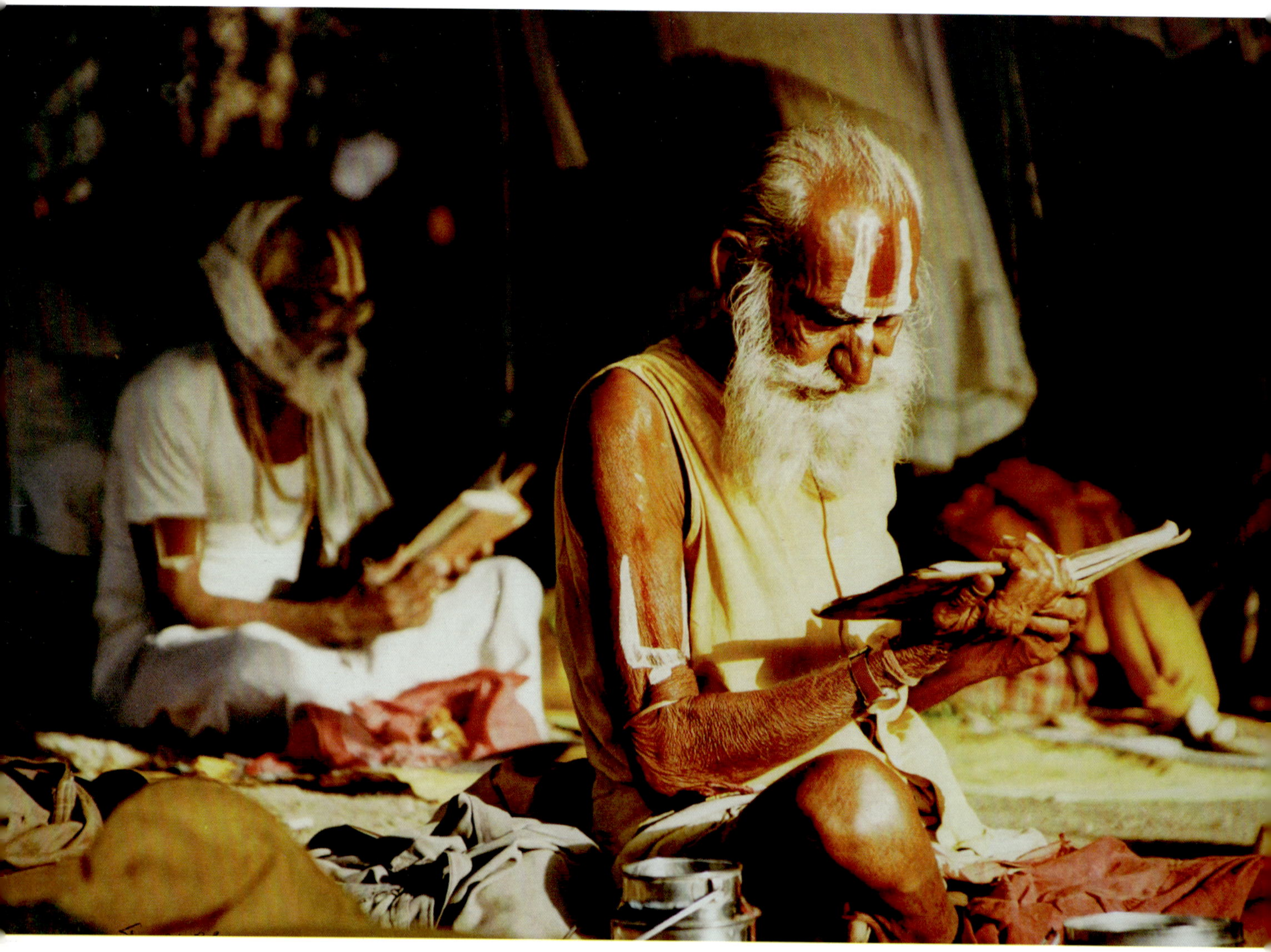

Sadhus' Studies

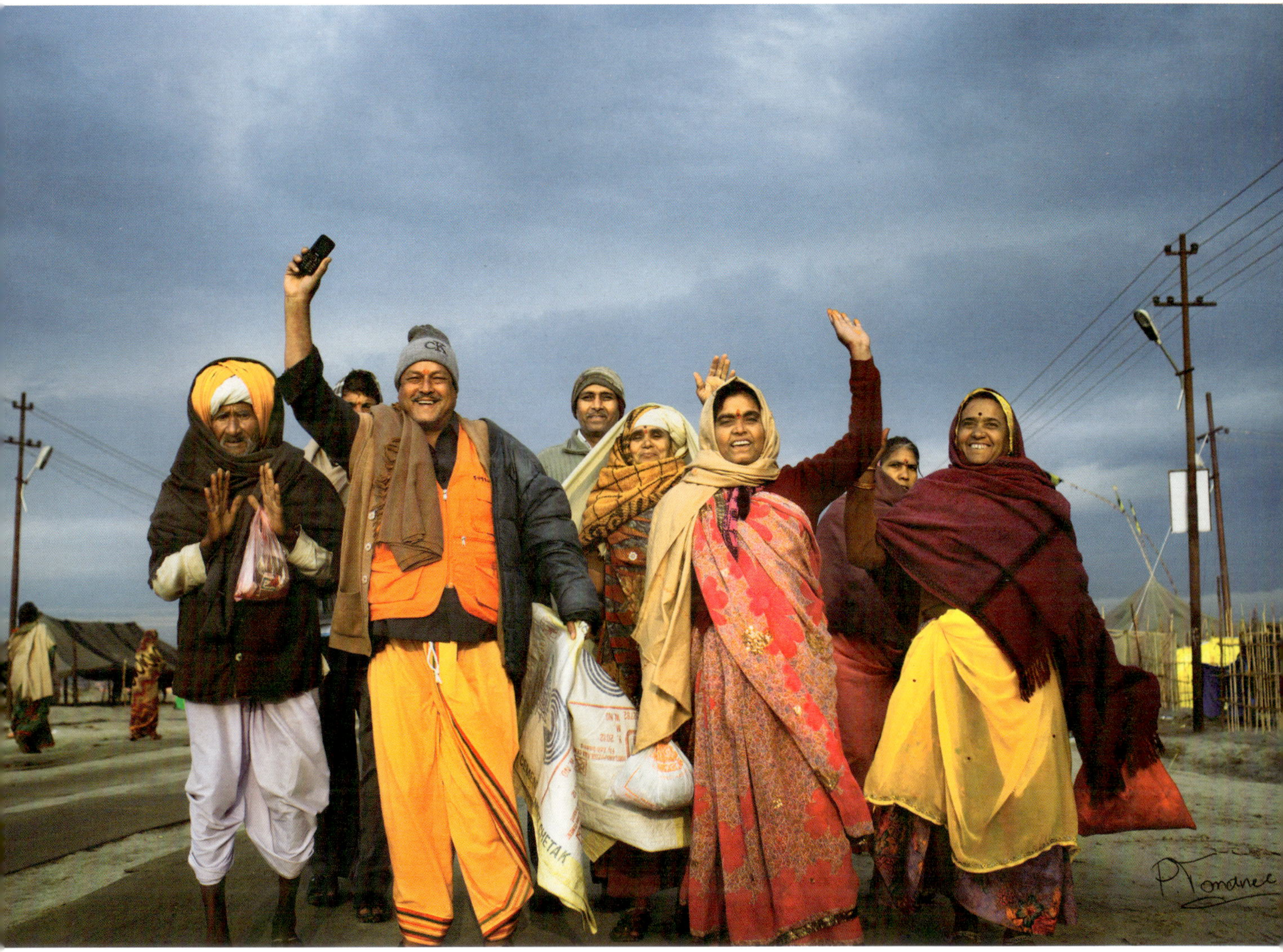

Pilgrims' Progress

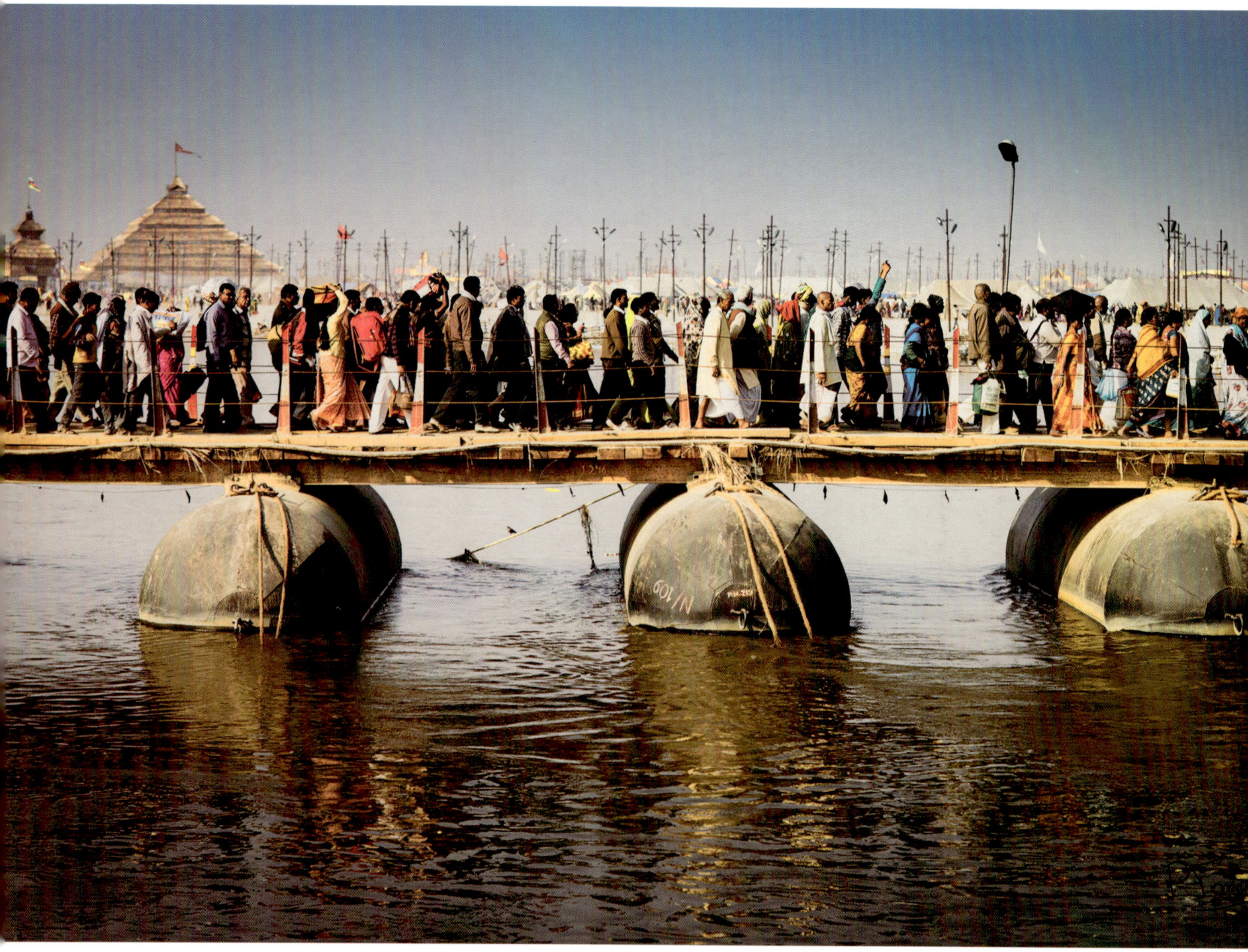

On the Way to the Confluence

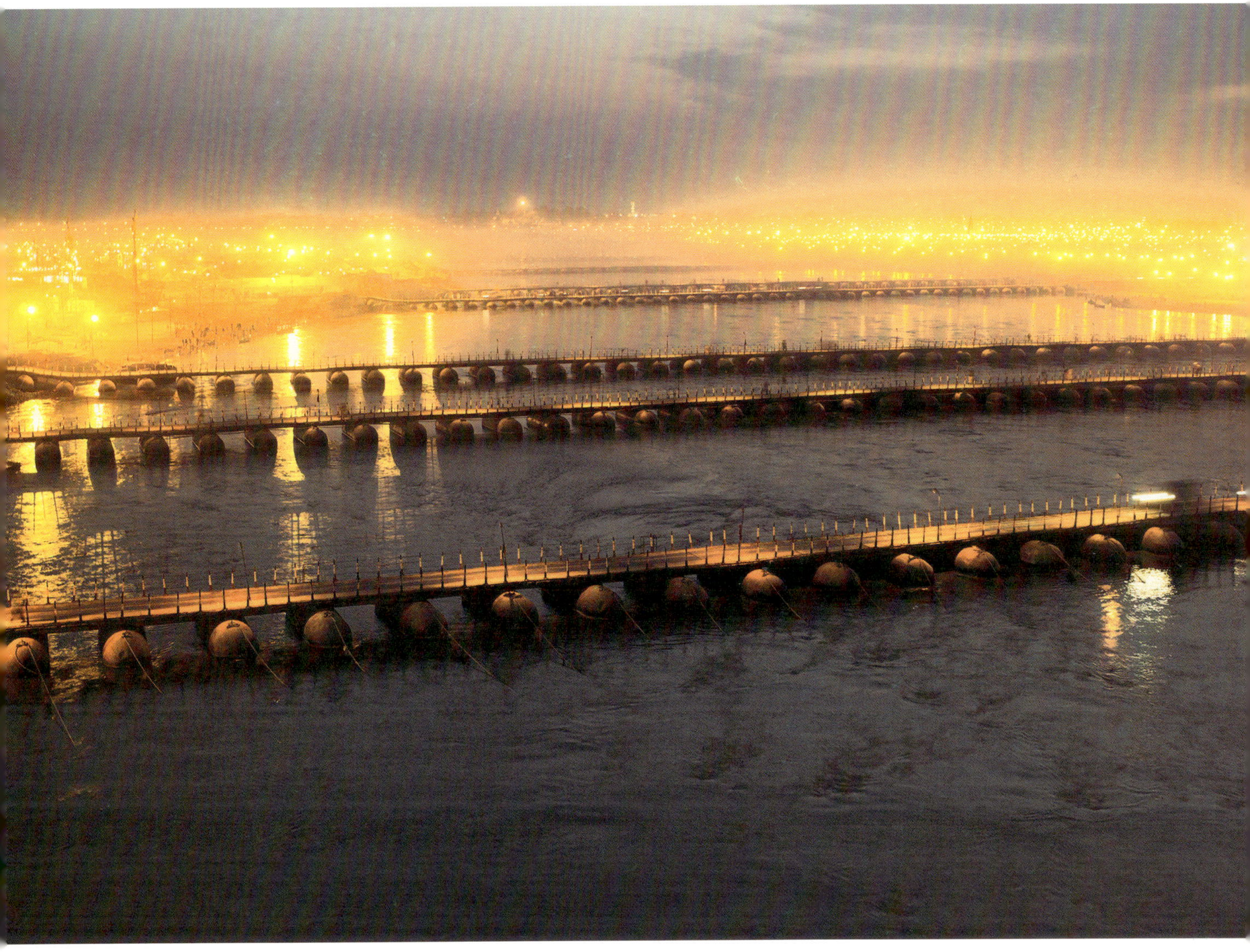

A View of River Ganges

VRINDAVANA

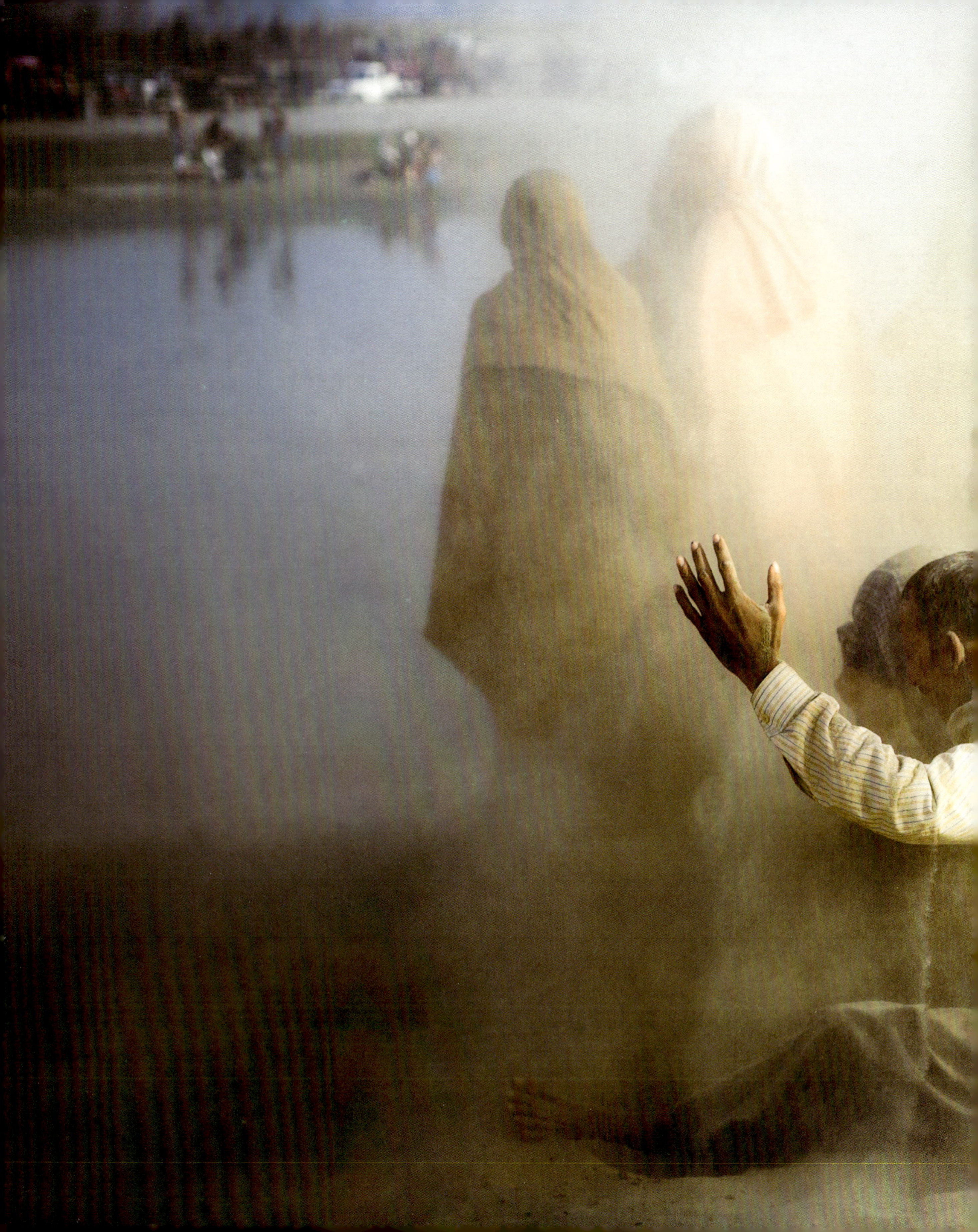

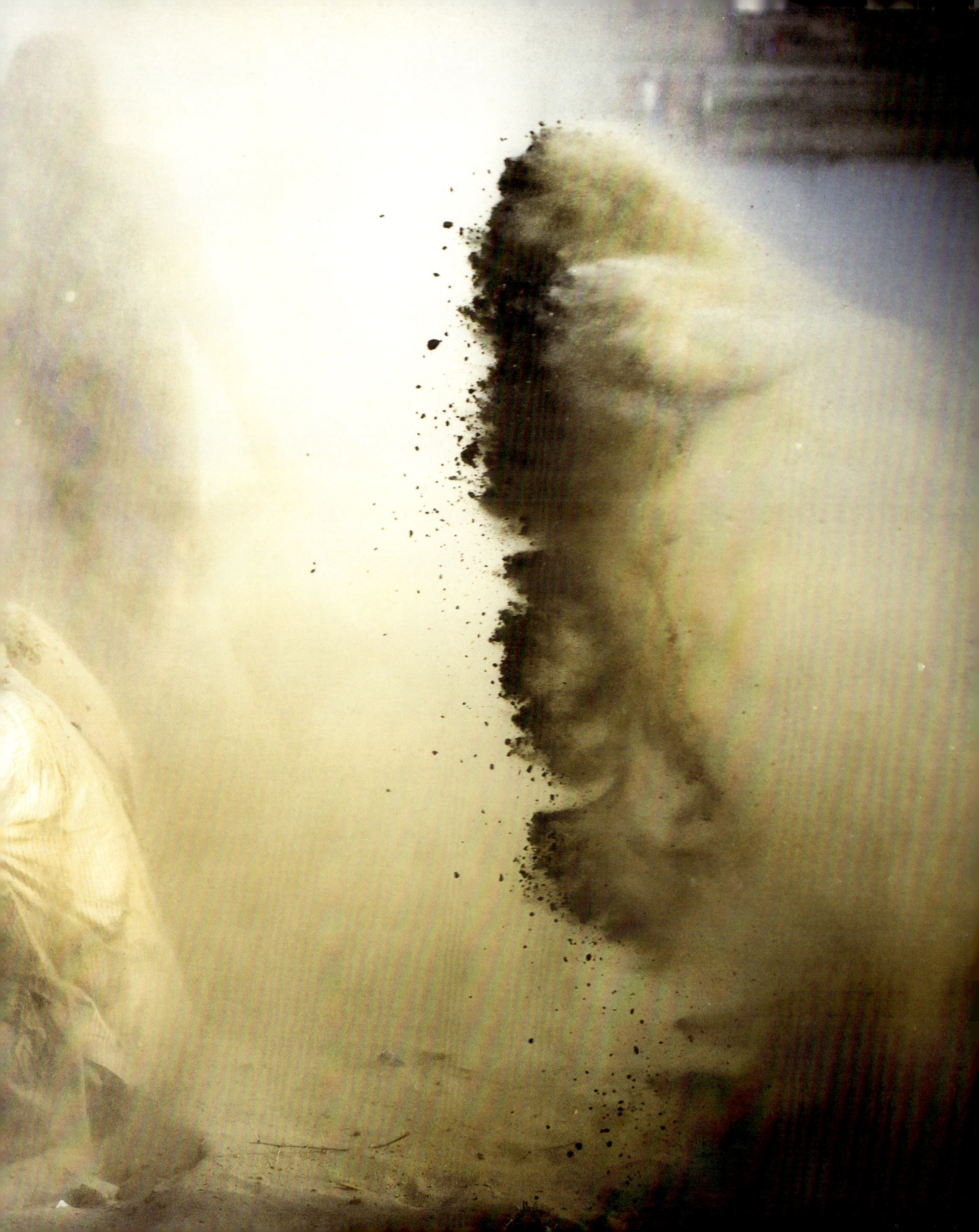

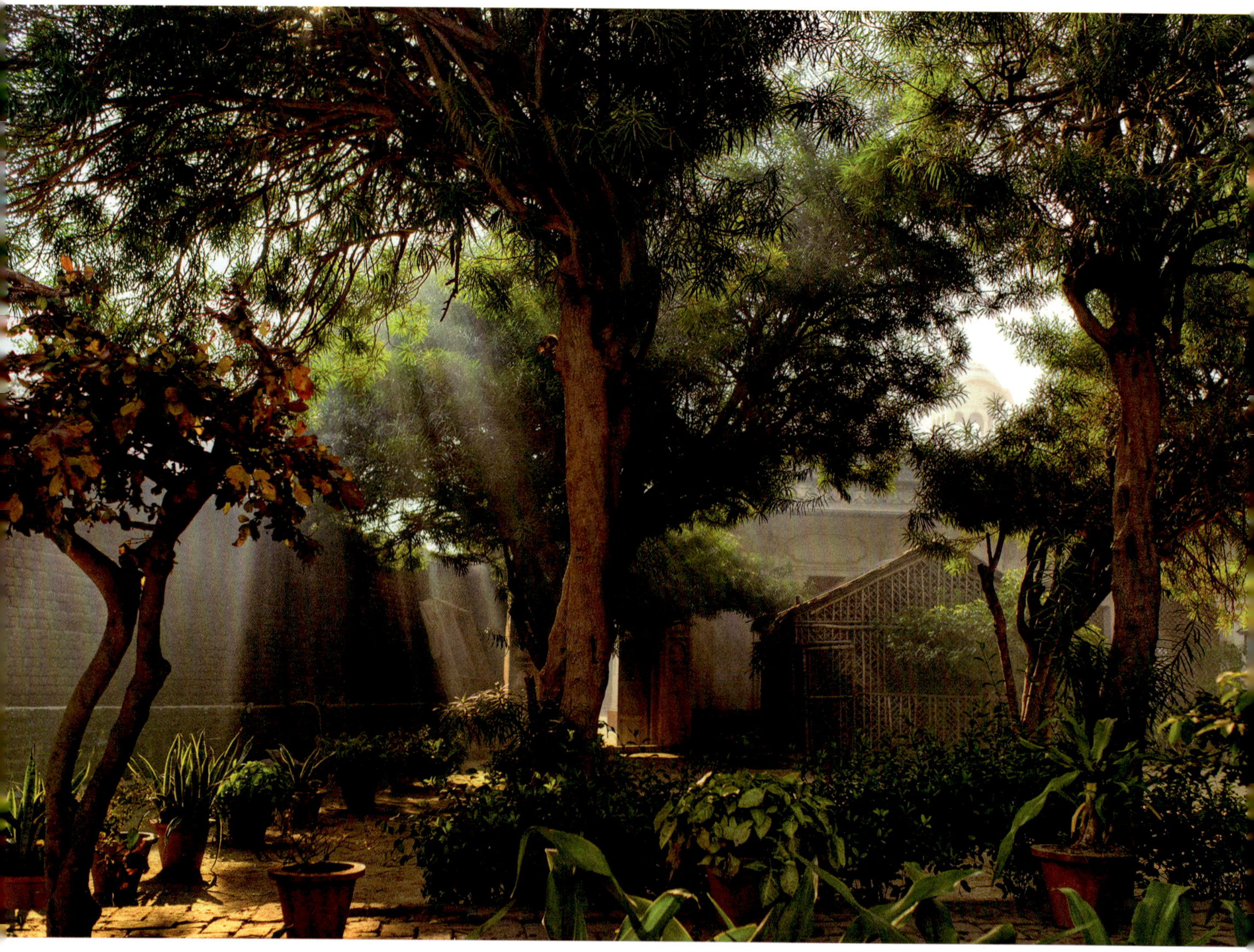

Bumblebee Garden

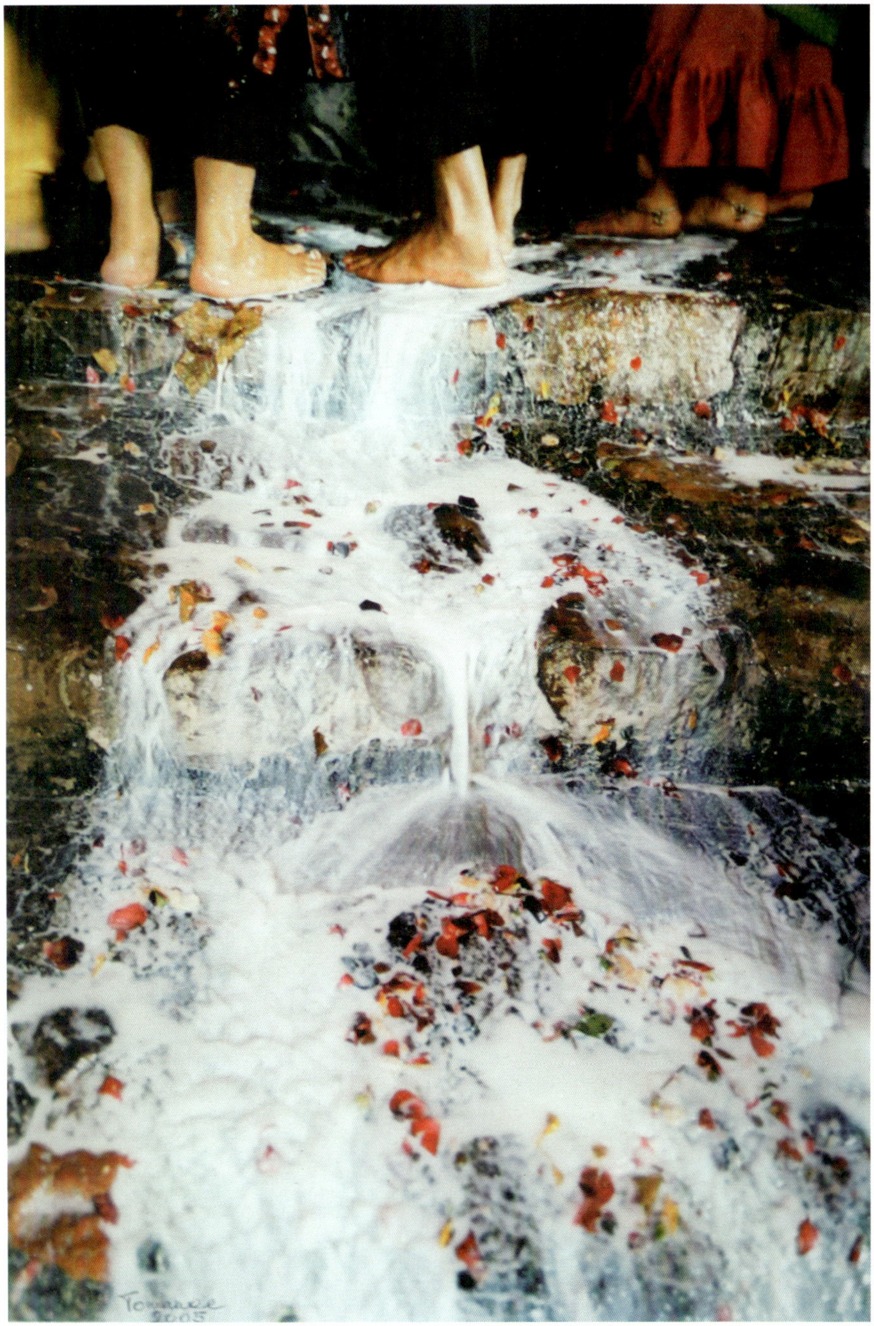

Milk Bath

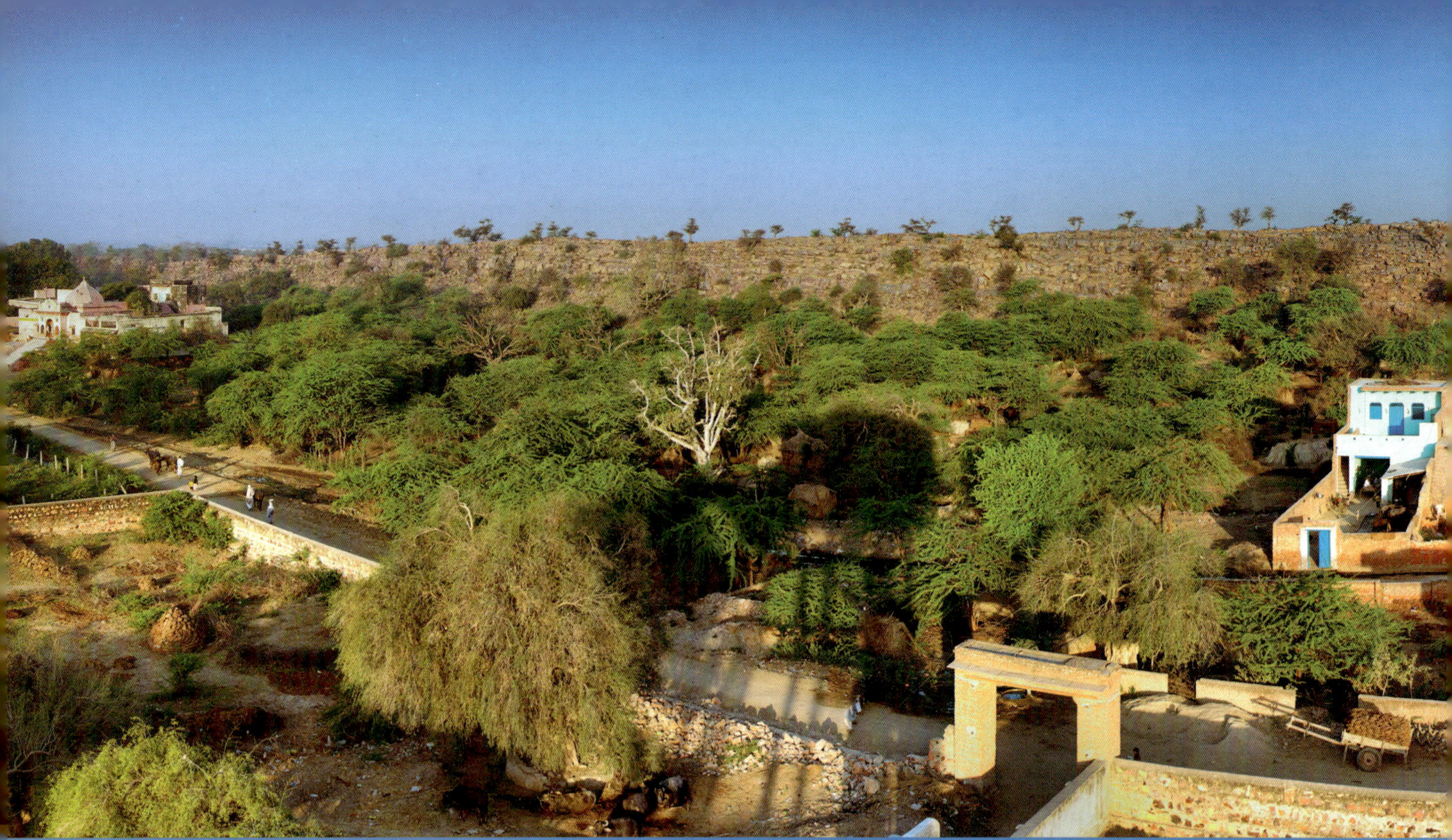

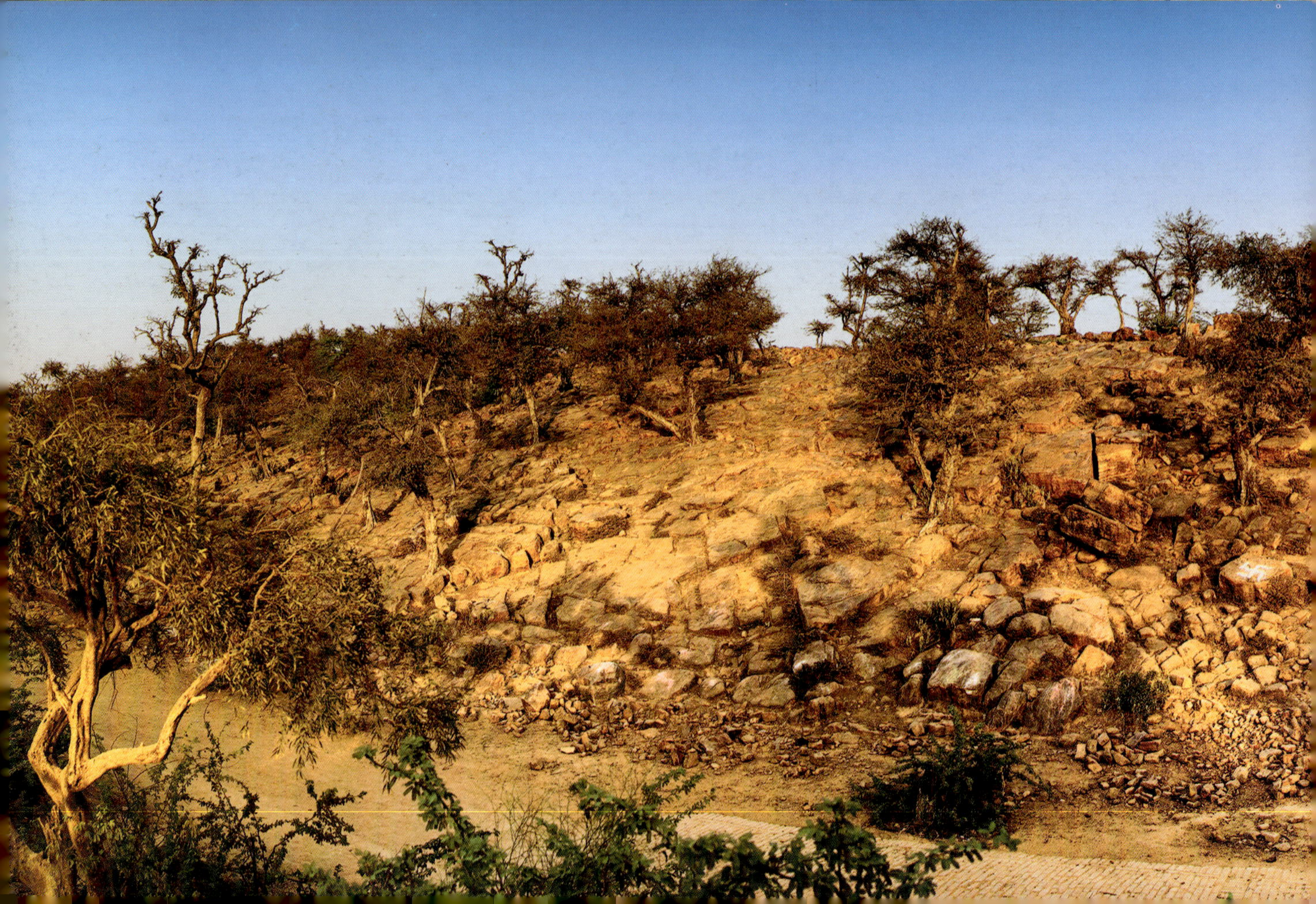

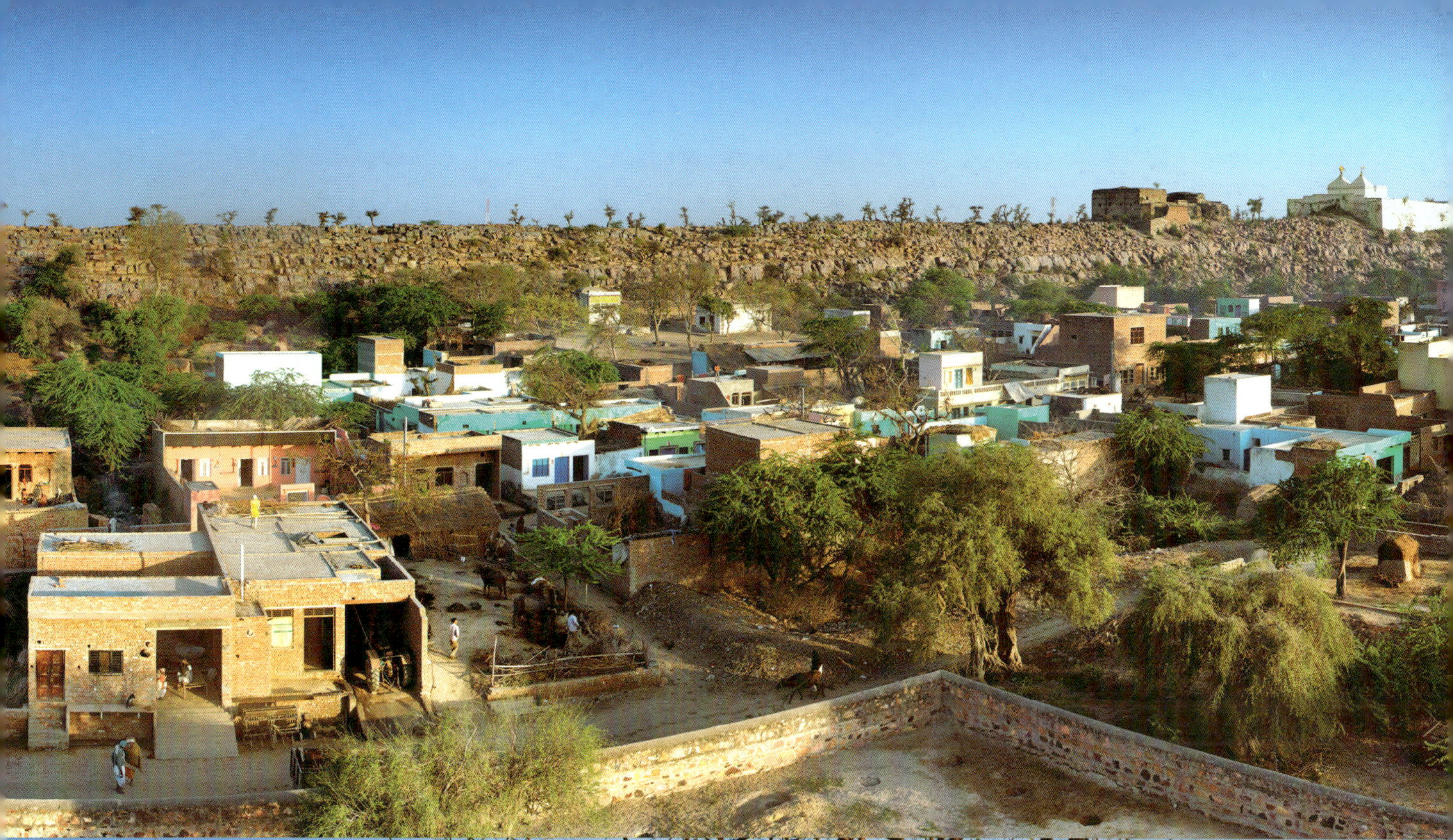

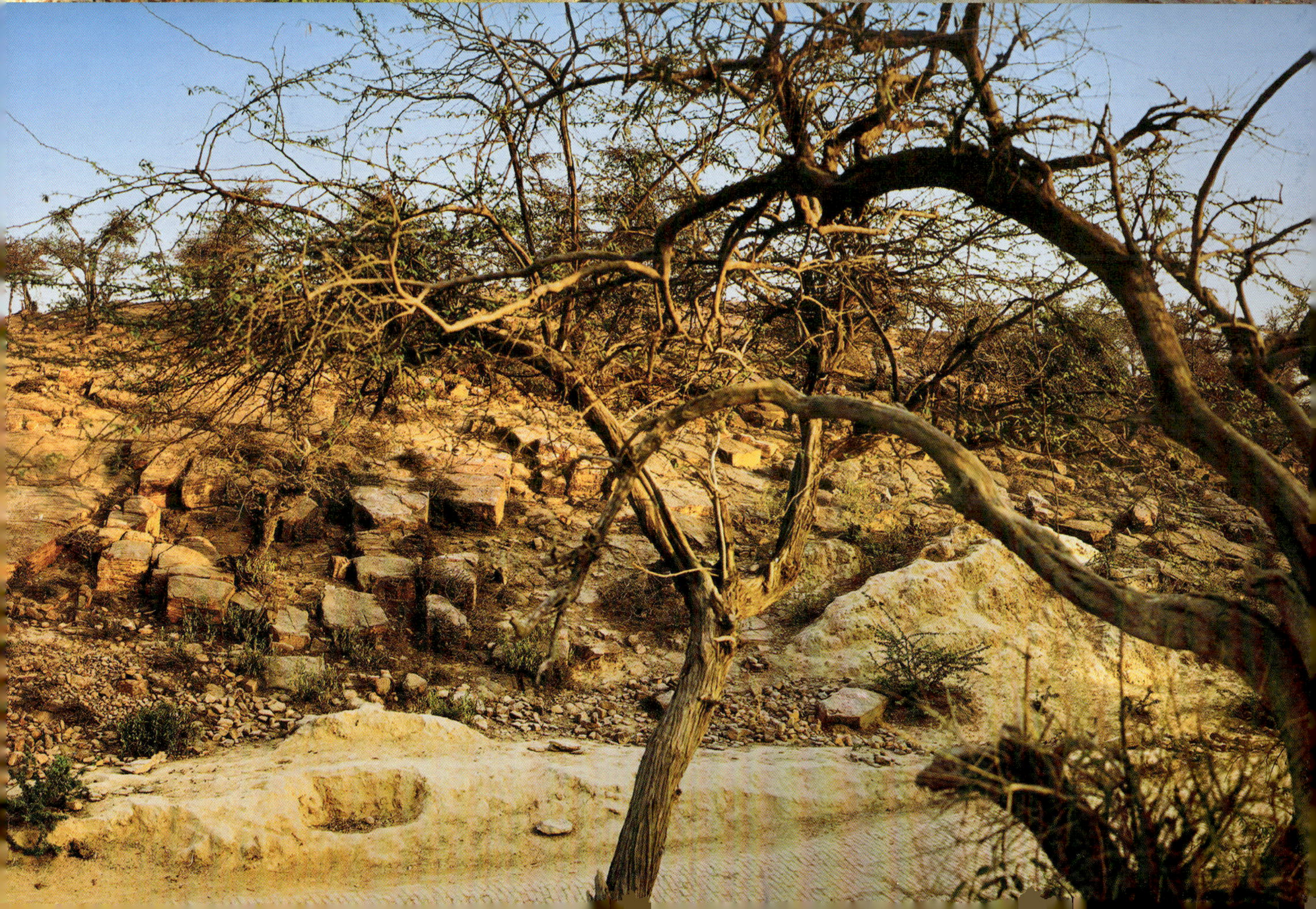

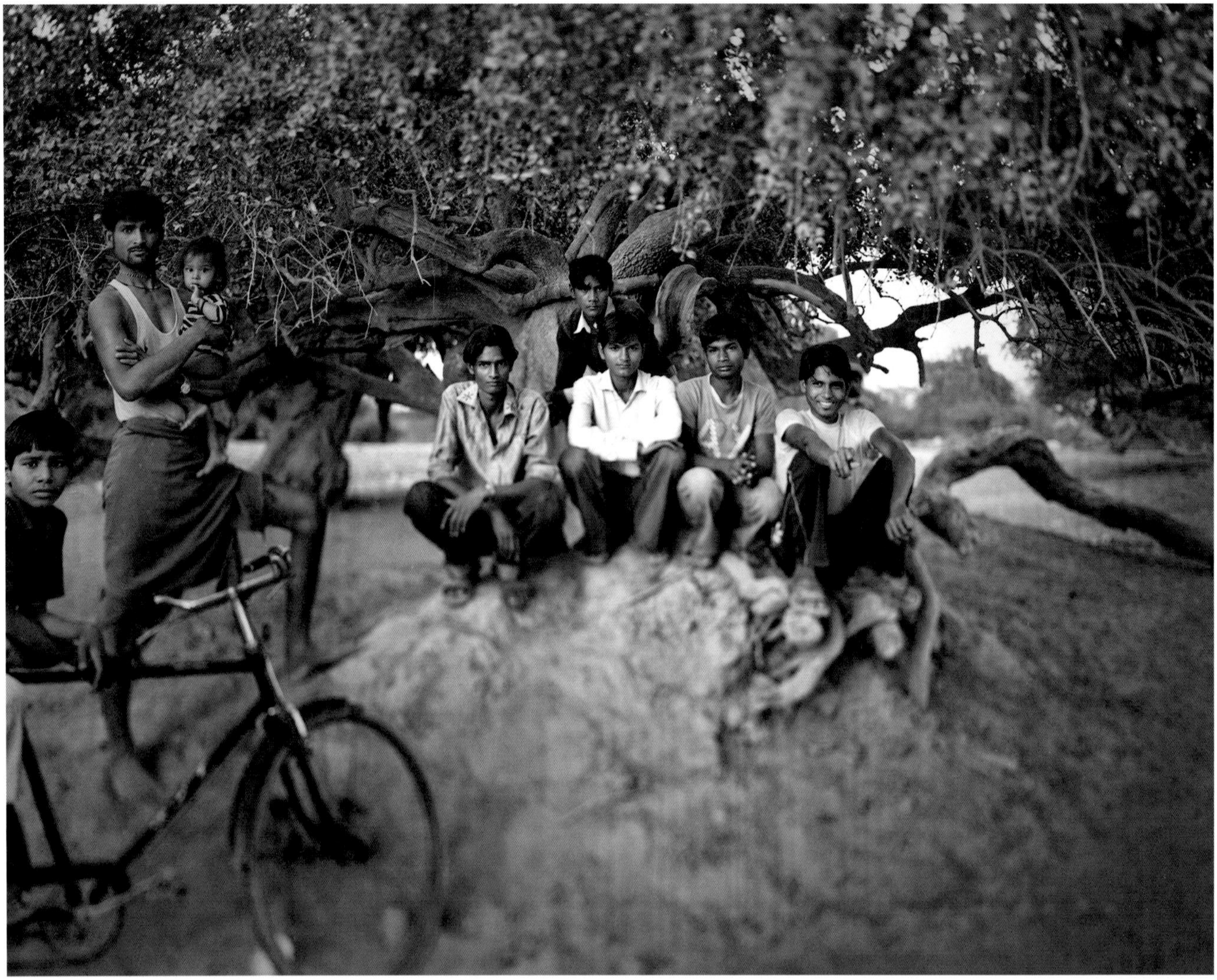

Vrijbasis in Belvan

Gopal and Young Bull >

< **Goverdhan Hill** (Uttar Pradhesh)
< **Goverdhan Hill** (Rajasthan)

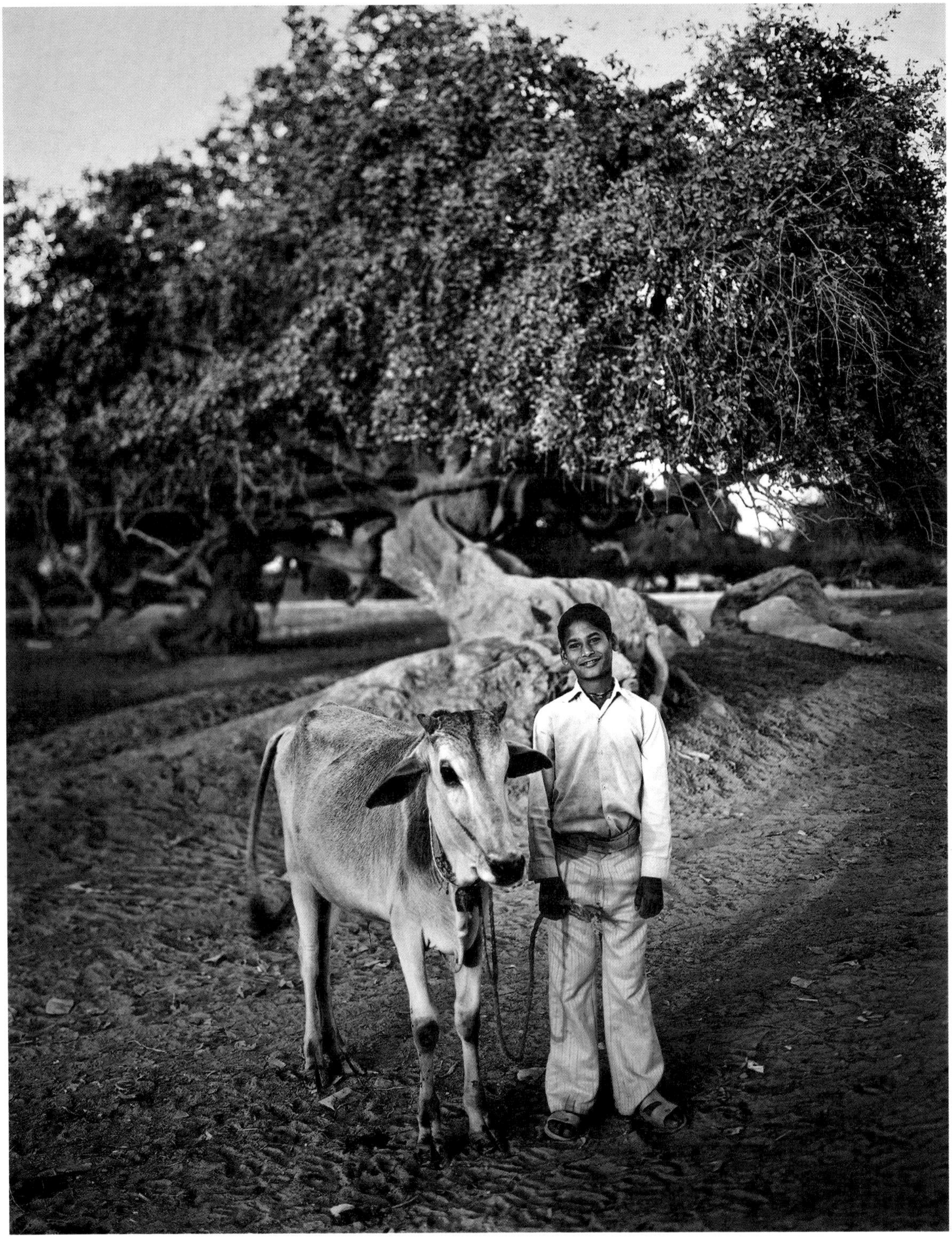

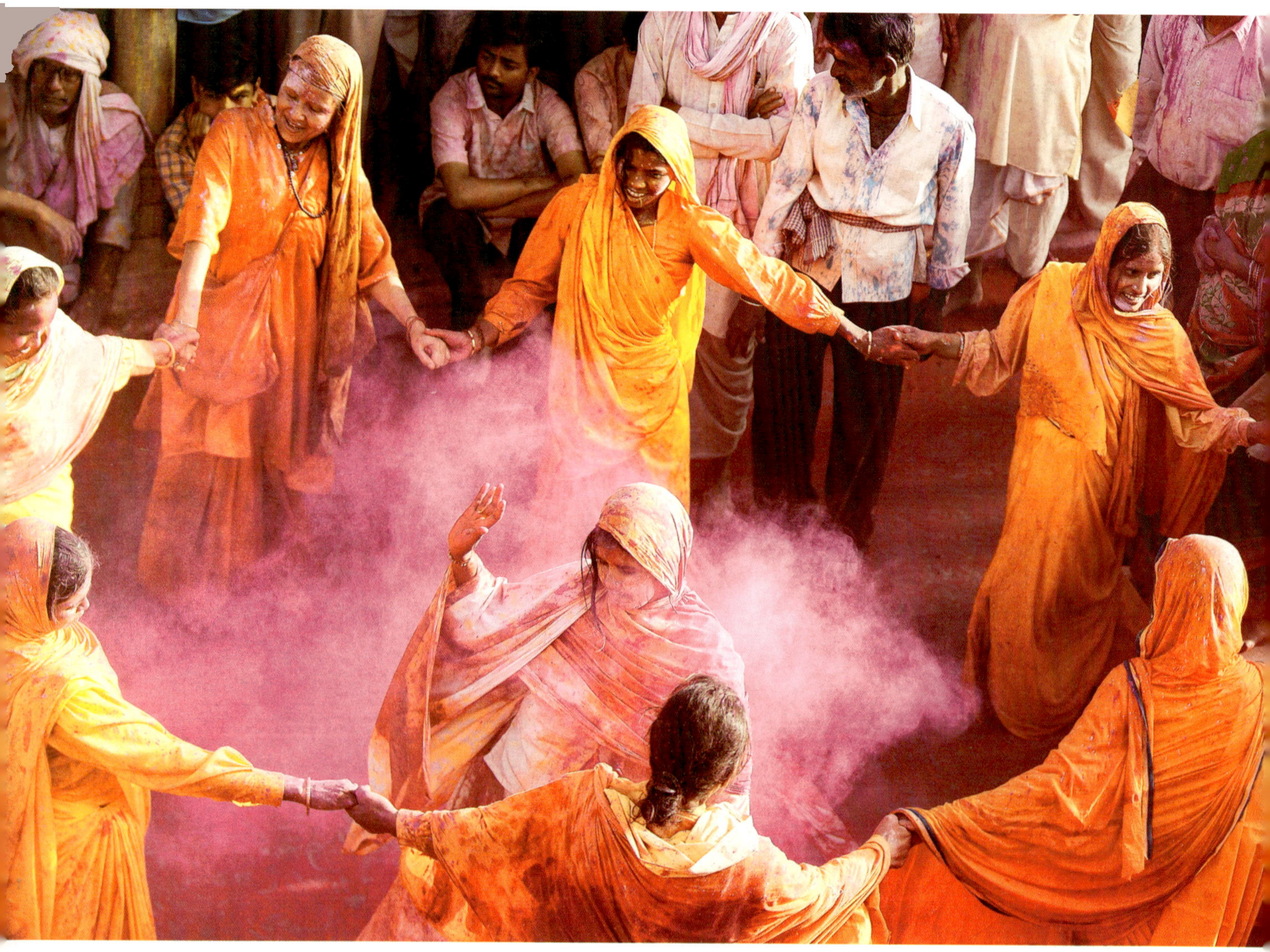

Pilgrims' Dance

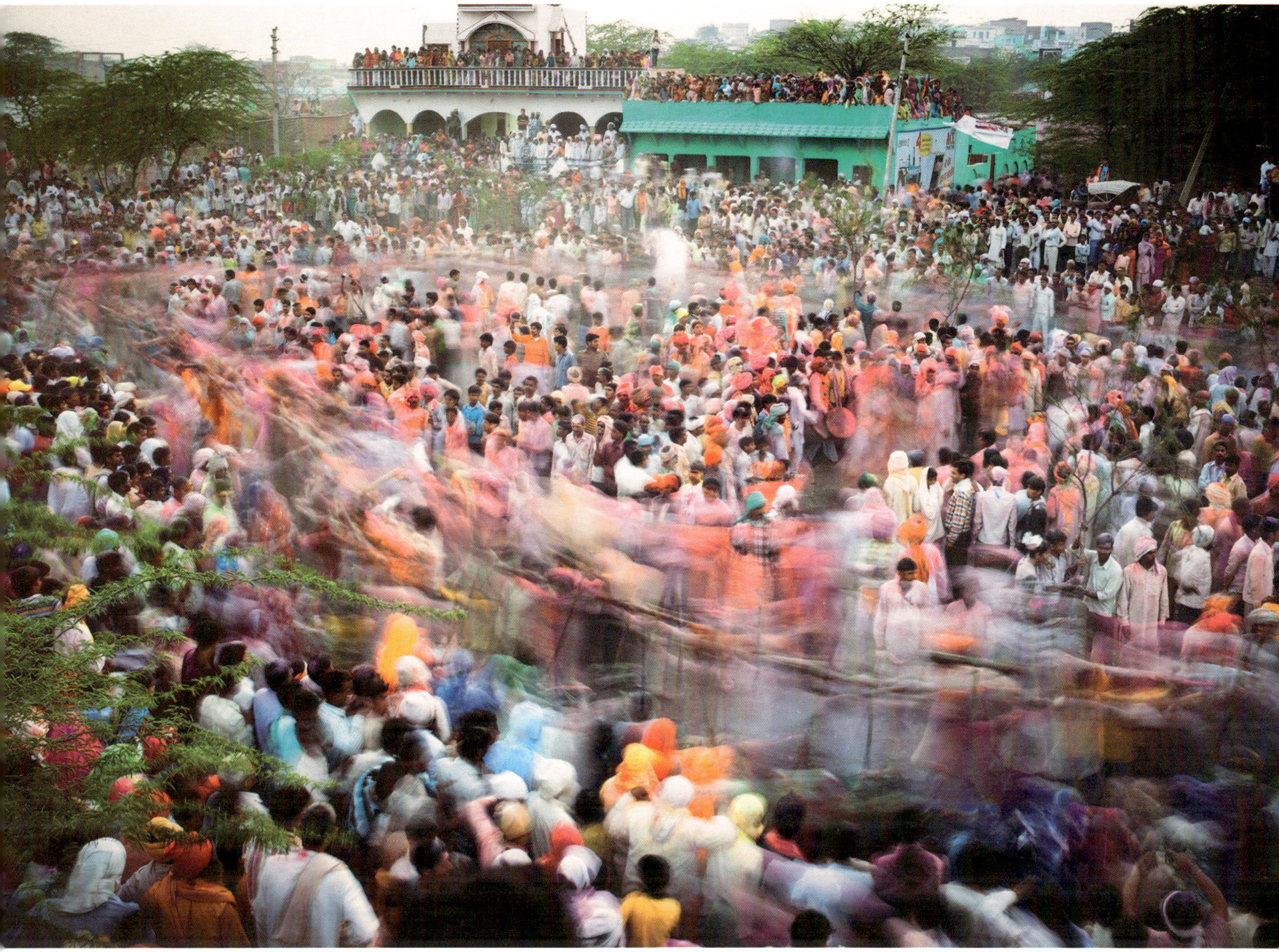

Dance Energy

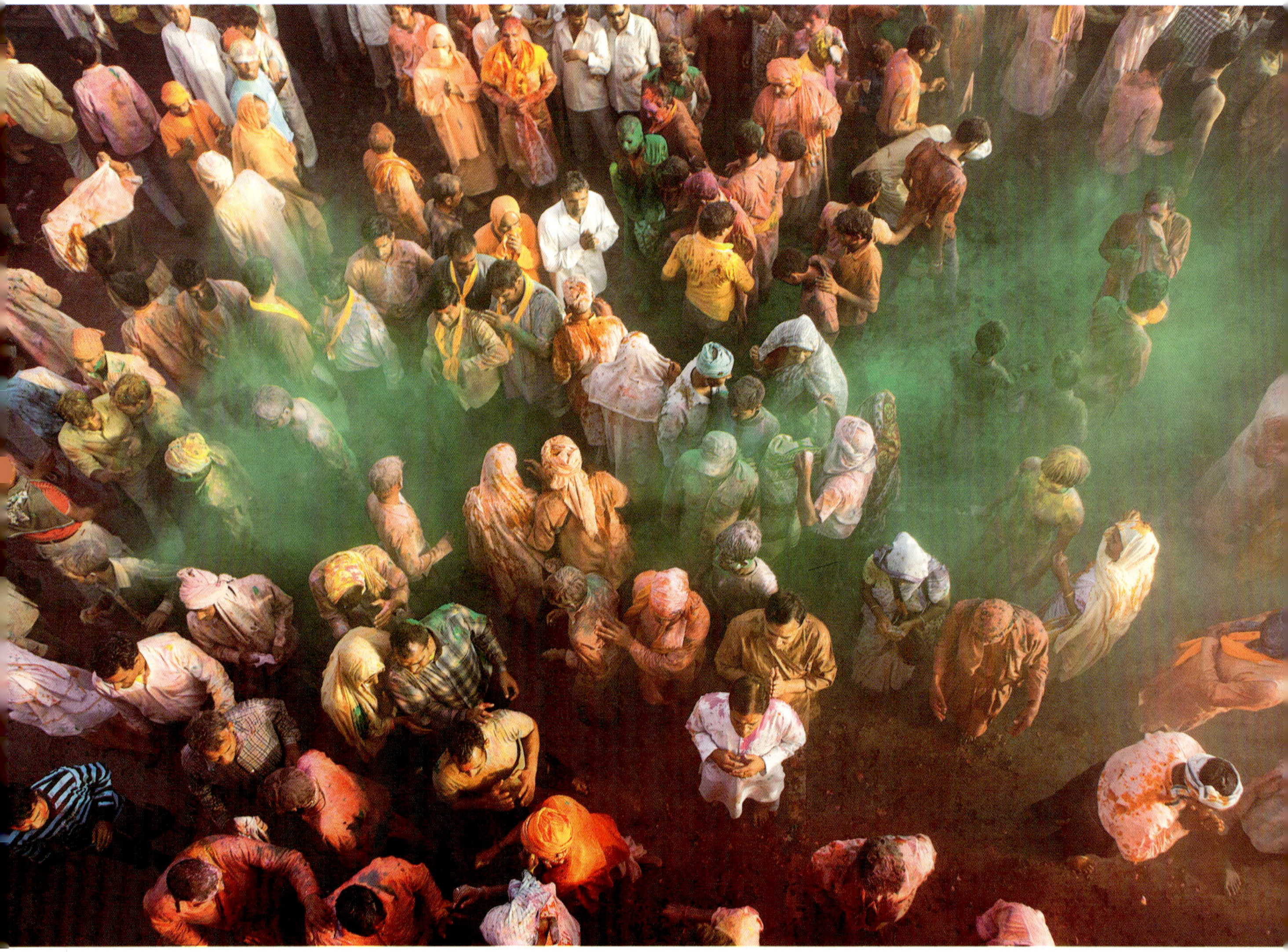

Holi Darshan

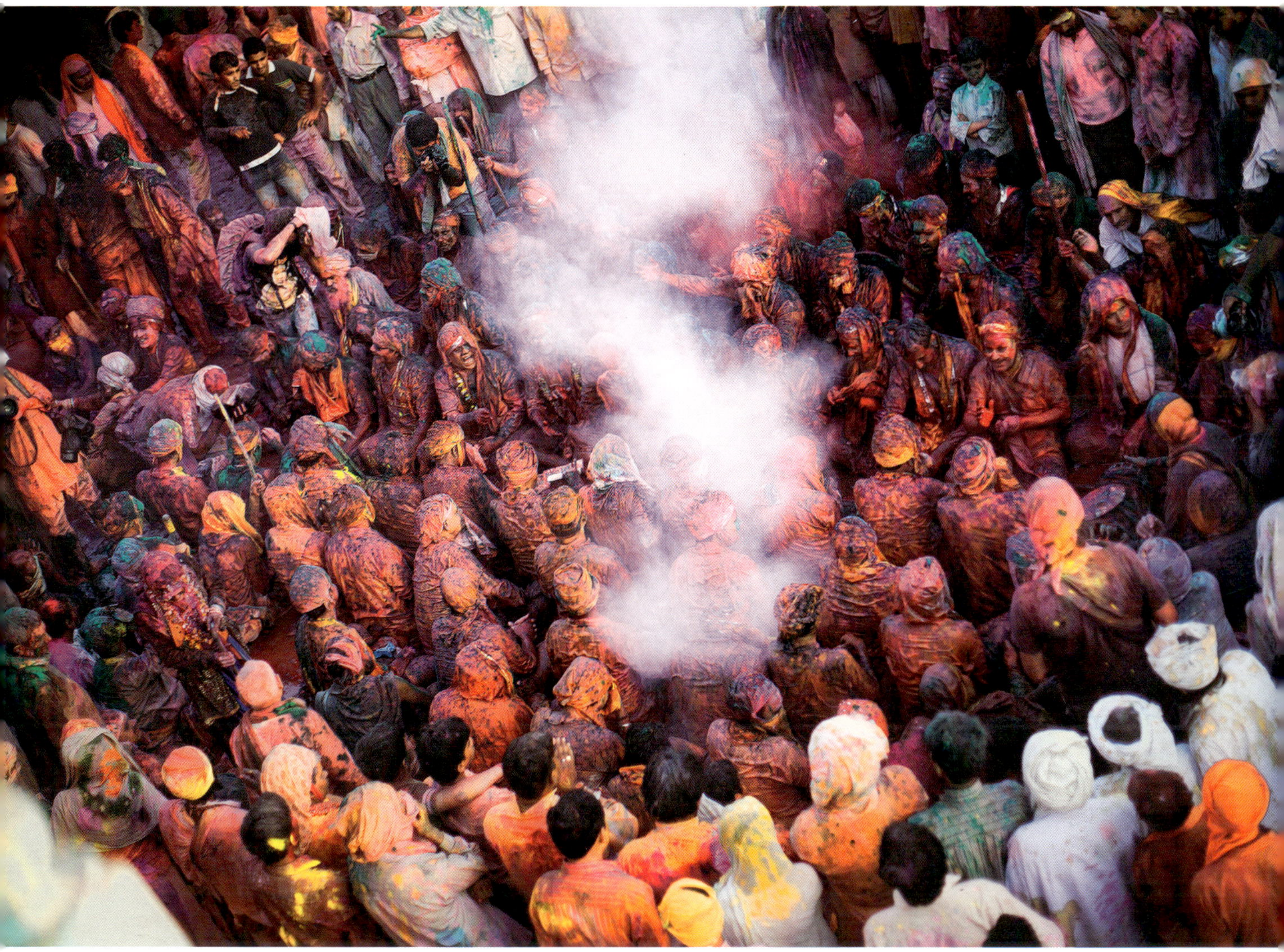

Enchanted Priests

Divine Celebration >

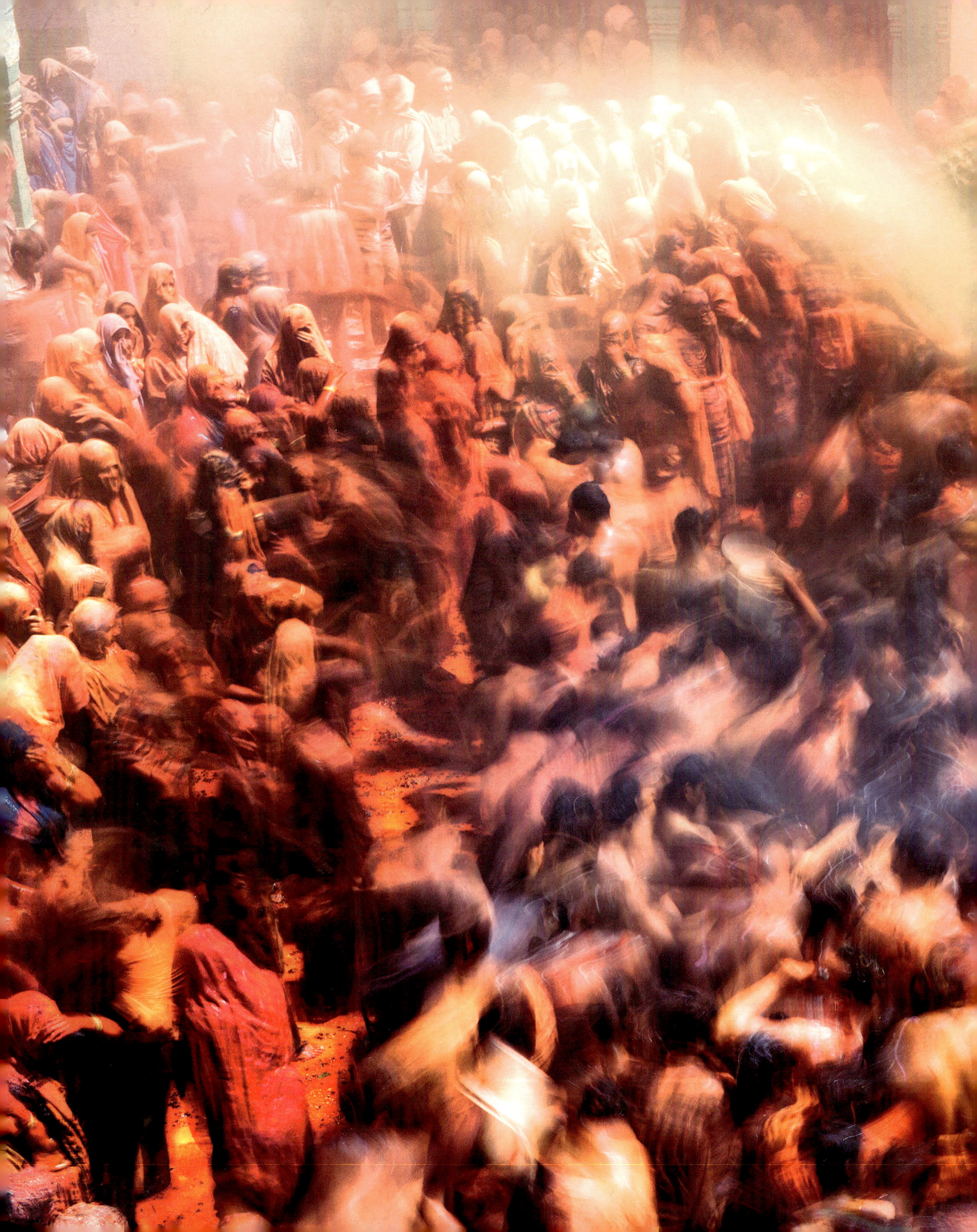

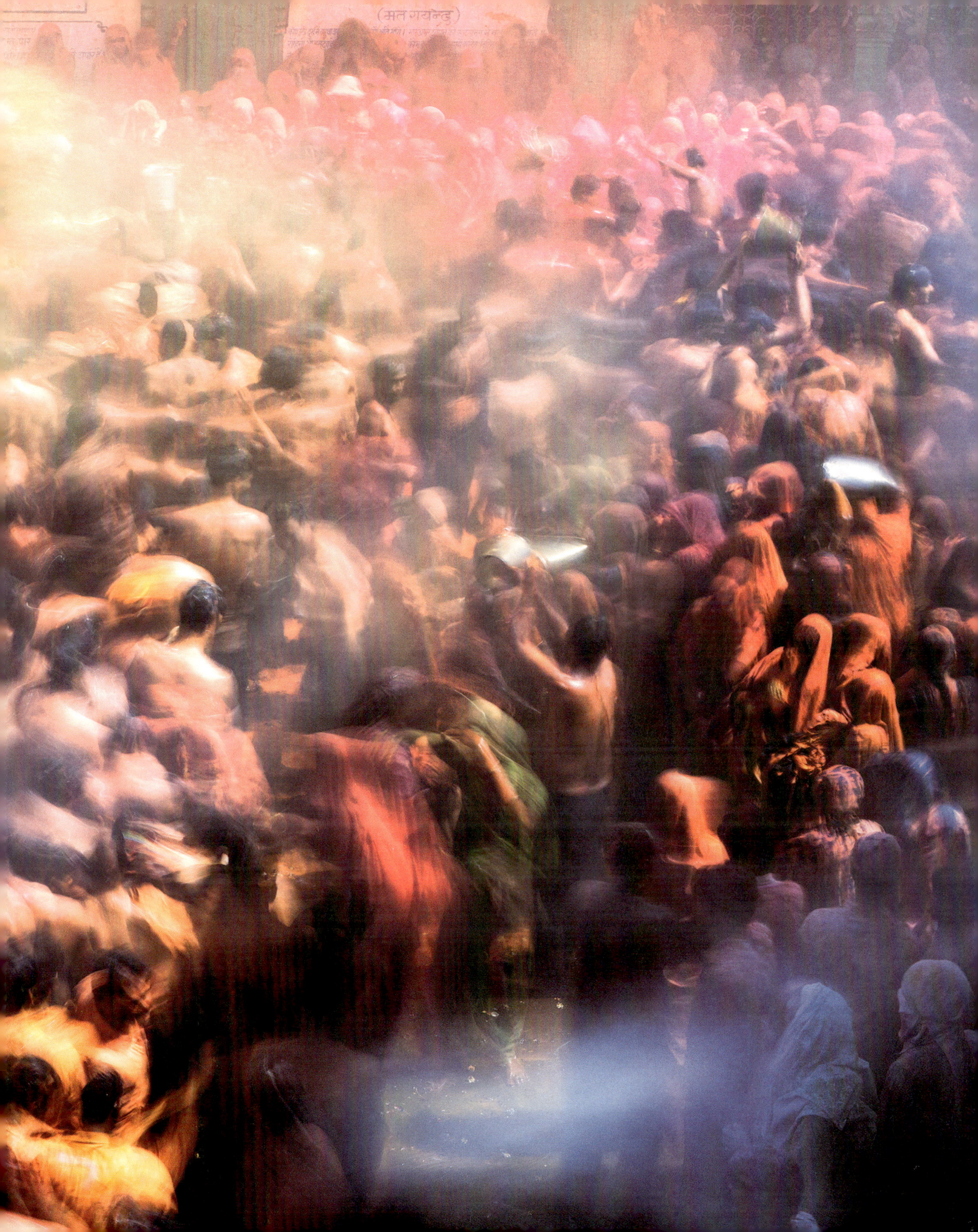

RASA LILA
SERIES

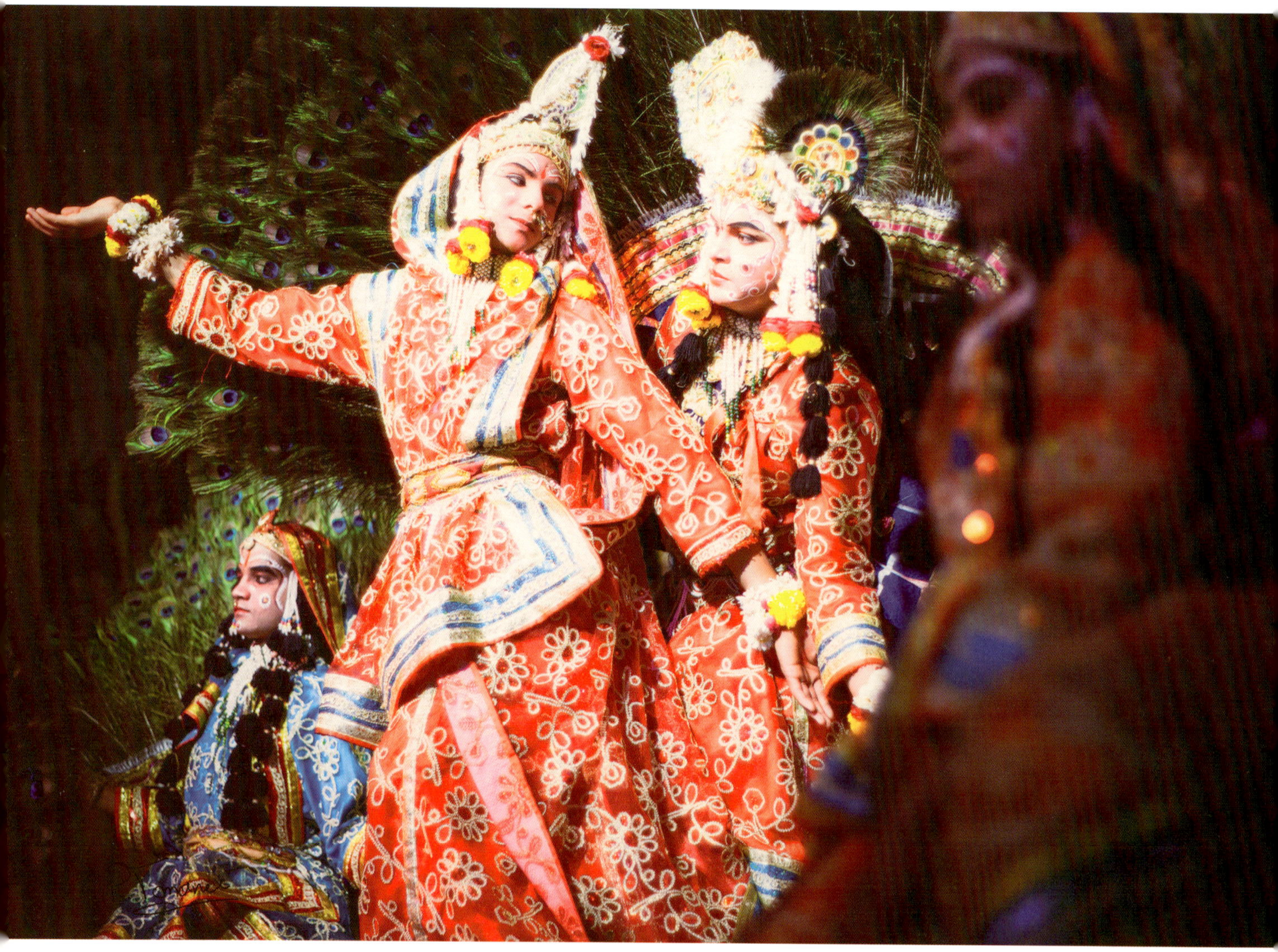

Krishna's Peacock Dance

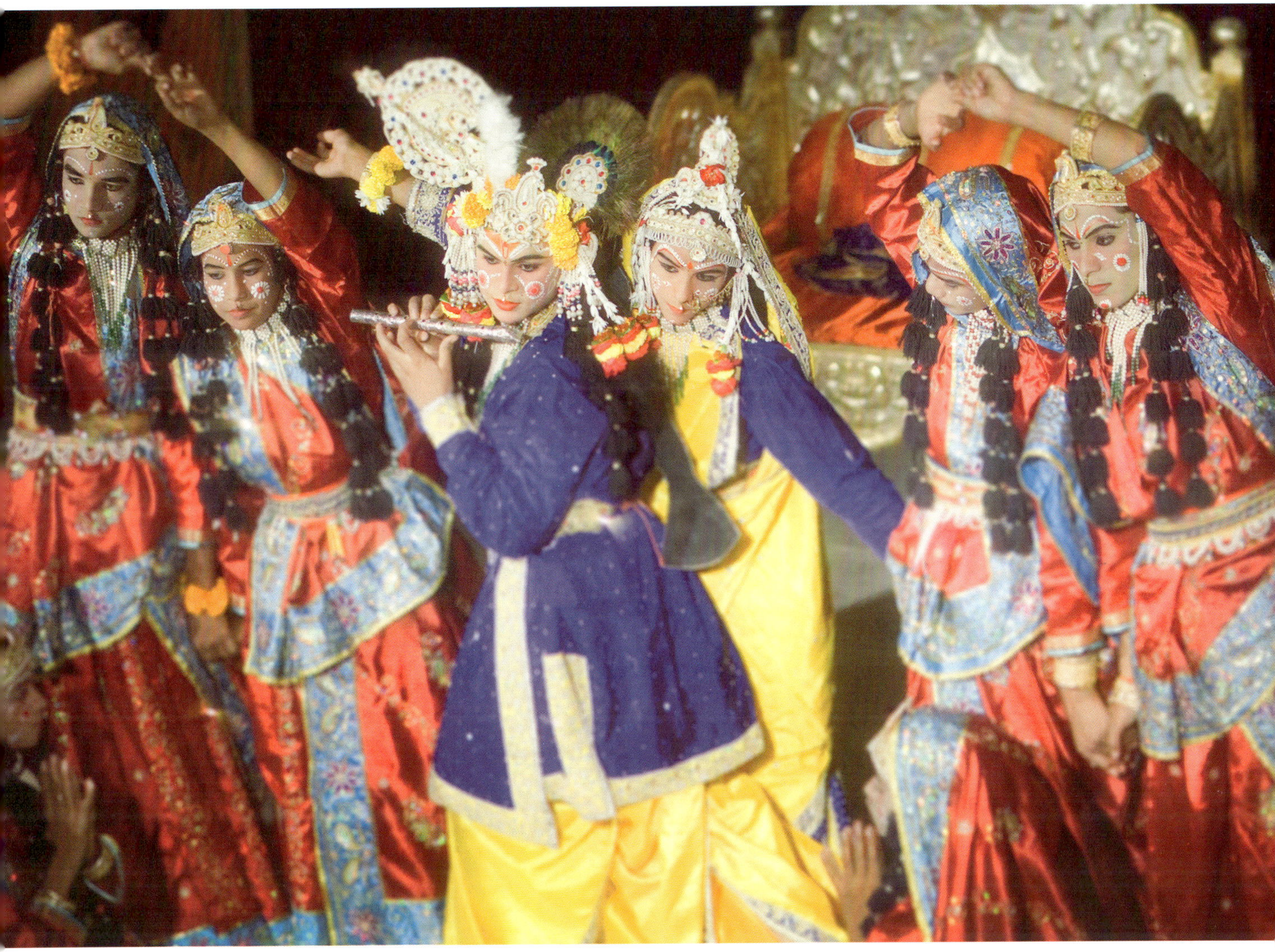

Rasa Lila

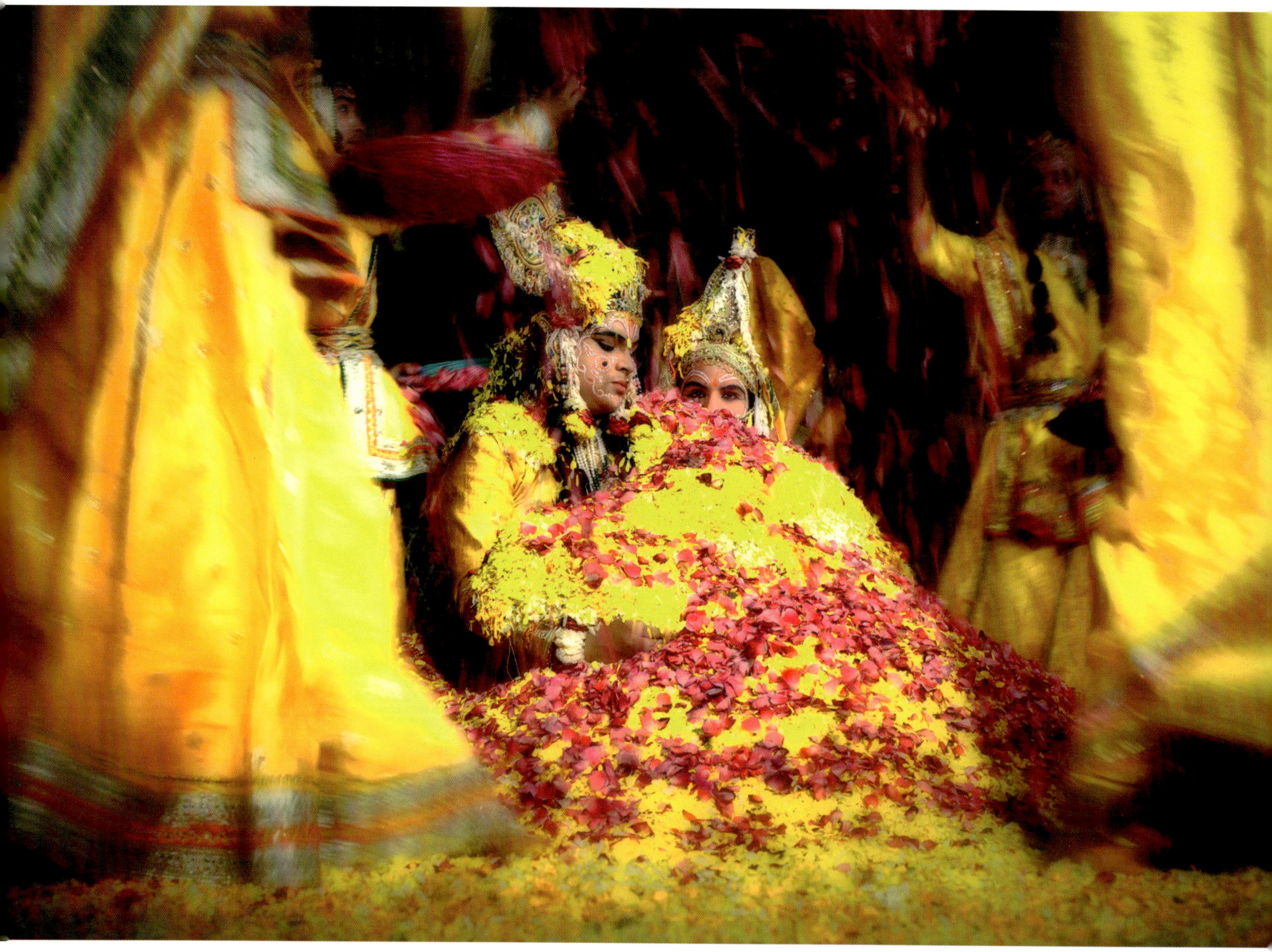

Radha Krishna Sacred Circle

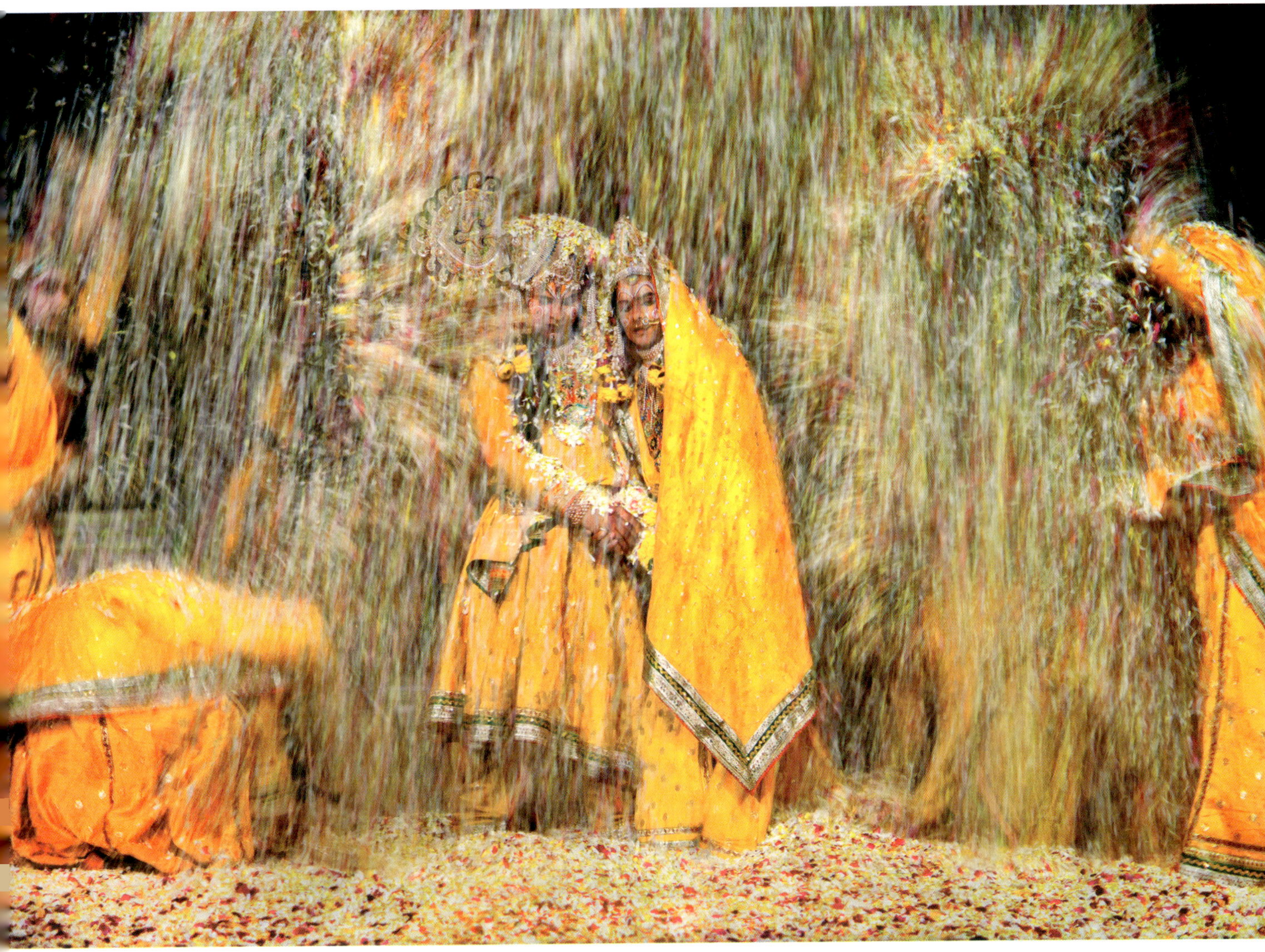

Rasa Lila Crescendo

RADHA GOVINDA SERIES

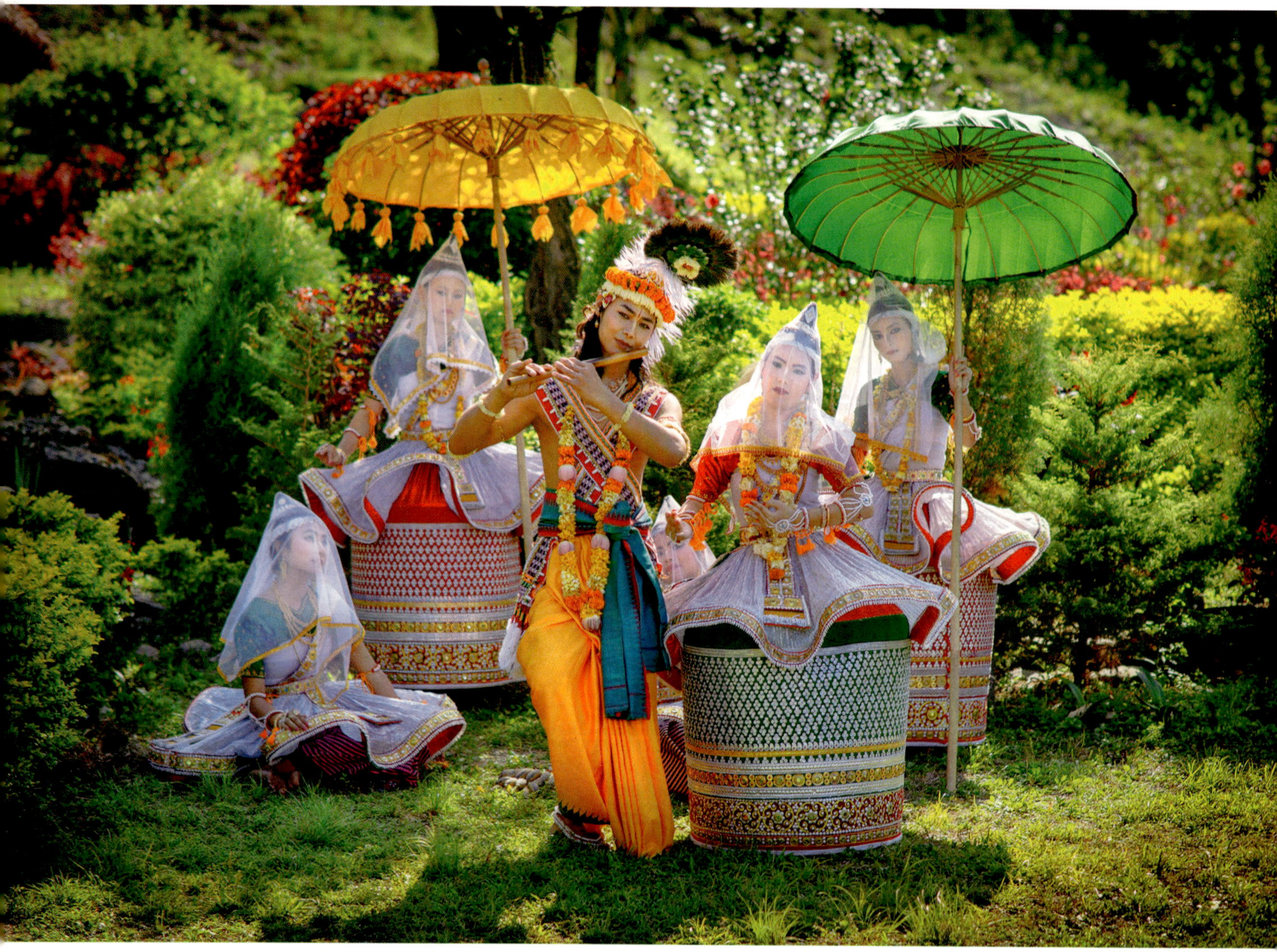

Govinda's Garden of Delight

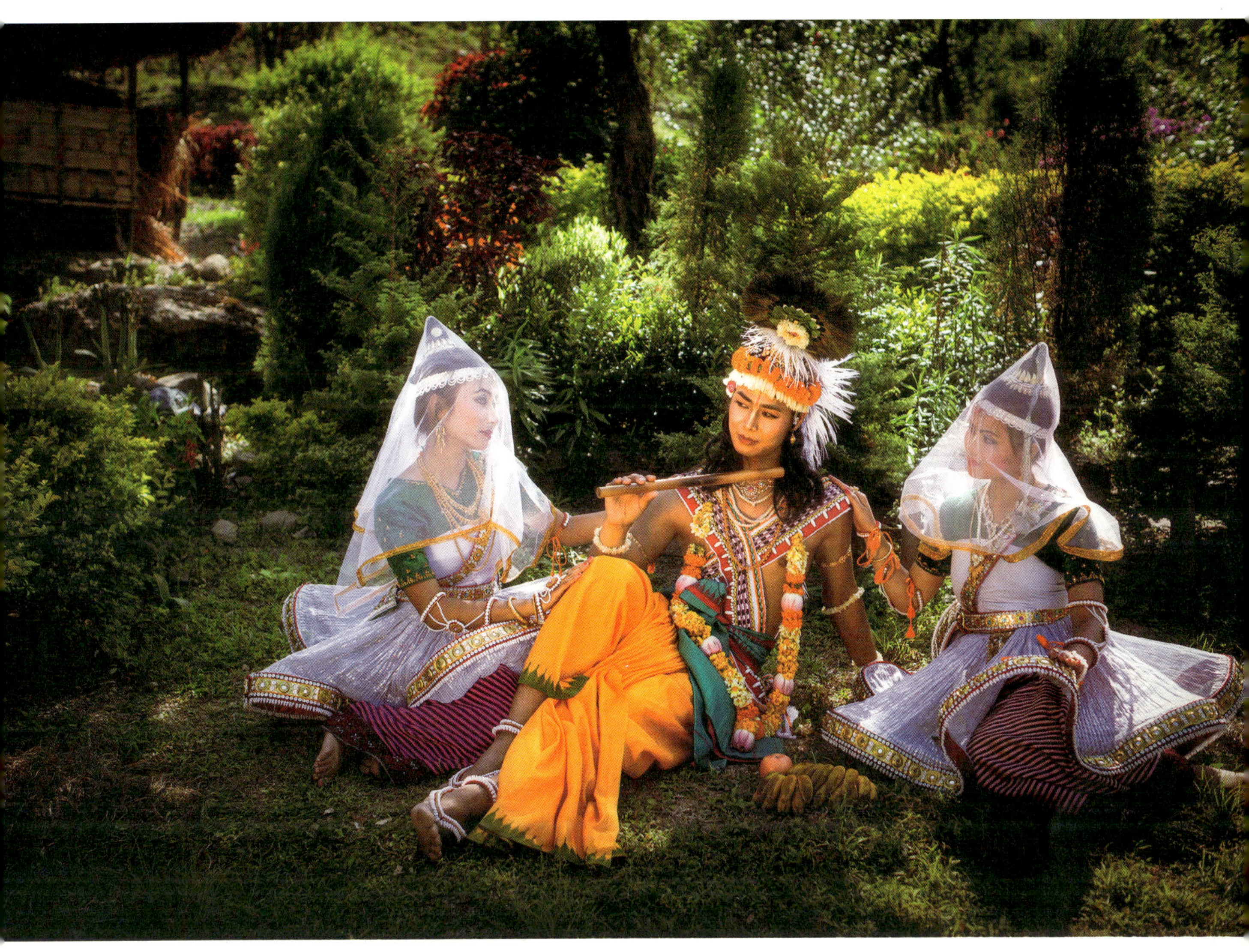

Govinda's Playground

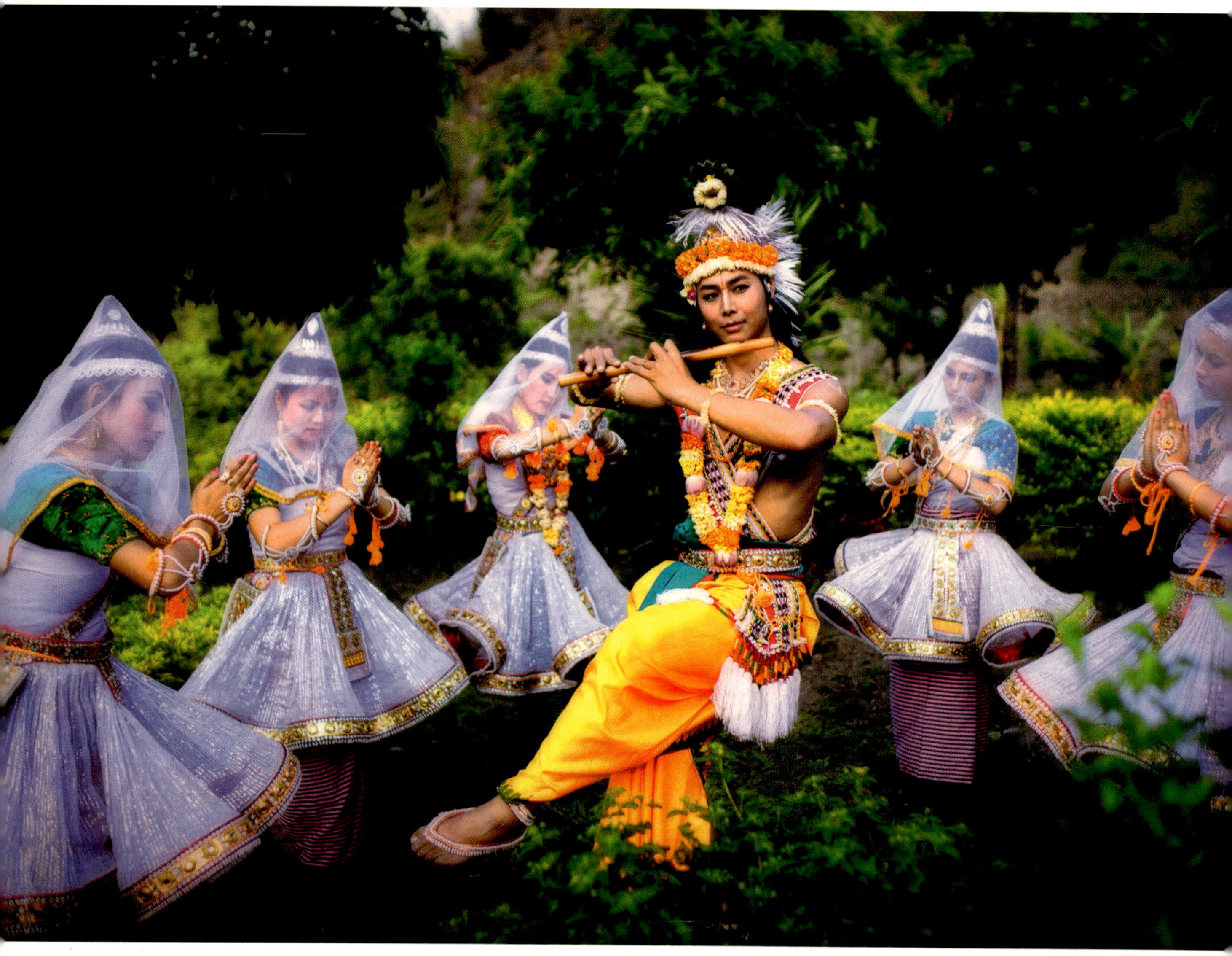

Rasa Lila Dance

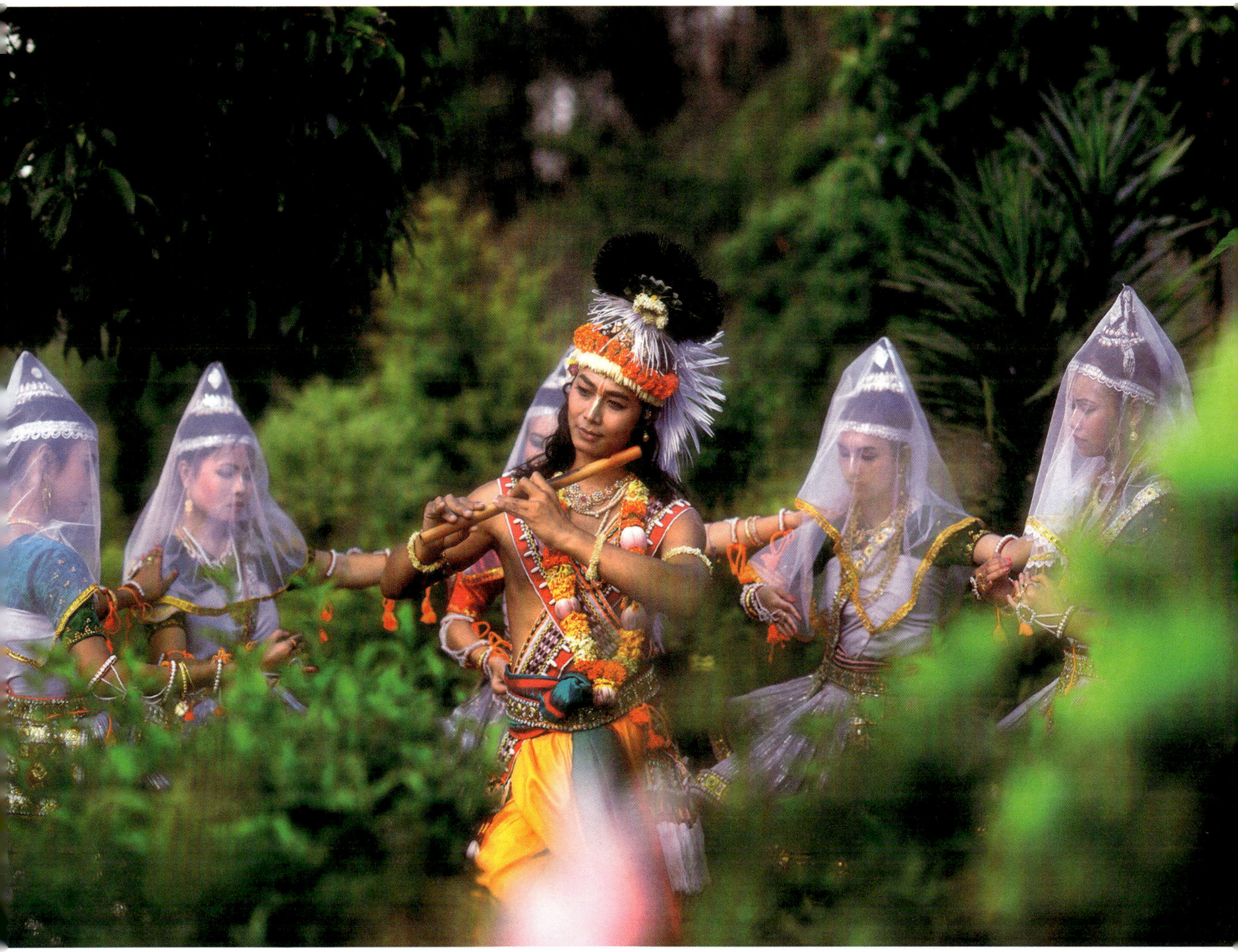

Sacred Garden (The best dance is through the Sacred Garden)

PHOTOGRAPHY & LOCATION NOTES

INTRODUCTION

On cloud nine
(112 x 76cm) page 2

This cloud appeared in the Kullu Valley in the Himalayas, in the land of Parashara Muni, a great yogin and father of Vyasa, who wrote the Vedas. Here Parashara practiced mystical yoga. The land is still charged with energy that inspires the imagination. The photograph's title was inspired by George Harrison's blissful album Cloud Nine.

Mohan, Brajesh and Raj
(62 x 44 cm) page 6

Devotees of Sri Radha, Krishna's consort, are prepared for the sacred Holi dance in a place called Jaav or Javat, near Vrindavana. Photographed inside Sri Radha Temple's colourful compound on a day when forgiveness is celebrated.

Keshi Ghat
(294 x 60cm) pages 12-13

The arched Keshi Ghat area, built besides the River Yamuna in the early seventeeth century by the Raja and Rani (king and queen) of Bharatpur, is where Krishna killed the giant horse Keshi when he attacked Vrindavana. In the foreground are construction materials for building a concrete bridge that would defile the area.

HIMALAYAS

Karttika Yatra (Stars rain)
(60 x 40cm) pages 18-19

This picture was taken during the holy month of Karttika, on the night of a full moon in October. At the foot of the Nara and Narayana mountain ranges lies the pilgrimage town of Badrinath, one of the four famous dhamas (abodes of God) in the Himalayas. There I received permission to spend a night on my own in the mountains from Bashkar Joshi, the local head priest. Joshi is a great admirer of Sri Chaitanya, the foremost spiritual leader in medieval Bengal. During our interview, he recited prayers written by Sri Chaitanya. Bashkar's disciple Shyam escorted me up the mountain at about 7 p.m., and two hours later we reached a point where I was left on my own. When the full moon appeared over Mount Nara, and her rays illuminated the foreground of the Narayana mountain range, I made several exposures, ranging from six to fifteen minutes. Then, between 2 and 4 a.m.,

I was hosted by Buddhimanta Yogi at Charana Paduka Cave, where he gave me an empty potato bag to rest on and a flask of hot herbal tea. Before sunrise, I climbed higher to shoot a time-lapse sequence for film and later, as I descended, I took the following photograph of Badrinath Valley.

A morning view of Badrinath Valley
(60 x 40 cm) pages 20-21

Fifty years ago there were no cement buildings here: most of the environmental damage to the landscape took place in the early 1980s. Ganga Bharati Goswami, an old yogi in Badrinath, described coming here on pilgrimage when he was sixteen and it was far less populated and more suitable for deep meditation.

Gangotri Peaks
(60 x 40cm) page 22

Three majestic peaks stand where the source of the Ganges is worshiped by sadhus. With the help of their disciples and supporters, they established ashrams that accommodate growing numbers of pilgrims. Sadly, beautiful stones from the river are being taken away and used for road construction without considering the consequences. Visitors experience subtle noise vibrations from the massive towers built by India's mobile network providers. Dr Harshvanti Bisht, among others, is an active scholar working to preserve this area.

Crown of Narayana
(60 x 40cm) page 23

From Badrinath to the village of Mana, pilgrims travel to behold Srila Vyasadeva's image in the cave where he compiled the Puranas and other Sanskrit works of literature. Walking to Mana, I could see many of the surrounding peaks. At this altitude, the weather can change within minutes – what looked like a nice sunny day in the morning had turned into a storm by noon. Massive and majestic clouds signalling rain enveloped the Narayana peaks, which amazingly resemble the shape of a king's crown. The temperature dropped and winds began to blow, carrying the rain.

Rudra Ganga Falls
(60 x 90 cm) page 24

To capture the details of this waterfall scene, I used a high dynamic range technique. Accompanied on this day by Swami Raghavendra, he explained to me that even this charming waterfall is not spared from being affected by a hydro-power station built nearby.

Sages of Lake Gauri
(101 x 167cm) page 25

This view was taken from a terrace at an ashram of devotees of Lord Rama. The shapes and colours, along with the spiritual atmosphere, commanded my respect. One can only imagine the power of the flow of the Ganges here in ancient times, when her waters reached the top of the rocks.

Gangotri Valley
(90 x 60 cm) page 26

Along the River Ganges, above Gangotri, beautiful views untouched by man's machines are still there for anyone who wishes to see them. Here the river, with a cave residence, is depicted. Natural objects are the main protagonists. Some caves are administered by ashram owners, and some are freely available for the practice of tapasya (austerities) and yoga.

Alakananda Valley
(60 x 40 cm) page 27

Dancing waves of the River Alakananda descending from Lake Satopanth, where Brahma, Vishnu and Shiva meet every Ekadasi to discuss universal affairs. The river flows through Badrinath and merges into the Ganges at Rudra Prayag. Its waters are cool and soothing, with a refreshingly sweet taste.

Dancing River
(44 x 62 cm) page 28

The River Yamuna, near its source just under the Lake of Seven Sages. This holy river, with waters of mighty power, can bring about in the joyful believer release from a painful death. As death can be very sad, it is considered a great merit to receive such a blessing from the divine Yamuna, who is none other than the daughter of the Sun.

Keshava Confluence
(90 x 45cm) page 29

At Keshava is the confluence (prayag) of the Rivers Saraswati and Alakananda. The clean waters of the River Saraswati offer pilgrims a refreshing holy bath. At the confluence, there is a comfortable place to stay overnight in a conveniently located small cave, with a front porch to make fire, if needed. According to oral traditions, taking a holy bath in the River Saraswati bestows upon one a mastery of the arts and fine speech. This is the path walked by the five Pandavas to Lake Satopanth, from where they gradually ascended to the heavens at the end of their earthly lives. The cave is occasionally inhabited by visiting sadhus to practice their yogic feats.

Yogini Forest
(112 x 76cm) page 30

A stream from the Yogini Falls gives life to the people of the Kullu Valley. The pure water is collected for use both in sacred functions and in homes. The Bhagavata Purana explains that nature is seen as God's body, and rivers, originating from the earth, are seen as God's veins. According to village elders the river is becoming polluted by chemical fertilizers used on apple trees growing in the area. Further scientific analysis would contribute to establishing the facts.

Yogini Waterfall
(112 x 76cm) page 31

The Yogini Waterfall is said by the people of the Kullu Valley to be the residence of sixteen of Lord Shiva's sixty-four female devotees (yoginis). The waterfall serves as a natural veil covering their ethereal bodies when they bathe. Since 2003, this site has been threatened by hydropower companies that want its waters. The Acharya family, a line of teachers and servants at the Sita-Rama Temple in Vashishta, confirmed that in March 2013 the Himachal Pradesh government ordered a stop to the hydroelectric project. Mr Acharya confirmed that the destructive works have stopped and the site has been vacated. The next step will be to order the power company to restore the sacred site to its original condition. Dr. Anup Thakur, a leader of the movement for protection of the Yogini Waterfall advisers that this case is still pending at the Shimla High Court at the time of publication. I feel proud to be part of the movement to protect the Yogini Waterfall.

Nila Kantha Valley
(60 x 40cm) pages 32-33

Mount Neela Kantha presides over Badrinath Valley. Neela means 'blue' and Kantha 'neck'. Here Lord Vishnu in a yogic pose is revered by Shaiva priests from the Namboodri community in Kerala, South India, whose members, starting in the eight century, were tasked with this service by Adi Shankaracharya.

SACRED PLACES

Moon over Orchha
(90 x 60 cm) pages 36-37

Orchha was a place of recreation established in 1501 by Maharaja Rudra Pratap Singh of the Bundelkhand Empire. Here the famed Sita Rama Temple is located, celebrating the extraordinarily beautiful forms of Sita and her prince, Lord Rama – elaborately decorated, served and worshipped by enthusiastic priests and pilgrims visiting all year round at large numbers.

Krishna Mandapam
(167 x 111cm) page 38

This relief sculpture is inspired by the pastimes of Krishna. The images manifested themselves through the hands of gifted sculptors, who were patronized by the royal government. Medieval visitors and tradesmen coming from overseas first saw these fine pieces of sculpture in the middle of the seventh century. The scenes depict Krishna milking a cow, Krishna embracing his father Nanda Maharaja, Krishna lifting the marvelous Govardhan Hill, and Krishna playing a flute. I took the picture when the first rays of sunlight began creating long shadows.

Jagat Shiromani Temple
(62 x 44) page 39

Raja Man Singh built this temple to Krishna in Amer, Rajasthan. Mira Bai, the celebrated medieval devotional poet, worshipped Krishna here. The outstanding design of the windows is set in intricately crafted interior decorations. Such design embellishments enhance prayers recited in such a visually spiritualized environment. Windows serve as a metaphor for a source of illumination and liberation. My goal was to recreate Mira Bai's desire to look out from a window and see the life of Krishna, as we see it in the previous photograph of Krishna Mandapam, for example.

The Chittorgarh Ruins
(111 x 76cm) page 40

The Chittorgarh Fort is located in south Rajasthan. Chittorgarh is a place of pilgrimage for Jains and Hindus. The architecture here incorporates designs inspired by both traditions. The builders paid remarkable attention to details in sculpting the forms, assured its correct positioning in the landscape and many other aspects of the art of building forts. Some forts, like Chittorgarh, were conceived as residences, fully accommodating the needs of everyday life.

The Tower of Victory
(111 x 76cm) page 41

The Mewar king, Rana Kumbha, built this nine-story tower around 1450 to commemorate his victory over the armies from Malwa and Gujarat in Chittorgarh. He dedicated the temple to Lord Vishnu, naming it Vijay Stambha. In this composition, I included a half moon. The moon is seen in the Bhagavata Purana as the eye of Lord Vishnu. In my work, it represents the idea of 'seeing and being seen' in a reciprocal process, an important element in the understanding of darshana philosophy.

Keshi Ghat Meditation
(60 x 40 cm) page 42

This photograph serves as a reminder and reflection upon one of the most charming river banks in all of India, nestled in Vrindavana, a small but important place of pilgrimage in northern India. During the arati ceremony, pilgrims chant songs in praise of the River Yamuna, while the chief priest offers flowers, incense, water and fire to the sacred river. It is also the customary to perform *kirtan* (ancient chants).

Dwaraka Yatra (Krishna Temple)
(111 x 76cm) page 43

This view of the Krishna Temple in Dwaraka has a special place in my heart. The Temple of Krishna in western Gujarat on the shore of the Arabian Sea has been there since the sixth century AD – or at least parts of it, like the inner chambers and nine main shrines. The nights were so pleasant when I visited that I used to sleep on a roof of the guesthouse and operate my camera from there. My ears would listen to distant sounds of mantras being chanted throughout the night, which permeated into my dreams and into my waking states. In recent years Dwaraka sadly is facing dramatic ecological change as the appreciation for clean and serene environment is dissapearing from the agendas of the modern day leaders in Gujarat.

Manikarnika Ghat
(111 x 76cm) pages 44-45

Among the works of architecture on the Ganges in Varanasi, the Durga-Shiva Temple is depicted here. Human bodies are continually being cremated on the river bank, as it is considered a blessing to die in Varanasi, which is also known as Kashi. The scriptures assure the pilgrims that no harm for one's sins will be harvested in the afterlife if they finish their earthly life here; instead the pilgrim of the heart is granted infinite bliss. Nowadays, the *ghats* of Kashi seem neglected, their former glory less visible. Unpalatable buildings and structures appeared in recent years offering cremation services, but lack the quality and refinement we see hints of in the architecture of this older one. I was fortunate to sail River Ganga during a power supply failure as I made this exposure. All the artificial lights installed there went off, then I could see flames of fire with disintegrating human bodies. Just as artificial light exposure is a cause of light pollution, harmful to the human eye and brain, it also tends to distort the perception of details on a photographic image.

PORTRAITS

Sita Rama Dasa
(40 x 60cm) page 48

Sita Rama lives at the Hanuman Ashram in Rudra Prayag. Our friendship began in 2004 on my first journey to Badrinath. When visiting again in 2006, I noticed that, next to the Hanuman Ashram and closer to the confluence of the Alakananda and Mandakini Rivers, foundations for a hotel had been laid and the road widened. Sita Rama and others were offered privilege by the contractors - a free construction of modern toilets for the ashram residents in exhange for the river side land. In 2009, the hotel's structure had taken over the landscape, and a cemented river bank replaced the natural river bank, with its round stones to rest on in prayer, its pebbles to massage the feet, and its fine sand to relax on after a long journey. In 2011, the cement began cracking and sharp stones appeared on the surface. A solid metal barrier – allegedly for health and safety purposes, but now broken – prevents pilgrims from having easy access to the river. Sita Rama said, "I can clearly see now that it was not good what has happened here. Nowadays, we have peace here only during winter months. The rest of the year is no longer suitable for our spiritual practice due to noise pollution. People have lost interest in taking a sacred bath because of the dangerous surface of the concrete river bank. We trusted the company to help us, but we are left only with their poor *karma* (activities)."

Sadhu Ramesh
(40 x 60cm) page 49

Sadhu Ramesh lives near Gangotri in the Himalayas. He revealed to me that he had renounced "the chains of family life" for the unbound way of life of a mendicant, a humble servant of the Lord, who has surrendered to circumstance. A pilgrim of the heart sees spiritual practice as the safest position for attaining a blissful soul in this present age of hypocrisy (*Kali Yuga*).

Raghavendra Swami
(60 x 40 cm) page 50

A friendly sadhu, Raghavendra Swami was one of the first pilgrims to permanently settle at Gangotri. He recalls arriving in Gangotri at the age of fourteen or fifteen. Over the years, he built the Ishavasya Ashram, the largest hermitage there. According to legend Hanuman himself appeared to Swami in a dream requesting to be worshipped by him there.

Krishnananda Dasa
(40 x 60 cm) page 51

A Vaishnava monk belonging to the Gaudiya school of thought, Krishnananda came on a pilgrimage to Vrindavana more than a decade ago. He decided to stay and become a servant at the Radha Gopinatha Temple, which is one of the six main temples in Vrindavana. This photograph was taken in the winter. Despite the harsh weather conditions, Dasa's eyes appear graceful. Dasa explained that chanting the Hare Krishna maha-mantra is a source of inspiration and warm bliss, keeping the devoted heart free from expereincing the cold.

Subhadra Devi
(112 x 76cm) page 52

Subhadra Devi is a devotee of the Ganges, living in the village of Mukhva. Subhadra Devi and her husband, Ramanuja Acharya Dasa, hosted me for the night before we all embarked on a pilgrimage to Gangotri. Before the winter begins, the deity is brought down from the mountains to Mukhva, and in the spring the diety is returned back again accompanied by devotees. Subhadra Devi cooked a sumptuous vegetarian meal in the kitchen on a simple wood-burning stove long after sunset for all the guests. We were moved by her devotional sense of service.

Rishi Ma
(112 x 76cm) page 53

Rishi Ma likes to see her life as a daily pilgrimage. What she appreciates most is the time she can spend in the Yogini forest with her cows. While they graze, Rishi Ma and other ladies discuss daily affairs or meditate or knit.

Janardan, Keshava and Kiran
(170 x 152cm) page 54

Janardan, Keshava and Kiran are followers of Swami Haridas, a medieval poet and one of the teachers of the classical composer Miyan Tansen, who served at the Court of King Akbar. Janardan (left) was a manager in an engineering company for ten years in Bengalore. When I created this photo with film camera Mamiya 7II of him and his spiritual friends, with their foreheads smeared with sandal paste, he had been living in Vrindavana for over a year already, having left his mundane work behind. Keshava and Kiran are young sadhus who found shelter in the ashram. They are learning to make spiritual friendship with ascetic sadhus to become one of them, if successful.

Meditating Sadhu
(90 x 60 cm) page 55

This likable elderly sadhu belongs to the same order of ascetics as Janardan, Keshava and Kiran. About forty years ago when his young family died in a tragic event, this sadhu decided to retire in Vrindavana to dedicate his life fully to prayer. He is very kind and does not seek unwanted attention from curious pilgrims. His plan now is to die in Vrindavana with Krishna's holy name on his lips.

Manohar Chaturvedi
(76 x 101cm) page 56

The Chaturvedi family line is said to have lived in Mathura in Lord Krishna's time. The Chaturvedis maintain a certain cultural identity in the Krishna bhakti tradition. Their daily practice is to chant the Gayatri and Gopala mantras from sunrise till noontime, then they return to household duties and their families. In the Vishram Ghat pilgrims rest as they walk about Mathura hearing about Krishna. According to the tenth book of the Bhagavad Purana, it was here that Krishna rested after wrestling and killing the tyrant king Kamsa. Under Krishna's government, a society based on respect and prosperity for every devotee of the Lord was established.

Murlidhar Chaturvedi
(76 x 101cm) page 57

This photograph was also taken at Vishram Ghat. Manohar Chaturvedi is another householder serving at the Vishram Ghat. Recently, the Chaturvedi community acted to protect the River Yamuna from the pollution caused by new petrochemical industries and slaughterhouses. They pray to have once again clean water in Mathura just like it is near the Yamuna's Himalayan source. I am waiting to see the Chaturvedis' prayer materialise.

Pujan Swami
(40 x 60cm) page 58

Pujan Swami is a devotee of Hanuman and chants "Jaya Sri Rama!" from six to nine in the morning in Dwaraka's twenty-four-hour kirtan. He has chanted for six years in the temple there. One day at the temple I forgot my bag, with a lens and some money in it. Two days later I realized it was missing. When I returned to the temple, the bag was in the same spot near the door where I had left it with all the belongings intact. I felt blessed.

Uma Shankar Goswami
(40 x 60cm) page 59

Uma Shankar Goswami and I met in Tupani village, twenty-five kilometres (15 miles) from Dwaraka. Tupani has a well called Carana Ganga that gives sweet water even though it is on the sea plains. History has it that Lord Krishna, with Srimati Rukmini, took sage Durvasa Muni here from Dwaraka. To cool Muni's desire for Ganga water, Krishna pushed his thumb into the earth and pure waters from Ganga flowed out. Two new friends I met in Dwarkhadish Ice Cream Shop one hot afternoon, spontaneously took me to Tupani village by motorbike, and thanks to Lord Dwarkhadish we spent a rewarding day together. In good Hindu tradition, Tupani village elders politely asked me to visit and stay anytime I needed in the future.

Jitendra Dasa (A Prayer to the Sun)
(167 x 111cm) page 60

A prayer to the Sun by the Badhva Brahmin, Jitendra Das, living in Maharashtra's holy town of Pandharpur. Maharashtra is renowned for the worship of Lord Panduranga (Krishna) and Rakhumai (Rukmini). The medieval saintly poets Tukaram and Eknath were active here. As a result of their activities, the Varkari Panth (the Pilgrims' Path) was established. The Varkari Panth, focusing on the worship of Vithoba, is considered an important Vaishnava line in India today, noted for its simple way of life based on ahimsa (non-injury) and bhakti (devotion).

Sadhu Param Das
(60 x 40 cm) page 61

Param Das represents another important Vaishnava line coming from an original medieval thinker Ramanujacarya from southern India. Param Das lives in Hanuman Cave in front of Orchha's huge pavilions with gardens. He attends to passing pilgrims or tourists by blessing them with a smile or a prayer. I sensed from him a spirit of detachment embellished with inner joy. He enjoyed being photographed.

DEITIES

Krishna Balarama
(60 x 40cm) pages 64-65

Two smiles light up the faces of the brothers Balarama and Krishna (the darker one).. Both are Govardhan shilas (sacred stones) from Govardhan Hill. The ornamentation of shilas is a devotional art form. These forms come from Govardhan Palace, administered by the Hare Krishna Movement, founded by His Divine Grace A.C. Bhaktivedanta Swami Prabhupada.

Radha Gokulananda
(168 x 102cm) page 66

This photograph depicts a shrine with various deities from Vrindavana, once worshiped by Srila Lokanatha Gosvami, Srila Baladeva Vidyabhushana, Srila Vishvanatha Chakravarti, and Srila Narottama Dasa Thakur. Formerly, all the deities in this temple – built by Vishvanatha Chakravarti – were worshiped separately.

Garuda Govinda
(167 x 101cm) page 67

The twelve hands hidden under Garuda Govinda's dresses are seen only during special ceremonies at this temple. The temple is located about five kilometres (3 miles) from Vrindavana, near the forest with black bees where dark clouds give ample rain. The large pond next to the temple area is covered by green lotus leaves. The place where this deity resides is called Chattikara, and there everyone is under the spell of Lord Krishna's love.

Krishna and Mira Bai Shrine
(168 x 102cm) page 68

Mira Bai, the celebrated medieval devotional poet, worshipped Krishna. This photograph shows Mira Bai next to Krishna, the place that would normally be occupied by Srimati Radharani. In the foreground of the picture, a pilgrim is offering incense and a *ghee* (clarified butter) lamp.

Shiva Mahadeva
(90 x 60 cm) page 69

Elaborately decorated for the Shiva Ratri festival, this image of Shiva Linga is worshipped at Vrindavana's Loi Bazaar. The Linga is dressed with matted hair, an attractive golden face, a crown, earrings and numerous other ornaments. I was welcomed by the priest to create this photograph on this special occasion and offered a donation for his spiritual pleasure. According the Bhagavata Purana, Shiva is considered to act as the protector of Vrindavana.

Bhagirati Devi
(40 x 60cm) page 70

Depicted is a deity, a personification of the holy River Bhagirati at the major Sri Krishna Temple in Udupi is attended to daily by pilgrims and priests. The deity is found in a secluded area in the right corner of the temple pond, which is called the Madhva's pond after its founder Sri Madhvacharya. The photograph was processed and layered with film emulsion, grain, and colour embellishment. The diffused vignette was created by a door frame.

Ganesha Puja
(40 x 60cm) page 71

Here we see worship of Ganesha, together with Krishna, on the day of Shivratri. Ganesha received the spirit of devotion for Lord Krishna from his father Lord Shiva. He is known for removing obstacles from one's life, and to worship him is especially recommended on Shiva Ratri.

Radha Vallabha
(40 x 60cm) page 72

Hit Harivamsa Goswami, a disciple of Gopala Bhatta Goswami, the founder of the Radha-Vallabha tradition, established the worship of this enchanting image of Sri Radha Vallabha in the sixteenth century. The devotees and priests tend to be friendly toward photographers, which is a relief when more and more often one hears, "Photo is not allowed."

Radha Ramana
(40 x 60cm) page 73

Sri Radha-Ramana is a deity self-manifested from a sacred stone. The deity appeared to the saintly scholar Sri Gopal Bhatta Goswami in the sixteenth century. At that location a temple was built to celebrate this charming form of Krishna. Pilgrims now travel from around the world to visit this sacred place in Vrindavana. Forty families in the line of the original founder currently take turns to provide the temple services.

KUMBHA MELA

Kumbha Mela Grounds
(112 x 76cm) pages 76-77

Tented camps line a thoroughfare at the Kumbha Mela in Prayag (also known as Allahabad). A dried-up confluence of the Ganges and Yamuna Rivers accommodates an entire city of tents and a few million sadhus and pilgrims. Kumbha Mela is the largest spiritual festival on Earth. According to early accounts, Kumbha Mela was designed to serve as a gathering to share hospitality, love and respect for one another since time immemorial. Many pilgrims wish to preserve this spirit of the festival in contrast to its steady commercialization. Gradually, over the past thirty-five years or so, it has been transforming the Kumbha Mela into more of a show, causing an ecological disaster instead of happiness.

Sadhus' Feats
(60 x 40 cm) page 78

These sadhus are entertaining on-looking guests with the fruits of their austerities. The austerity of celibacy or the mastery over one's genitals, is perhaps the most desirable one for a sadhu, as it provides a key to the doors of liberation from the iniquities of the world. At Kumbha Mela, *sadhus* display their daily practices publicly. Among other daily practices – or *sadhana* – are *japa* yoga (chanting of the holy names), practice of *asanas* (postures), cooking, dancing and – for some – inhaling marihuana smoke to expand consciousness.

Sadhus' Camp
(60 x 40 cm) page 79

One of the cultural activities at Kumbha Mela is visiting the camps of fellow companions. This view is from inside of a large tent of friendly sadhus during their afternoon relaxation. When I arrived in the tent, the sadhus made a small fire and I asked them how they see the Kumbha Mela festival and what significance it has for their practice. They were generally happy, but many would feel even happier if the sound amplification were abandoned.

Sadhu Naga Giri
(75 x 75 cm) page 80

A brave devotee of Lord Shiva who embraced the naga (naked) way of life many years ago, Naga Giri is attending his third Kumbha Mela. I was attracted by his face, from which I could read a mood of detachment, prior to photographing him.

Sadhvi Narayani
(75 x 75 cm) page 81

Sadhvi Narayani's eyes and mine met minutes after her Kumbha Mela bathing ceremony. I found her face intriguing and peaceful. We stood silently for some moments, then I nodded my head and waited to have her approval to take a photo. Sadhvi Narayani nodded her head in return and raised her hand to offer a blessing, a signal for me to focus the lens and photograph her.

Vandana Devi
(75 x 75 cm) page 82

Vandana Devi, a recently married young mother, arrived with her son at Kumbha Mela to spend three days with her new family. She felt fortunate to visit the festival and sung a traditional prayer in praise of pilgrimage to me after photographing her at the Sita Rama Temple, which overlooks the riverbed from a nearby hill.

Syama Bihari
(75 x 75 cm) page 83

Syama Bihari came to Kumbha Mela on a pilgrimage from Vrindavana, where he resides in an ashram near the River Yamuna. He is of brahminical descent from Kanpur, and at the Kumbha Mela he lives in small tent with his Vaishnava mother. We would meet and walk the Kumbha Mela grounds. He helped tremendously with the interpretation of the Hindi and Sanskrit languages.

Sadhus' Studies
(30 x 20 cm) page 84

This image shows two pilgrims in their camp at the Kumbha Mela. Study of the scriptures is considered to be one of the principal practices on the devotional path. Such morning meditation enhances good insight into the yogic way of life.

Pilgrims' Progress
(112 x 76 cm) page 85

Cheerful pilgrims consider Kumbha Mela the most special festival, because everyone is welcomed and can visit without invitation. People from all over India and the rest of the world arrive here to be blessed by the nectar of immortality once dropped by the demigods at the confluence.

On the Way to the Confluence
(112 x 76 cm) page 86

Pilgrims are crossing pontoon bridges to reach and bathe at the confluence of the Yamuna, Ganges, and Saraswati Rivers. Electric pylons and lamps cover an area of about fifty-eight square kilometers (22 square miles) making it larger than Allahabad. As the River Ganges is today considered unsafe to be bathed in, richer Kumbha Mela campers source clean water from pipes available for rent throughout the riverbed from a company.

A View of River Ganges
(108 x 72 cm) page 87

This evening scene from the Kumbha Mela festival in Allahabad evokes a great feeling when viewing the area. The electricity supply during the festival drains from the entire state the limited quota provided by the Indian government. If light comes from within, sun, moon or the stars, one may wonder to whom it is worth spending so much money on supplying so many electrical lamps? Sacred sound comes from a mouth directly to the ears of the learner quietly, often secretly, so why is it then necessary to have millions of loudspeakers installed for the festival, blasting sounds night and day? The photograph can be considered a blessing, as it offers the viewer a sterilised version of reality.

VRINDAVANA

Soul of Sand
(60 x 40cm) pages 90-91

Caught in a shower of sand on the bank of the River Yamuna. The image shows the atmosphere experienced by pilgrims in Vrindavana, and something of their attitude toward life's everyday joys and sorrows.

The Bumblebee Garden
(60 x 40 cm) page 92

Srimati Radharani's famous poetic talk with a humming bumblebee took place here. This image shows a bamboo hut in a garden, conceived as a natural place for meditation and, if you look carefully, you can spot a squirrel in the tree. Sometimes, Radharani would experience ecstatic feelings for Krishna caused by separation from him and the next moment she would feel neglected by him. The entire poem with a humming bumblebee, with all its charming details, appears in the tenth book of the Bhagavata Purana.

Milk Bath
(30 x 20 cm) page 93

One of the first photographs I created in 2004, while wandering around Govardhan Hill. The sacred milk bath takes place in the village of Jatipura. It is accompanied by enthused participants, who chant songs in praise of the hill so loved by the residents of Vrindavana. The milk used for the bath is sold by milkmen, and it tends to be diluted with water. After the milk offering follows the flower service, incense and a final bath in clear water. Even though photography is strictly discouraged, somehow I managed to record this scene on this particular day by the grace of Govardhan.

Goverdhan Hill
(355 x 101 cm) page 94-95 upper part

This panorama of Govardhan Hill facing east covers a range of 180 degrees. Govardhan Hill is considered sacred in the Hindu tradition. Hindus worship the hill by circumambulating it and by offering prayers, prostrating themselves, and offering grains and fruits. A camera was mounted and operated from a water tank approximately thirty-five meters (100 fee) high. Govardhan Hill straddles the border between Uttar Pradesh and Rajasthan.

Goverdhan Hill
(350 x 95 cm) pages 94-95 lower part

This panorama presents the Rajasthan side of Govardhan Hill facing west. Govardhan Hill is the mythical hill once lifted by Krishna to protect the helpless people of Vrindavana against torrential rains. This side is less populated and still remains somewhat rural. This can no longer be said about the part of the hill nestled in Uttar Pradesh. A concrete road has been constructed with houses along it, many ponds have been filled with dangerous cement, and plastic bags have become an inseparable element of the rural landscape.

Vrijbasis in Belvan
(40 x 30 cm) page 96

These residents of Vrindavana, known as Vrijbasis, readily agreed to be photographed with a large-format camera. Photographer Abhinav Goswami prepared a 5x7 camera with film and I calculated the tilt/shift degrees of the bellows and exposure value. Focusing at eye level, I wanted to change the perspective of the foreground and upper part of the image – the tree crown. We made two exposures and this came out beautifully sharp – exactly how I wanted it, thank God.

Gopal and the Young Bull
(40 x 30 cm) page 97

When we were in the Belvan area, a likable boy with his bull appeared. Looking so photogenic, I approached him to se if it would be possible to take a photo. His cheeks went red and he agreed. After the photograph, we enjoyed refreshments together before bidding each other farewell. For this photograph a large format film camera was used.

Pilgrims' Dance
(60 x 35 cm) page 98

About thirty five kilometers (20 miles) from Belvan lies the village of Nandagaon with its famed Temple of Krishna Balarama. Here each year the Holi festival takes place in great splendour. Inspired perhaps by divine madness, this group of ladies came from Vrindavana to dance together for Krishna and Balarama. Photographed from the temple roof, this image sequence has been recorded as part of the film *Rasa Yatra*.

Dance Energy
(167 x 101 cm) page 99

Jaav is another Holi venue with a specific form of devotion. A big sacred circle dance is filled with energy, extraordinary passion and colours. Within the large circle, another dance is performed, which represents the notion of samsara, the cycle of birth, death and rebirth.

Holi Darshan
(60 x 40cm) page 100

These Holi players are having darshana (sacred vision) of the two brothers Krishna and Balarama, as part of the Holi celebrations. Krishna and Balarama used to play here with their friends on top of Nandishwara Hill, where their temple is built. It is located in the Mathura district.

Enchanted Priests
(60 x 40) page 101

In the centre of the composition invited village elders sit with temple priests. They chant devotional songs in the midst of splashes of colour and water. The chanters have their song-book. Among them, if you look carefully, you can see a number of young photojournalists in their search for a good photograph.

Divine Celebration
(167 x 101 cm) pages 102-103

Near Nandagaon, another important place on a pilgrim's map is the village of Dauji, where the Holi atmosphere is probably the most ecstatic and sublime. At Dauji, the image of Balarama, Krishna's elder brother is worshipped. Devotees and pilgrims join in a dance and circumambulate the temple shrine of the unpredictable Balarama.

RASA LILA SERIES

Krishna's Peacock Dance
(112 x 76 cm) page 106

In this Rasa Lila dance, Radha Krishna are dressed in a red outfit, with gopis dressed in blue and decorated with peacock feathers. It was photographed during the Holi festival, as part of a devotional performance at the Jai Singh Ghera Ashram, located near Radha Ramana Temple, in 2011. Just as Krishna is seen as the king of dancers among the charming Hindu gods, similarly the peacock is seen in Vrindavana culture as the best dancer in the kingdom of birds, beautifully enacted by the Vrindavana-based Swami Fateh Krishna dance troupe.

Rasa Lila
(60 x 40 cm) page 107

Accompanied by live music, these musicians are singing devotional tunes with melodious voices for the pleasure of Radha Krishna. Every scene has its own dramatization and form. The decorations complement the sacred mood, with musical instruments guiding each scene with a unique rhythm.

Radha Krishna Sacred Circle
(60 x 40 cm) page 108

In this scene gopis and gopas (Krishna's friends) circle the divine couple while offering a shower of rose petals. The rose shower lasts until Radha and Krishna are completely covered by a small mountain of flowers. Then circumambulation stops, and we see the divine couple arise from the flower petal mountain to dance.

Rasa Lila Crescendo
(62 x 37 cm) page 109

The grand finale of a Rasa Lila dance creates an intoxicating, sweet atmosphere with red and yellow colours from the aromatic rose petals. The crescendo lasts several minutes. After Radha and Krishna have been showered with flowers, the audience then takes part by showering friends and relatives with the rose petals and making everyone dance in devotional ecstasy.

RADHA GOVINDA SERIES

This series was inspired by the dances found in the ancient kingdom of Manipur. Among the eight Indian classical dances the Manipuri art form is considered by some art connoisseurs to be the most refined. In 1972, Manipur became a full State of the Indian Federation. Devotion in Manipur is interwoven into the lives of its people, despite its economic and cultural decline.

The wonderful performing artist Manju Elangbam, in the role of Govinda, also became the teacher for the team of young dancers and, out of love for the photography project, dedicated time and energy to it. The supporting roles of Krishna's friends (gopis) were cast from Imphal's Bhaktivedanta Mission School, namely Sarju Devi, Pinky Devi, Hemlata Devi and Princy Devi. The rehearsals for this enactment took four weeks.

Govinda's Garden of Delight
(90 x 60 cm) page 112

Govinda's Playground
(90 x 60 cm) page 113

Rasa Lila Dance
(60 x 40 cm) page 114

Sacred garden (The best dance is through the sacred garden)
(60 x 40 cm) page 115

ACKNOWLEDGMENTS

Approaching Maha Shivaratri
(60 x 40) page 135

This photograph was taken from the Viswamitra Muni Shrine in Gokarna, a sacred place in southern India, the night before the Maha Shivaratri festival, for which pilgrims travel from all over Kerala and Karnataka. In Gokarna, Ganesha, one of Lord Shiva's children with a crescent moon nested in his hair, is worshipped in an amazing way. He is given daily offerings of vegetables, rice, fresh coconuts, bananas, guavas and lotus flowers.

ॐ

Param Tomanec
January 2015
Oxfordshire, England

BIOGRAPHY

In 2009, Param was appointed Artist-in-Residence at the Oxford Centre for Hindu Studies (OCHS), a Recognised Independent Centre of the University of Oxford. His still photography and moving pictures are used at universities around the world for courses on Indian life, culture and art. Works of his are in the permanent collection of the Museum of Sacred Art and growing number of private collections. Param collaborates with Insight Editions, a publisher based in California, USA. Since 2014 he serves as Visiting Artist at the OCHS. For the next nine years Param will be working on his feature film project. He is a life long vegetarian and activist.

Learn more about Param's photography : www.paramtomanec.com

EXHIBITIONS

2010 group show, Biographica, Foyer Gallery, London & Piramal Gallery, Mumbai
2011 group show, Govinda Festival, Jaipur Temple Palace
2011 solo exhibition, Meller Merceux Gallery, Oxford
2013 solo exhibition, Museum of Sacred Art, Belgium
2014 solo exhibition Indiart Gallery, Brussels
2015 group show, Lalit Kala Academy, Delhi

PUBLICATIONS

Param's photography appeared across art books, journals and periodics. He frequently publishes academic and artistic collaborations focusing on Indian culture, philosophy and beyond.

ACKNOWLEDGMENTS

My thanks go to the friends and teachers at the Oxford Centre for Hindu Studies. Without their continuing enthusiasm and encouragement these pages would remain unmanifested. Namely Dr. Kenneth R. Valpey for guiding me through the philosophies of India. Dr. Rembert Lutjeharms from Oxford University for assistance with Sanskrit and Bengali languages. Shaunaka Rishi Das for supporting my activities. Zach Hester for copy editing. Annette Kahmann for text edit. I am grateful to Cunilal Acharya of Vashishta for hosting me on location scouting in Himalayas. Thanking for great memories to all friends in Vrindavana, and for tolerating the demands of my photography during the image acquisition.

Approaching Maha Shiva Ratri